The Peop

Hosea
Joel
Amos

Paul E. Eickmann

NORTHWESTERN PUBLISHING HOUSE
Milwaukee, Wisconsin

Second edition, 2002

Cover art by Frank Ordaz.
Interior illustrations by Glenn Myers.

Covers of first edition volumes and certain second edition volumes
feature illustrations by James Tissot (1836–1902).

Library of Congress Card 88-62756
Northwestern Publishing House
1250 N. 113th St., Milwaukee, WI 53226-3284
© 1989 Northwestern Publishing House
Published 1989
Printed in the United States of America
ISBN 0-8100-1182-4

CONTENTS

ILLUSTRATIONS

EDITOR'S PREFACE

The People's Bible is just what the name implies—a Bible for the people. It includes the complete text of the Holy Scriptures in the popular New International Version. The commentary following the Scripture sections contains personal applications as well as historical background and explanations of the text.

The authors of The People's Bible are men of scholarship and practical insight, gained from years of experience in the teaching and preaching ministries. They have tried to avoid the technical jargon that limits so many commentary series to professional Bible scholars.

The most important feature of these books is that they are Christ-centered. Speaking of the Old Testament Scriptures, Jesus himself declared, "These are the Scriptures that testify about me" (John 5:39). Each volume of The People's Bible directs our attention to Jesus Christ. He is the center of the entire Bible. He is our only Savior.

The commentaries also have maps, illustrations, and archaeological information when appropriate. All the books include running heads to direct the reader to the passage he is looking for.

This commentary series was initiated by the Commission on Christian Literature of the Wisconsin Evangelical Lutheran Synod.

It is our prayer that this endeavor may continue as it began. We dedicate these volumes to the glory of God and to the good of his people.

INTRODUCTION TO
THE MINOR PROPHETS

The minor prophets and their times

Hosea is the first of the 12 minor prophets. The writers of the last dozen books of the Old Testament in our English Bible received this name because their writings are much shorter than the books of Isaiah, Jeremiah, Ezekiel, and Daniel, the so-called major prophets. Jewish scribes customarily wrote the books of Isaiah, Jeremiah, and Ezekiel each on a separate scroll. They copied all 12 books from Hosea to Malachi on a single scroll. In Hebrew the minor prophets are simply referred to as "the Twelve."

We do not know exactly why these 12 books were arranged in their present order, nor do all Bible manuscripts follow the same arrangement. Hosea and Amos, two of the first three minor prophets, worked in Israel's Northern Kingdom under King Jeroboam II, who ruled from 793 to 753 B.C.* Haggai and Zechariah dated their books to the second year of the Persian king Darius, 520 B.C., and Malachi, the last of "the Twelve," probably prophesied about 450 B.C. Thus the order of the 12 books is roughly chronological. Perhaps, however, the Jews used some other principle of arrangement as well. They may have placed Hosea first, for example, because his book was the longest of the minor prophets.

---

* Dates in this volume are according to E. Thiele, *A Chronology of the Hebrew Kings* (Grand Rapids: Zondervan, 1977).

The Holy Spirit inspired these 12 books over a period of more than three hundred years. Those centuries were some of the most eventful times in the history of God's Old Testament people. The Northern Kingdom reached the pinnacle of its earthly glory under King Jeroboam II. Yet within less than one generation after Jeroboam's death, the Assyrians dismembered the Israelite territories. In 722 B.C. they captured Samaria, the capital of the Northern Kingdom, and carried off King Hoshea and a large part of the Israelite population into a captivity from which they never returned. "So the LORD was very angry with Israel and removed them from his presence" (2 Kings 17:18).

Jerusalem, the capital of the Southern Kingdom—also called Judah—escaped destruction at the hands of Sennacherib's Assyrian army about 700 B.C., only to fall before the forces of Nebuchadnezzar, King of Babylon, in 586 B.C. The Babylonian exile of the Jews, their return from captivity, the building of the second temple, and the people's subsequent life under Persian rule: all of these took place during the period from Hosea to Malachi. The so-called major prophets (Isaiah, Jeremiah, Ezekiel, and Daniel) also ministered during this same period from the eighth to the fifth century B.C.

The Bible tells some of the history of those times in 2 Kings chapters 14 to 25, 2 Chronicles chapters 26 to 36, and in the books of Ezra, Nehemiah, and Esther. Sometimes the prophets themselves describe events and conditions during their ministries. The history of the prophets' times helps us understand the messages they brought from the Lord to his people. Knowing something about the original setting of the prophets' words also aids us in properly applying their messages to ourselves and our own times.

Applying the message of the prophets

The Lord originally sent his prophets to deliver his Word to the people of Israel, his Old Testament church. Christians, through Spirit-worked faith in Jesus, are also his people, his New Testament church. Therefore we will recognize that in the words of the Old Testament prophets, God is speaking to us as well. The messages of these ancient servants of the Lord expose our sin. They instruct us about God-pleasing fruits of faith. Above all, they testify of Jesus Christ, the only Savior of both Jews and Gentiles (John 5:39).

Yet we must also recognize the differences between ancient Israel and ourselves today. Israel was not only God's Old Testament church but also a nation among the nations of the world. When the prophets addressed their people, they spoke to them not only as a congregation of sinners waiting for their Savior but also as the total society of a nation, responsible for upholding fairness in social relations and requiring justice in the courts. Such civil functions are fulfilled today by local, state, and national governments, not by the Christian church.

When the Lord Jesus Christ sent his church into the world, he gave us the commission to "preach the good news to all creation" (Mark 16:15). Proclaiming the gospel is the mission of the Christian church. We are also to teach those who become Christ's disciples to obey everything he has commanded (Matthew 28:20). This includes instruction in Christian living, which disciples of Jesus will practice in their total lives, including when they function as citizens of their states and nations.

While the Christian church is called to proclaim the good news of the forgiveness of sins according to the Scriptures, government has another function. The Bible calls government God's servant to commend those who do right and to

3

punish the wrongdoers, even by using the sword if necessary (Romans 13:1-7). To guide government he has given all people the light of reason and a knowledge of his law written in their hearts (Romans 2:14,15). Jesus did not give his church authority over civil governments. He did not put the Christian church into the world to tell legislators what laws to pass, administrators how to enforce the laws, or judges what sentences to impose.

How, for example, should we apply the words of Amos when he condemns the merchants of the Northern Kingdom for greed and dishonesty? "[When will] the Sabbath be ended that we may market wheat?" they ask, and then they take advantage of their poor customers, "skimping the measure, boosting the price and cheating with dishonest scales . . . selling even the sweepings with the wheat" (8:5,6). Amos as the Lord's prophet is exposing the selfishness of the rich merchants among God's people.

We would be mistaken in our application of this passage if we used it to justify our congregations conducting a campaign to force businesses to close on Sunday. Further, it is not part of our mission as a church to protect consumers from dishonest weights and measures or inferior merchandise in the local stores. Those are functions of society at large or, specifically, of our governments.

We rightly apply this word of God to ourselves when we let it expose human selfishness. These passages condemn our covetous hearts when we adopt the standards of the world and value making money above worshiping our God and Savior. It illustrates the Seventh Commandment, forbidding us to take advantage of our neighbor in business. It instructs us as forgiven sinners to bear witness to our Christian faith by practicing honesty when we buy and sell. It reminds us that we worship the Lord not only by hearing his Word and singing his praises but also by practicing justice and right-eousness among our fellowmen in our communities.

The books of "the Twelve" are minor in length only, not in the importance of their content. Like the rest of the God-breathed Scriptures, the books of the minor prophets are "useful for teaching, rebuking, correcting and training in righteousness" (2 Timothy 3:16).

Hebrew poetry

The prophets wrote some of their messages in prose. Most of their writing, however, is poetry. Hebrew poetry does not have rhyme, and its rhythm is usually quite irregu-lar. The main feature that makes Hebrew poetry different from prose is parallelism.

There are three main types of parallelism. In the most common type, a second line restates the thought of the first, usually in other words. For example, the second line of Hosea 2:2 reads, "for she is not my wife"; line 3 continues, "and I am not her husband." One line may be followed by a second line that *contrasts* with it. There is an example in the last lines of Hosea 2:13: " '[She] went after her lovers,/ but me she forgot,' declares the LORD." Or the thought of a sec-ond line *develops* what is said in the first. In Hosea 2:4, for example, line 2 gives a reason for the statement made in line 1: "I will not show my love to her children,/ because they are the children of adultery."

Parallelism aids our interpretation of the text. In Hosea 9:3, for example, the prophet describes Israel's future exile: "Ephraim [Israel] will return to Egypt/and eat unclean food in Assyria." He does not mean that some of the Israelites will be exiled to Egypt, others to Assyria. The Israelites went into exile in Assyria, where they were not able to observe the dietary and sacrificial regulations of

God's law, as the second line says. The first line, which is parallel to the second, tells the people that their Assyrian captivity will be as burdensome to them as if they had returned to their ancient slavery in Egypt. Thus, if one line of Hebrew poetry is unclear to us, the parallel line may help to explain it.

INTRODUCTION TO HOSEA

Author

The Bible does not mention the prophet Hosea outside his own book. There he calls himself "son of Beeri" (1:1) to distinguish himself from other Israelites with the same given name. He shares his name, which means "salvation," with Hoshea, the last king of Israel (the Hebrew consonants in both names are the same). The first three chapters of his book tell us some intimate details of the prophet's marriage and family life.

Hosea repeatedly mentions Ephraim, another name for the Northern Kingdom (Israel), and he calls the Israelite monarch "our king" (7:5). On the other hand, he mentions the Southern Kingdom (Judah) seldom and Jerusalem never. It is plain from these and other details of his book that Hosea is prophesying in Israel, the Northern Kingdom, which must also be his homeland.

The prophet's times

David's son Solomon ruled as the last king of an undivided Israel. Already during Solomon's reign (970–930 B.C.) an Ephraimite named Jeroboam rebelled against the king (1 Kings 11:26-40). When Solomon's son Rehoboam estranged many of his people with threats of a harsh regime, ten northern tribes seceded from the nation. Jeroboam succeeded in making himself king of the ten tribes. That left

Rehoboam to rule only Judah and Benjamin from David's capital, Jerusalem (1 Kings 12:1-20).

Jeroboam kept his people from returning to Jerusalem and giving their allegiance to Rehoboam by erecting golden calves in Bethel and Dan, cities at the southern and northern boundaries of his kingdom. "He said to the people, 'It is too much for you to go up to Jerusalem. Here are your gods, O Israel, who brought you up out of Egypt'" (1 Kings 12:28). This wicked king built other shrines on high places in Israel and appointed priests of his own choosing, even though they were not Levites as the law of Moses required. In addition, King Jeroboam instituted his own festival and offered sacrifices on the altar at Bethel.

Jeroboam wanted to retain the worship of the Lord in his kingdom, even though he erected calf images, established altars, appointed priests, and instituted a festival in disobedience to God's written law. His people were already worshiping Canaanite deities such as Baal and Asherah on their high places, and before long it seems that the worship at Bethel and Dan was also "baalized." We know from archeology that bull-calf images like those that Jeroboam erected represented Baal in Canaanite religion. Thus through Jeroboam's wicked leadership, idolatry invaded the official worship of the Northern Kingdom.

We gain some idea of the direction taken by Israelite religious life from the Bible's accounts of the ministries of the prophets Elijah and Elisha about a hundred years before Hosea prophesied. The Israelite king at that time, Ahab, married Jezebel, a Phoenician princess. Queen Jezebel supported 450 prophets of Baal and 400 prophets of Asherah (1 Kings 18:19). It is no wonder that in his discouragement the prophet thought he was the last faithful spokesman of the Lord. God revealed to Elijah that there were still seven thousand Israelites whose knees had not bowed down to Baal (1 Kings 19:18) and reminded him that his Word was still at work in Israel (verses 11-18).

The great world powers of those times were Egypt to the southwest and Assyria to the north and east of Canaan. After the reign of Jeroboam I, Egypt played little part in Canaanite affairs. The powerful Assyrian king, Shalmaneser III, forced Jehu of Israel to pay tribute about 841 B.C., but a period of about a century followed when Assyria made no strong moves to assert its influence in Canaan.

Assyrian weakness or indifference allowed the expansion of Israel's neighbor to the north, the Aramean kingdom centered in Damascus. The Arameans—also called Syrians—dominated their Israelite neighbors for a number of decades. Of King Jehu's son Jehoahaz, for example, we read that "nothing had been left of the army of Jehoahaz except fifty horsemen, ten chariots and ten thousand foot soldiers, for the king of Aram had destroyed the rest and made them like the dust at threshing time" (2 Kings 13:7).

A more formidable and active king on the Assyrian throne meant trouble for the Arameans of Damascus. When Adadnirari III of Assyria invaded Aram but did not press on into Canaan, the Israelites under Jehoash, son of Jehoahaz, seized their opportunity and revolted. "Jehoash son of Jehoahaz recaptured from Ben-Hadad son of Hazael the towns he had taken in battle from his father Jehoahaz. Three times Jehoash defeated him, and so he recovered the Israelite towns" (2 Kings 13:25).

Jeroboam II, son of Jehoash, was probably the strongest leader the Northern Kingdom ever had. Ruling from 793 to 753 B.C., Jeroboam II "was the one who restored the boundaries of Israel from Lebo Hamath to the Sea of the Arabah" (2 Kings 14:25). Hamath lay north of Aram, and its territory bordered on the Euphrates; "the Sea of the Arabah" is the Dead Sea. At the same time King Uzziah (also called Azariah) was building up the territories and prestige of Judah, the Southern Kingdom. The boundaries of the two Israelite kingdoms almost matched in extent the united empire of David and Solomon. To all outward appearances, those were prosperous times for the Lord's Old Testament people.

Unfortunately, however, the visible glory of the kingdom of Israel did not imply inward spiritual health. Like Jehu, Jehoahaz, and Jehoash before him, Jeroboam II "did evil in the eyes of the LORD and did not turn away from any of the sins of Jeroboam [I] son of Nebat, which he had caused Israel to commit" (2 Kings 14:24). The prophet Amos paints a vivid picture of conditions in Israelite society during the times of Jeroboam II. The high-living rich exploited the poor. Merchants took dishonest profits. And money controlled the courts of law. Crowds filled the religious shrines, but the life of the people showed that their hearts were far from the Lord.

Israelite religion

From the denunciations of the prophets and from biblical archeology, we get a good idea of Israelite worship at Hosea's time. In the shrines at Bethel and Dan, and perhaps also at such border sanctuaries as Gilgal and Beersheba, priests continued to bring sacrifices. The calf images erected by Jeroboam I as visible representations of the Lord's presence still stood at Bethel and Dan. We can be sure that there were still Israelites who were true believers in the Lord and in his promised Savior, just as in Elijah's time a century before (1 Kings 19:18). At Bethel and Dan, however, and on many high places throughout the land, the people combined the worship of the true God with Canaanite religion, essentially a fertility cult.

The Canaanites believed that El, whose name means "god" or "a god," was the father of the gods and his consort Asherah was the mother of 70 deities. Most active of these deities were Baal and Ashtoreth (Astarte). The Canaanites pictured Baal riding on thunderheads and hurling lightning bolts. They believed that Baal blessed them with the early rain each fall to make plowing possible. They asked him to send the continuing winter and spring rains to green up their pastures and to make their land bear crops. By worshiping these deities, the Canaanites thought they could insure the fertility of fields and flocks.

A Canaanite "high place" would have an altar for Baal. A sacred stone standing near the altar might represent the presence of the god. Also near the altar would stand a wooden Asherah pole, representing the goddess. Cult prostitutes might be found at the Canaanite shrines. By having intercourse with them as an act devoted to the deities, the worshipers tried to insure that their fields would be fertile, their cows would calve, and their ewes would drop healthy lambs. When the Israelites adopted the deities of the land, they practiced such ritual prostitution and also another horrible feature of Canaanite worship: human sacrifice. "They shed innocent blood, the blood of their sons and daughters, whom they sacrificed to the idols of Canaan, and the land was desecrated by their blood. They defiled themselves by what they did; by their deeds they prostituted themselves" (Psalm 106:38,39).

That was the sort of worship that became mingled with the faith of the people of Israel. It is not hard to see why the prophets used adultery as a metaphor for the people's unfaithfulness to the Lord, their Creator and Savior. This picture is an important feature of the book of Hosea.

Outline and summary of Hosea

Hosea's book is composed of two unequal parts:

1. The prophet's marriage to Gomer: a picture of the Lord's faithful love for unfaithful Israel (1–3).
2. The prophet's message: a call to repentance in view of the coming judgment (4–14).

The prophet's message is very difficult to outline in detail. In the commentary that follows, chapter and paragraph headings, often quotations from the text, will serve as subheadings for the two main divisions of the book.

Very frequently Hosea's preaching alternates between threat and promise, judgment and mercy, law and gospel. "The Book of Hosea contains some of the most passionate denunciations and threats that the OT [Old Testament] knows (e.g., 13:7,8,15,16). But the distinctive note in Hosea is his portrayal of the God who loves when all possibility of loving has rightly ceased, the God who loves 'again' (3:1), the injured Husband who forgives the unforgivable (chapters 1-3), the father whose 'heart recoils within' Him, whose 'compassion grows warm and tender' (11:8) for the wayward child whom He led with cords of compassion in his youth (13:3,4), the Healer who hurts in order to restore with compassionate skill and with a love that does not die, simply because it is the love of God and not of man (7:1; 11:3; 14:4; cf. 5:13; 6:1)."*

---

* M. Franzmann, *Concordia Self-Study Commentary* (St. Louis: Concordia, 1971), 588.

PART ONE

The Prophet's Marriage
(1:1–3:5)

The prophet's wife

1 The word of the LORD that came to Hosea son of Beeri during the reigns of Uzziah, Jotham, Ahaz and Hezekiah, kings of Judah, and during the reign of Jeroboam son of Jehoash king of Israel:

²When the LORD began to speak through Hosea, the LORD said to him, "Go, take to yourself an adulterous wife and children of unfaithfulness, because the land is guilty of the vilest adultery in departing from the LORD." ³So he married Gomer daughter of Diblaim. . . .

Hosea presents the credentials for his prophetic ministry: his words are "the word of the LORD." He dates his prophecies with the name of Jeroboam (II), son of Joash (Jehoash) king of Israel, who reigned from 793 to 753 B.C., and with the names of four Judean kings. The reign of Uzziah, the first Judean king mentioned, roughly matches the period of Jeroboam II. Hezekiah, the last of the four, comes to the throne about 715 B.C. Thus the preaching of Hosea extends over 40 years or more, from the glory years of Jeroboam II until after the fall of Samaria, the capital city of the Northern Kingdom, in 722 B.C.

Why would a prophet who works in the Northern Kingdom mention several Judean kings but only one king of Israel, omitting the names of Zechariah, Shallum,

Menahem, Pekahiah, Pekah, and Hoshea, the last six rulers of the Northern Kingdom? Perhaps Hosea is reminding his listeners that the kings of Israel who rule in Samaria have actually usurped the throne from the legitimate royal line, the kings of the house of David who rule in Jerusalem.

The beginning of the Lord's call to Hosea is startling, to say the least. Even before the prophet begins to preach, the Lord calls him to proclaim his message with his own body and life. By worshiping the Canaanite deities, the people of Israel are committing spiritual adultery against the Lord, who has been a faithful husband to them. Instead of responding to him with equal faithfulness, they are "prostituting themselves" to other gods (Judges 2:17). In the life-sermon that the Lord calls Hosea to deliver, the prophet represents the Lord, faithful in his love for his people. Unfaithful Gomer illustrates the nation of Israel. Her "children of unfaithfulness" represent the individual Israelites.

Gomer may be a common harlot, but it is also possible that she is a cult prostitute at a Canaanite shrine. (Some think that Canaanite girls regularly served the deities in this way for a time before their marriage.) Since the Lord calls Gomer's offspring "children of unfaithfulness," it appears that not Hosea but one of Gomer's lovers is the father of some or all of them. Hosea is to accept them as his own. What deep devotion the Lord calls for and receives from the prophet for the sake of his ministry to the people of Israel! Hosea is called to love the unlovable, as the Lord himself does.

Before we object with "How could Hosea possibly marry such a woman?" we need to remind ourselves that Gomer represents Israel. If we look beneath the surface of our own lives, we realize that we also have been unfaithful to our God. We have no more claim on his love than Gomer had on the love of her husband Hosea. Yet the Lord does love us. "When we were still powerless, Christ died for the ungodly. Very rarely will anyone die for a righteous man, though for a good man someone might possibly dare to die. But God demonstrates his own love for us in this: While we were still sinners, Christ died for us" (Romans 5:6-8). Not only in his message but also in his marriage, Hosea proclaims the good news of the Lord's gracious love for undeserving sinners like us.

The prophet's children

And she conceived and bore him a son.

⁴Then the LORD said to Hosea, "Call him Jezreel, because I will soon punish the house of Jehu for the massacre at Jezreel, and I will put an end to the kingdom of Israel. ⁵In that day I will break Israel's bow in the Valley of Jezreel."

⁶Gomer conceived again and gave birth to a daughter. Then the LORD said to Hosea, "Call her Lo-Ruhamah, for I will no longer show love to the house of Israel, that I should at all forgive them. ⁷Yet I will show love to the house of Judah; and I will save them—not by bow, sword or battle, or by horses and horsemen, but by the LORD their God."

⁸After she had weaned Lo-Ruhamah, Gomer had another son. ⁹Then the LORD said, "Call him Lo-Ammi, for you are not my people, and I am not your God."

Each of Gomer's three children receives a symbolic name. The first son is called Jezreel. This was the name of a city north of Mount Gilboah. To the west and northwest, the rich Valley of Jezreel, including the Plain of Esdraelon, leads toward the Mediterranean. To the east the valley narrows as it descends to the Jordan. Jezreel was a residence of Israel's kings (1 Kings 21:1).

At Jezreel, Jehu, great-grandfather of Jeroboam II and the founder of his dynasty, murdered Ahab's son Joram, his

15

predecessor on the Israelite throne. Jehu ordered the queen mother, Jezebel, thrown down from her window into the street below. At the gates of Jezreel, Jehu piled up the severed heads of Ahab's 70 princes. "So Jehu killed everyone in Jezreel who remained of the house of Ahab, as well as all his chief men, his close friends and his priests, leaving him no survivor" (2 Kings 10:11). Although God made Jehu king in Joram's place, he did not sanction such bloodshed. The assassination of Zechariah, son of Jeroboam II and Jehu's great-great-grandson, will punish Jehu's brutality, bringing his dynasty to a bloody end (2 Kings 15:8-12).

Only a few years after Hosea's son Jezreel is born, the Assyrians, as instruments of the Lord's judgment, will "break Israel's bow," bringing the nation's military power to an end. We do not know from the books of Kings the name of the place where the Assyrians won their decisive battle before the siege of Samaria. The Lord may well be telling Hosea in verse 5 that his judgment will bring defeat on Israel in the Valley of Jezreel, the same place where Jehu by his bloody acts established the greatest dynasty of the Northern Kingdom.

Thus the Lord "brings princes to naught and reduces the rulers of this world to nothing. No sooner are they planted, no sooner are they sown, no sooner do they take root in the ground, than he blows on them and they wither, and a whirlwind sweeps them away like chaff" (Isaiah 40:23,24).

The Lord calls Hosea's next child, a daughter, Lo-Ruhamah, meaning "not loved" (verse 6). God's time of grace for the Northern Kingdom as a whole is coming to an end. Through his prophets Elijah and Elisha, the Lord earlier pleaded with his people to repent, but they stubbornly resisted his Holy Spirit and would not listen. Now the time of grace for the nation is past, though individual Israelites may still hear the prophet's warning and return to the Lord.

Judah, the Southern Kingdom, has not sunk quite so far into idolatry and disobedience. Besides, the Lord will never revoke the unconditional promise he made to King David: "Your house and your kingdom will endure forever before me; your throne will be established forever" (2 Samuel 7:16). A remnant of the chosen people will remain in Judah for the sake of this covenant promise, which will finally be fulfilled in the rule of David's greater Son.

Like Joshua's conquest of Canaan, "You did not do it with your own sword and bow" (Joshua 24:12), the deliverance of Judah will be the Lord's free gift. In fact, Jerusalem will fall to the Babylonians (586 B.C.) and the Jews will go through the bitter experience of exile. Yet for the sake of his promise, the Lord will bring them back to their land and reveal his salvation there in the coming of the promised Savior.

The Lord names Gomer's second son Lo-Ammi, meaning "not my people" (verse 9). The boy's name repeats a message of judgment for the people of Israel. No longer can they call themselves God's chosen ones. No longer can they call the Lord their God. By their idolatry and disobedience to his law, they have broken the covenant that they sealed with the Lord at the foot of Mount Sinai.

At Sinai the Lord said to his people, "You yourselves have seen what I did to Egypt, and how I carried you on eagles' wings and brought you to myself. Now if you obey me fully and keep my covenant, then out of all nations you will be my treasured possession. Although the whole earth is mine, you will be for me a kingdom of priests and a holy nation" (Exodus 19:4-6). Israel responded: "We will do everything the LORD has said" (Exodus 19:8).

The Lord warned his Old Testament people through Joshua when they entered the Promised Land: "If you violate the covenant of the LORD your God, which he commanded you, and go and serve other gods and bow down to them, the LORD's anger will burn against you, and you will quickly perish from the good land he has given you" (Joshua 23:16). Israel did not heed the warning. Now, therefore, not the Lord's blessing but his curse rests on them. He will fulfill all the threats connected with the Sinai law covenant (Leviticus 26:14-29). Israel is no longer his people, and he will not be their God.

The history of Israel stands as a warning sign for believers of all time. Will we learn from the Lord's dealing with his Old Testament people not to mingle false religion with the truth, to be guided by every word that proceeds from the mouth of God, and to make good use of our time of grace? "Today, if you hear his voice, do not harden your hearts. . . . See to it, brothers, that none of you has a sinful, unbelieving heart that turns away from the living God. But encourage one another daily, as long as it is called Today, so that none of you may be hardened by sin's deceitfulness" (Hebrews 3:7-13).

A promise of future blessing

¹⁰"Yet the Israelites will be like the sand on the seashore, which cannot be measured or counted. In the place where it was said to them, 'You are not my people,' they will be called 'sons of the living God.' ¹¹The people of Judah and the people of Israel will be reunited, and they will appoint one leader and will come up out of the land, for great will be the day of Jezreel.

2 "Say of your brothers, 'My people,' and of your sisters, 'My loved one.'

Here for the first time, we meet a characteristic feature of the book of Hosea: a sudden alternation from threat to promise, from law to gospel.

As an adulterous wife breaks her marriage vow, the people of Israel have broken the covenant they made with the Lord at the foot of Mount Sinai. Long before the Sinai law covenant, however, the Lord made another agreement with Abraham: "I will surely bless you and make your descendants as numerous as the stars in the sky and as the sand on the seashore" (Genesis 22:17). This was a gospel covenant, antedating the Sinai law covenant. The gospel covenant with Abraham included the promise of the Savior: "Through your offspring all nations on earth will be blessed" (Genesis 22:18).

Hosea 1:10–2:1 presents the fulfillment of this promise in Old Testament terms. The people will become God's children again. The divided kingdom will be reunited under one leader, the promised Messiah. The whole nation will again go up from the land to the temple at Jerusalem, as in the days of the undivided kingdom: God's people will worship him together.

That will be the great "day of Jezreel" (1:11). Instead of referring to the bloodshed and destruction that took place at Jezreel, the Lord is playing on the meaning of the city's Hebrew name, "God will sow." The future age in his kingdom will be a time for planting and growing, fruit-bearing and harvesting.

In his New Testament revelation, God himself explains the meaning of such promises. Not the blood of Abraham flowing in our veins but the faith of Abraham created in our hearts makes us children of God. "You are all sons of God through faith in Christ Jesus, for all of you who were baptized into Christ have clothed yourselves with Christ. . . . If you

19

belong to Christ, then you are Abraham's seed, and heirs according to the promise" (Galatians 3:26-29).

Believing Jews and believing Gentiles form the one, undivided people of God, the holy Christian church (Ephesians 2:11-22). Their one leader, master, and King is David's Son and David's Lord, Jesus Christ (Matthew 22:41-45). Unlike the Old Testament worship in the temple, their service of God is not bound to Jerusalem. Their worship pleases God if it is offered "in spirit and truth" (John 4:19-24). The Lord will send his disciples to sow his Word and to harvest people's souls for him, so that believers of every nation will become his beloved people. "Once you were not a people," Peter reminds us, "but now you are the people of God; once you had not received mercy, but now you have received mercy" (1 Peter 2:10). The apostle Paul quotes Hosea 1:10 in Romans 9:26 to make this same point.

In passages like Hosea 1:10–2:1, the sun of God's grace shines even more brightly than elsewhere, surrounded as it is with the dark clouds of approaching judgment for the kingdom of Israel. Both the Lord's holiness and his love are perfect. Yet his fatherly heart would rather exercise mercy than judgment. "Where sin increased, grace increased all the more" (Romans 5:20). That is the kind of God we have.

Israel rebuked

> [2] **"Rebuke your mother, rebuke her,**
> **for she is not my wife,**
> **and I am not her husband.**
> **Let her remove the adulterous look from her face**
> **and the unfaithfulness from between her breasts.**
> [3] **Otherwise I will strip her naked**
> **and make her as bare as on the day she was born;**
> **I will make her like a desert,**
> **turn her into a parched land,**
> **and slay her with thirst.**

> ⁴ **I will not show my love to her children,**
>   **because they are the children of adultery.**
> ⁵ **Their mother has been unfaithful**
>   **and has conceived them in disgrace.**
> **She said, 'I will go after my lovers,**
>   **who give me my food and my water,**
>   **my wool and my linen, my oil and my drink.'"**

The prophet appeals to his children to rebuke their mother for her unfaithfulness to him. She has not acted like a wife. Therefore he will no longer be her husband. He appeals to Gomer to stop looking lustfully at other men and offering her body to them. Instead of depending on her faithful, loving husband to feed her, clothe her, and give her drink, she has been chasing after her lovers and giving them credit for providing what she needs. If this adulterous conduct continues, the punishment will be total disgrace. Everyone will see her shame, because her husband will take everything away from her, even her clothing. Left without food or drink, she will die of thirst. Her children will share in her disgrace. They have no claim on her husband's love, because they are not his children.

Again, Hosea represents the Lord in his faithful love for his people, and treacherous Gomer represents unfaithful Israel. The Lord's deep love for his people does not mean that he overlooks the idolatry that is tearing his beloved Israel away from him. The believers among his people ought to be rebuking their nation ("your mother," verse 2) for following idols. Israel is attributing to Baal, the Canaanite storm god, the blessings for which the nation ought to be thanking the Lord: rain, the fruits of the fields and olive groves, the products of the flock. The nation deserves to lose all these blessings, to become a parched and thirsty desert. The Israelites have forfeited the love of God because of their devotion to idols.

The Lord's love for his people is beyond all understanding. One measure of his love is that he rebukes their sin. He will not let them go their foolish way, because their way leads to death. He rebukes—because he cares. His love should be the model for ours. Sometimes we may need to speak to one of our fellow church members and say, "Your iniquities have separated you from your God" (Isaiah 59:2). Christians will rebuke their Christian brothers and sisters who fall into sin—because they care about them and want them to be saved.

Israel punished

> ⁶ "Therefore I will block her path with thornbushes;
> I will wall her in so that she cannot find her way.
> ⁷ She will chase after her lovers but not catch them;
> she will look for them but not find them.
> Then she will say,
> 'I will go back to my husband as at first,
> for then I was better off than now.'"

The Canaanite gods were local deities. That must have been one of their appealing qualities for the Israelites when they entered the land from the desert. In the wilderness they had been herdsmen. In Canaan they would raise grain, grapes and olives, as well as flocks and herds. Baal, Asherah, and Ashtoreth were already in place as fertility deities of the land. The Israelites forgot the Lord's stern command: "Break down their altars, smash their sacred stones, cut down their Asherah poles and burn their idols in the fire. For you are a people holy to the LORD your God. The LORD your God has chosen you out of all the peoples on the face of the earth to be his people, his treasured possession" (Deuteronomy 7:5,6).

If the Israelites will not give up their national devotion to the Canaanite gods, the Lord will take them where

Canaan's gods cannot go: back through the thorny wilderness into captivity. The prophet is speaking about the exile of God's people. Already in the reign of King Pekah (752–732 B.C.) Tiglath-Pileser king of Assyria "took Gilead and Galilee, including all the land of Naphtali, and deported the people to Assyria" (2 Kings 15:29). In 722 B.C. "the king of Assyria captured Samaria and deported the Israelites to Assyria. He settled them in Halah, in Gozan on the Habor River and in the towns of the Medes" (2 Kings 17:6). The harsh experience of exile will bring some of the Israelites to their senses. They will realize that, compared with life in exile, they were better off when the Lord was feeding them and leading them through the wilderness before they came to Canaan.

Sometimes only the bitter taste that remains after sinning is enough to bring us up short so that we return to the Lord. A person who is addicted to alcohol or other drugs loses health, family, and friends. A fornicator loses the freshness of youth and faces a lonely old age. A cheat finds that in the long run, he has cheated himself permanently out of his good name and self-respect. In such straits they may think back to a time when they enjoyed the love of God and the respect of their fellowmen. Like the prodigal son (Luke 15:17) they come to their senses and realize, "I was better off then than now." Sometimes God's children come home again on that rough and thorny way.

The Lord will take his gifts away

> [8] "She has not acknowledged that I was the one
> who gave her the grain, the new wine and oil,
> who lavished on her the silver and gold—
> which they used for Baal.
> [9] "Therefore I will take away my grain when it ripens,
> and my new wine when it is ready.

Baal

I will take back my wool and my linen,
> intended to cover her nakedness.
¹⁰ So now I will expose her lewdness
> before the eyes of her lovers;
> no one will take her out of my hands.
¹¹ I will stop all her celebrations:
> her yearly festivals, her New Moons,
> her Sabbath days—all her appointed feasts.
¹² I will ruin her vines and her fig trees,
> which she said were her pay from her lovers;
I will make them a thicket,
> and wild animals will devour them.
¹³ I will punish her for the days
> she burned incense to the Baals;
she decked herself with rings and jewelry,
> and went after her lovers,
> but me she forgot,"

> > > declares the LORD.

Moses warned the people of Israel on the border of the Promised Land, "When you have eaten and are satisfied, praise the LORD your God for the good land he has given you. Be careful that you do not forget the LORD your God, failing to observe his commands, his laws and his decrees that I am giving you this day" (Deuteronomy 8:10,11). It was because they forgot the Lord and his deliverance that the Israelites brought their sacrifices to Baal on the high places and no longer went to worship at the Lord's temple in Jerusalem. It was because the people were willing to forget the Lord that Jeroboam I and his successors on the throne of Israel could enforce their command to worship at Bethel and Dan.

The Lord will impoverish his people by taking away their food and clothing and all the products of the land. Israel will not escape his judgment. Surely the Baals will not save it:

25

"No one will take her out of my hands," the Lord says (verse 10). All the religious festivals—the annual pilgrimage festival proclaimed by Jeroboam I and the other holy days that Israel retained after separating from Judah—will cease, because the exiled people will no longer live in the land of Canaan.

In Canaanite religion, people burned their incense, offered their sacrifices, and performed their ceremonies with the thought that the god would respond to their worship by giving them abundant harvests and healthy flocks. As Baal's worshipers committed fornication with his prostitutes at the high places, so the god was supposed to respond by impregnating their fields with the autumn and winter rains. This was the religion adopted by Israel: she said her vines and her fig trees were "her pay from her lovers" (verse 12). As in all humanly devised religions, man did something for the god, and the god was supposed to respond with his blessings.

When Israel went into captivity, the neglected vineyards and fig trees were overgrown like a thicket. Instead of flocks and herds, wild animals inhabited the land. When the Assyrians settled heathen immigrants in the territory of Samaria, the Lord "sent lions among them and they killed some of the people" (2 Kings 17:25). He took back the blessings he had showered on Israel with his gift of the Promised Land. "All this took place because the Israelites had sinned against the LORD their God. . . . They worshiped other gods and followed the practices of the nations the LORD had driven out before them, as well as the practices that the kings of Israel had introduced" (2 Kings 17:7,8). "She . . . went after her lovers, but me she forgot," declared the Lord (verse 13).

It is easy to pray, "In all times of our tribulation, help us, good Lord." But the good Lord teaches us to pray for help in all the times of our prosperity as well. Especially in those times, we can easily forget him. The Israelites forgot the Lord in "a good and spacious land, a land flowing with milk and honey" (Exodus 3:8), which he had given them according to his promise. The warning God gave to his ancient people is as much in place for his well-off people today: "You may say to yourself, 'My power and the strength of my hands have produced this wealth for me.' But remember the LORD your God, for it is he who gives you the ability to produce wealth" (Deuteronomy 8:17,18).

Israel restored

> ¹⁴ "Therefore I am now going to allure her;
> I will lead her into the desert
> and speak tenderly to her.
> ¹⁵ There I will give her back her vineyards,
> and will make the Valley of Achor a door of hope.
> There she will sing as in the days of her youth,
> as in the day she came up out of Egypt.
> ¹⁶ "In that day," declares the LORD,
> "you will call me 'my husband';
> you will no longer call me 'my master.'
> ¹⁷ I will remove the names of the Baals from her lips;
> no longer will their names be invoked.

Sometimes when a marriage has sailed into rocky waters, the couple may repair their relationship by starting the voyage all over again. The husband courts his wife, and she responds as if he were wooing her for the first time. In the Lord's relationship with Israel, all the wrong is on Israel's side and all the undeserved love and care come from him. Yet even though Israel has gone her own uncaring way, the Lord woos her all over again. He pictures himself as a lover inviting his beloved to take a walk with him, so that he can

27

speak tenderly to her. Why? Israel forgot the Lord. "Therefore I am now going to allure her," he says (verse 14). Just because she has forgotten him, he goes after her. He loves her so much that he will not let her go without making every attempt to win her back.

Here is another side of Israel's exile. The same action of the Lord that punishes the Israelite nation for its stubborn idolatry is also a loving effort to win back the hearts of the individual members of his people. In grace the Lord will restore to a penitent people the vineyards that his just judgment took away.

The Valley of Achor—Achor means "trouble" or "disaster"—was the place where Achan was stoned after he disobediently took for himself clothing, silver, and gold from the condemned city of Jericho (Joshua 7). Achor thus comes to represent trouble as a result of disobedience. The exile—trouble because of Israel's disobedience—will be for some of the people of Israel an entrance to hope, because the Lord will use it to lead them to repentance. A repentant people will respond to the Lord's goodness with the first love that some of them showed when they followed his leading out of Egypt.

By Hosea's time the worship of the Lord at Bethel and Dan has become so "baalized" that the people even call the Lord "my Baal," which means "my master" (verse 16). Those Israelites who repent of their idolatry will respond to the Lord by recognizing him as the lawful, loving husband he has proved himself to be. He revealed his name, "the LORD," "I AM," through Moses (Exodus 3:14,15), and he wants to be remembered as the faithful and loving LORD of the covenant. Repentant Israelites will not call him "my Baal."

It is not hard for us to understand the judgment aspect of Israel's exile. Crime and punishment belong together. But

Hosea teaches us that in the heart of God, love burns hotter than anger. Even in the very act of punishing Israel's idolatry, he looks for repentance in his people. Even when he uproots them from the Promised Land, he is lovingly calling back the lost and working for the day when repentant Israelites will find their first love again.

Christians can testify that the fire of God's love burns just as hot today. He may tear a life to pieces, but he does so in order to heal. He injures in order to bind up the wounds (6:1). There is simply no limit to his promise that *"in all things* God works for the good of those who love him, who have been called according to his purpose" (Romans 8:28). The rebellious ingratitude of the whole sinful world could not extinguish his love, of which we sing: "Oh, love beyond all telling, that led you to embrace in love, all love excelling, our lost and fallen race!" (Christian Worship [CW] 18:2)

The Lord's great day of salvation

¹⁸ **"In that day I will make a covenant for them**
　　with the beasts of the field and the birds of the air
　　and the creatures that move along the ground.
Bow and sword and battle
　　I will abolish from the land,
　　so that all may lie down in safety.
¹⁹ **I will betroth you to me forever,**
　　I will betroth you in righteousness and justice,
　　in love and compassion.
²⁰ **I will betroth you in faithfulness,**
　　and you will acknowledge the LORD.

"In that day" the Lord will make a new covenant between his people and all the animals in creation. Disharmony between man and God, resulting from the fall into sin, also resulted in disharmony between man and nature. The ground was cursed and now produces thorns and thistles, and the animals are not willingly subject to fallen man. Instead, birds and beasts harm the crops and flocks. But "in that day," man and animals will live in harmony. The animals will be completely subject to man in that peaceful kingdom (see Isaiah 11:6-9).

The fall into sin also brought disharmony between men. Bow and sword—or bomb and missile—and battle give evidence of that disharmony in every age of the world's history. Israel experienced it in Hosea's time when the king of Assyria about 732 B.C. dismembered the kingdom of Pekah and made most of it into Assyrian provinces (2 Kings 15:29). But "in that day," everyone will be able to sleep safely, because God will have abolished war and weapons. "Nation will not take up sword against nation, nor will they train for war anymore" (Isaiah 2:4).

The deepest disharmony in the world is that between man and his Creator. The evidence is all around Hosea's people in their lack of faithfulness and love, in their refusal to acknowledge God, in the cursing, lying, murder, stealing, and adultery that fill their cities (4:1,2). But this enmity between man and God will also be ended "in that day." It will be like a new marriage, a betrothal ceremony in which God will promise himself to his people for life. As the bride-price, he will endow his people with his gifts, which will also totally transform their life with one another: righteousness, justice, steadfast love, and compassion will be found in Israel, because God's people will "acknowledge the LORD" (verse 20) as their faithful husband.

When will that day dawn? "That day" or "those days" are other ways of saying "the day of the LORD." That day will be a day of the Lord's judgment (Joel 2:31; Amos 5:18-20) and a day of his salvation (Joel 3:18-21; Amos 9:11-15). "Surely

the day is coming; it will burn like a furnace. All the arrogant and every evildoer will be stubble, and that day that is
coming will set them on fire. . . . But for you who revere
my name, the sun of righteousness will rise with healing in
its wings" (Malachi 4:1,2). "That day" is a prophetic way of
describing the time when God will come as Savior and
Judge.

The promises about "that day" are fulfilled in the coming
of Jesus. "God was reconciling the world to himself in
Christ" (2 Corinthians 5:19), and so he put an end to the
disharmony that disrupted his creation. "He comes to make
his blessings flow far as the curse is found" (CW 62:3). The
everlasting blessings of that reconciliation will be fully
revealed when Jesus comes again in glory. In Hosea's
words, he will betroth himself to his people forever.
"Blessed are those who are invited to the wedding supper
of the Lamb!" (Revelation 19:9) Thus the prophet's expression "that day" takes in the whole New Testament era and
eternity beyond.

> [21]"In that day I will respond,"
>   declares the LORD—
> "I will respond to the skies,
>   and they will respond to the earth;
> [22] and the earth will respond to the grain,
>   the new wine and oil,
>   and they will respond to Jezreel.
> [23] I will plant her for myself in the land;
>   I will show my love to the one I called 'Not my
>   loved one.'
> I will say to those called 'Not my people,' 'You are
>   my people';
>   and they will say, 'You are my God.'"

In a number of passages, the prophets describe the
blessings of the Messiah's kingdom with a picture of natural

plenty. Joel says that "the mountains will drip new wine, and the hills will flow with milk; all the ravines of Judah will run with water" (3:18). According to Amos, the harvest will be so bounteous that the reaper will still be at work when the plowman begins to get the land ready for the next year's crop (9:13). Hosea pictures the Lord responding with his Word to the waiting heavens, so that they can send down the rain; the heavens respond to the earth's need for moisture; and the earth responds to the need of the grain, vineyards, and olive trees for water and nourishment. Finally, grain, wine, and oil respond to the need of Jezreel ("God sows"), the name of Hosea's son, here representing the Lord's redeemed people.

God's people themselves will be planted in the land, never to be uprooted again (Amos 9:15). There will be a total reversal of Israel's fortunes, shown by a renaming of the prophet's other two children, who also represent the people of Israel. "Not loved" will now be named "Beloved," and "Not my people" will be named "My people," and they will confess to the Lord, "You are our God" (verse 23).

Should we expect that the Lord Jesus Christ will provide us with abundant grain, wine, and olive oil in his kingdom? As he is not an earthly king (John 18:36), so the blessings of his kingdom are not ordinary earthly food and drink. He himself, the Bread of Life, is what our souls need (John 6:35). His Word supports spiritual life, and his gospel, the assurance of everlasting life, makes our hearts glad. We have everything we need because he has said that he will never leave us or forsake us (Hebrews 13:5). The prophet illustrates the spiritual blessings of the kingdom of God in terms of the earthly blessings of Old Testament Israel.

Should we expect that the Jewish people will be "planted" in the land of Canaan in the last times? Some teachers would say so. But the children of Abraham to whom this promise is made are the ones to whom Paul says: "You are all sons of God through faith in Christ Jesus. . . . If you belong to Christ, then you are Abraham's seed, and heirs according to the promise" (Galatians 3:26,29). Paul also quotes Hosea 2:23 in Romans 9:25 to teach the same truth. To all Christians, Jews, and Gentiles, Peter repeats the promise of blessing given through Hosea: "Once you were not a people, but now you are the people of God; once you had not received mercy, but now you have received mercy" (1 Peter 2:10).

Hosea's reconciliation with his wife

3 The LORD said to me, "Go, show your love to your wife again, though she is loved by another and is an adulteress. Love her as the LORD loves the Israelites, though they turn to other gods and love the sacred raisin cakes."

²So I bought her for fifteen shekels of silver and about a homer and a lethek of barley. ³Then I told her, "You are to live with me many days; you must not be a prostitute or be intimate with any man, and I will live with you."

⁴For the Israelites will live many days without king or prince, without sacrifice or sacred stones, without ephod or idol. ⁵Afterward the Israelites will return and seek the LORD their God and David their king. They will come trembling to the LORD and to his blessings in the last days.

Hosea's wife, Gomer, has left him. She has entered an adulterous union with someone else. If we were startled by the Lord's first command to the prophet, "Go, take to yourself an adulterous wife" (1:2), this second command surely goes beyond all human understanding. If a woman was divorced and then was married to another man, the law of the Lord said that her first husband was not to take her back again (Deuteronomy 24:1-5). Such conduct was not to be sanctioned in Israel. Yet the Lord directs Hosea not only to provide for adulterous Gomer again but even to love her.

Again the prophet's love illustrates the love of God. Israel has turned to idols—Baal, and the calf of Bethel—not just once but many times. They love to eat or offer sacred raisin cakes—apparently a part of Canaanite idol worship. (In Jeremiah 7:18 the women bake bread cakes for a goddess, the "Queen of Heaven.") When the Lord rebuked his people, they refused to listen to his prophets. Yet he still cares about them, provides for them, loves them. Here Hosea buys back his wife from her lover by paying the price of a slave for her: about 6 ounces of silver and 9 or 10 bushels of barley. With Hosea's purchase of Gomer, the Lord is picturing his faithful love that remains constant through all of Israel's unfaithfulness.

Why did the Lord choose Israel at the beginning of her national history? "It was because the LORD loved you and kept the oath he swore to your forefathers that he brought you out with a mighty hand and redeemed you from the land of slavery, from the power of Pharaoh, king of Egypt" (Deuteronomy 7:8). Why does the Lord call Israel back and, so to speak, chase after she when she has abandoned him? His abiding love for his people makes him willing to go to all lengths to make them his own again.

The command the prophet gives his wife to save herself only for him is explained in the next verse. The Israelites in their exile will no longer have a king or princes of their own. Because they will be uprooted from Canaan, they will not be able to participate in Canaanite worship either. They will not be able to make their sacrifices to Baal. They will not visit the symbols of the deities in Canaan, the sacred stones like the one at Bethel (Genesis 28:18,19) or at the heathen high places. They will not use the ephod, the priestly garment

(Exodus 28:6-8) employed for consulting the will of God (1 Samuel 23:9-12), which also developed into some sort of idol (Judges 8:27). Nor will they worship the Canaanite teraphim or household gods (see Genesis 31:34). In their exile they will also be separated, of course, from the prescribed sacrifices and worship of the true God in the temple at Jerusalem.

What will be the purpose of this separation from both true and false worship? Israel needs to learn that the Lord does not send his salvation in response to man's sacrifices. God saves freely, out of his mercy and undeserved love. His deliverance of the remnant of his people from the exile will lead them to come trembling in awe to seek him, his promised blessings, and his promised Savior, the Son of David (2 Samuel 7:11-16). It is not man's worship that brings salvation down from God. Rather, the Lord stoops down from heaven with his grace and salvation. Thus he and his free gifts inspire true worship.

Except for an isolated reference ("your mother"—4:5), this is the end of the story of Hosea's marriage. It is suggested by some Bible students that Hosea did not actually marry Gomer but that the Lord's command was symbolic. Some have asked: if the Lord did not permit a priest to marry either a prostitute or a divorced woman (Leviticus 21:7), how could he let his prophet Hosea marry a woman like Gomer?

The Lord who made a rule for priests could disregard his rule when he gave a special mission to his prophet Hosea. Such details as the name "Gomer, daughter of Diblaim" (neither name has any special meaning), the conception of her children, and the price the prophet paid to buy her back make it seem quite plain that the events actually occurred. The prophet, his wife, and their real marriage

35

symbolize the Lord, his people the Israelites, and the relationship between them. Gomer is an adulterous wife; Israel has been unfaithful to the Lord. The Lord loves his people with an everlasting love; Hosea loves Gomer faithfully and makes every effort to keep her for his own.

Through our disgust with foul and fickle Gomer, can we sense in some small way how sin, any and all sin, must appear in God's sight? We have our own pet sins and they live with us constantly, like dogs or cats in our houses. By no means, however, can God see our sins as if they were harmless pets in his family. Any sin can separate us from God, because it shows that something else is more precious to our hearts than our Father and his will. Covetousness, for example, is idolatry, and "because of such things God's wrath comes on those who are disobedient" (Ephesians 5:6). Can we learn to recognize in adulterous Gomer a picture of our foul and fickle selves? That is hard for us to see, and hard to admit when we see it, because "the heart is deceitful above all things and beyond cure. Who can understand it?" (Jeremiah 17:9)

The Scriptures use many comparisons for the love of God. His love for those who fear him is as great as the heavens are high above the earth (Psalm 103:11). He has compassion on his people as a father has compassion on his children (Psalm 103:13). Surely among all those comparisons one of the most vivid pictures of God's love for sinners is the real-life love of the prophet Hosea for unworthy Gomer. Only in the life and death of Jesus do we see more plainly God's eternal purpose "to seek and to save what was lost" (Luke 19:10).

Thus the first three chapters of the book of Hosea illustrate what Paul says: "Christ died for the ungodly" (Romans 5:6) and "Christ Jesus came into the world to save sinners—of whom I am the worst (1 Timothy 1:15). Hosea illustrates the undeserved love of God for each of us: "Love that found me—wondrous thought!—found me when I sought him not" (CW 385:2).

PART TWO

The Prophet's Message
(4:1–14:9)

The Lord's charge against Israel

4 Hear the word of the LORD, you Israelites,
because the LORD has a charge to bring
against you who live in the land:
"There is no faithfulness, no love,
no acknowledgment of God in the land.
² There is only cursing, lying and murder,
stealing and adultery;
they break all bounds,
and bloodshed follows bloodshed.
³ Because of this the land mourns,
and all who live in it waste away;
the beasts of the field and the birds of the air
and the fish of the sea are dying.

The Lord summons all of the people of Israel into court to answer charges. The Israelites are not dependable in carrying out their obligations. They do not show faithful love and loyalty by keeping the promises they make to one another. They refuse to acknowledge the Lord as their God. Instead, they disregard his will in word and deed so that all kinds of sins pollute the land he gave his people. The judge pronounces his sentence: there will be a great drought, so that the animals of the land, air, and water will die.

One God, the Lord, stands behind both the moral law and the laws of nature. His one harmonious rule extends over all things. Sun and clouds, vegetation and animals obey his Word without fail, but sinful mankind disregards his commandments. Even the nation he especially chose and blessed refuses to acknowledge him. The Lord uses his rule over nature to reprove Israel's rebellion. Through Moses he warned at Mount Sinai, "If you will not listen to me and carry out all these commands, and if you reject my decrees and abhor my laws and fail to carry out all my commands and so violate my covenant, then I will do this to you. . . . I will break down your stubborn pride and make the sky above you like iron and the ground beneath you like bronze. Your strength will be spent in vain, because your soil will not yield its crops, nor will the trees of the land yield their fruit" (Leviticus 26:14-16,19,20).

Many people today recognize neither moral law, summed up in the Ten Commandments, nor the laws of nature, such as the physical principles that govern the weather, as evidence of the Creator's authority. They believe that people accept moral law only because it is their social tradition or because they were trained that way in their childhood. They may also think that the laws of nature are just a matter of multiple physical causes and effects.

Scripture teaches that one God, the same Lord who spoke through Hosea and the other prophets, commands righteousness in his law, declares sinners righteous because of Christ's perfect righteousness and also totally controls the natural universe—land, sea, air, and outer space. He may bless or he may withhold blessing. Jesus says, "*All* authority in heaven and on earth has been given to me" (Matthew 28:18). Do we remember this truth as we read our daily paper and watch the evening news? Do we remember it when we pray?

The Lord will punish people and priests

⁴ "But let no man bring a charge,
  let no man accuse another,
for your people are like those
  who bring charges against a priest.
⁵ You stumble day and night,
  and the prophets stumble with you.
So I will destroy your mother—
⁶   my people are destroyed from lack of knowledge.

"Because you have rejected knowledge,
  I also reject you as my priests;
because you have ignored the law of your God,
  I also will ignore your children.
⁷ The more the priests increased,
  the more they sinned against me;
  they exchanged their Glory for something disgraceful.
⁸ They feed on the sins of my people
  and relish their wickedness.
⁹ And it will be: Like people, like priests.
  I will punish both of them for their ways
  and repay them for their deeds.

We know that the Hebrew scribes worked with painstaking care and even counted the letters when they copied the Scriptures by hand before printing was invented. Yet in quite a few verses of Hosea, perhaps more than in any other book of the Old Testament, the Hebrew text seems to have suffered in the course of being copied and recopied by the scribes. Further, Hosea writes in an abrupt style, so that we may not always follow the intended connection between sentences. Verses 4 and 5 of chapter 4 are difficult to understand. It is plain, however, that verse 6 and following are addressed to the priests in Israel. We therefore interpret verses 4 and 5 in a way that fits their connection with verse 6.

When we meet difficult verses in the Scriptures, we try to understand them in their context and in the light of other clear passages.

The priests of Israel, as leaders of the people's worship, bear a special responsibility for the sins that fill the land, described in the first verses of this chapter. "The lips of a priest ought to preserve knowledge, and from his mouth men should seek instruction—because he is the messenger of the LORD Almighty" (Malachi 2:7). When the people of Israel live immoral lives, they themselves are to blame. Yet the people's sinful actions are like witnesses bringing charges against the priesthood, because the priests are their teachers and examples.

Israel's other spiritual leaders are the prophets. The prophets in Israel, except for the few true spokesmen of the Lord such as Hosea and Amos, prophesy by Baal (Jeremiah 2:8). Both the unfaithful priests and the false prophets are blind guides leading the blind. Instead of showing the people the Lord's straight path, they "stumble day and night" (verse 5): they constantly fail to give the people clear guidance concerning God's will and a good example of a God-fearing life. The Lord will destroy Israel for lack of spiritual knowledge. In verse 5 the nation is referred to as the "mother" of the individual Israelites, recalling Gomer and her children in chapters 1 to 3.

The priests are guilty of more than simple ignorance. They are willfully rejecting the knowledge of God that he has given them in his Word. Such leaders disqualify themselves as servants of God, and the Lord, accordingly, rejects them. Since they go their own way in willful disobedience to the law of Moses, the Lord says that he will ignore their children. The hereditary priesthood will come to an end.

Jeroboam I "appointed priests for the high places from all sorts of people. Anyone who wanted to become a priest he consecrated for the high places" (1 Kings 13:33). Perhaps the kings in Hosea's time are continuing this practice. But as the number of priests multiplies in Israel, their larger numbers mean only an increase of idolatry and immorality, not a more widespread worship of the true God. Instead of serving the Lord, the true glory of Israel, Israel's spiritual leaders serve "something disgraceful"—Baal and Ashtoreth (verse 7). By enjoying their portion of the offerings the people bring to the calf-shrines and high places, the priests are feeding on the wicked idolatry of Israel and relishing it. "Like people, like priests" (verse 9): the people and their spiritual leaders are alike in their idolatry, and the Lord will punish them in the same way. All of them will suffer his punishment together.

Comparing his prophet to a "watchman for the house of Israel," the Lord told Ezekiel: "Hear the word I speak and give them warning from me. When I say to a wicked man, 'You will surely die,' and you do not warn him or speak out to dissuade him from his evil ways in order to save his life, that wicked man will die for his sin, and I will hold you accountable for his blood" (Ezekiel 3:17,18). And in the New Testament, the Lord tells us that our spiritual leaders keep watch over us "as men who must give an account" (Hebrews 13:17).

While all of us should make it our purpose to know the Lord and the teaching of his written Word, our pastors and teachers bear an especially heavy responsibility before God. Shepherds who ignore the Word can lead many sheep to ruin. Luther could have been commenting on many of today's religious leaders when he wrote in one of his hymns:

> With fraud which they themselves invent
> Thy truth they have confounded;
> Their hearts are not with one consent
> On Thy pure doctrine grounded.

> While they parade with outward show,
>> They lead the people to and fro,
>> In error's maze astounded.
>>>> (The Lutheran Hymnal [TLH] 260:2)

On the other hand, faithful pastors and teachers instruct us in the pure Word of God. They call us to repent of our sins, and they speak the word of forgiveness to penitent sinners. Through the good news that they preach and the sacraments they administer, God himself reaches down to us from heaven with his gracious gifts of forgiveness and everlasting life. Such leaders deserve to be followed and honored as ambassadors of Christ. We pray that our Savior would give us faithful pastors and teachers, so that we and our children will not be eternally "destroyed from lack of knowledge," as Israel was.

A people without understanding will come to ruin

¹⁰ "They will eat but not have enough;
> they will engage in prostitution but not increase,
because they have deserted the LORD
> to give themselves ¹¹to prostitution,
to old wine and new,
> which take away the understanding ¹²of my people.
They consult a wooden idol
> and are answered by a stick of wood.
A spirit of prostitution leads them astray;
> they are unfaithful to their God.
¹³ They sacrifice on the mountaintops
> and burn offerings on the hills,
under oak, poplar and terebinth,
> where the shade is pleasant.
Therefore your daughters turn to prostitution
> and your daughters-in-law to adultery.

¹⁴ "I will not punish your daughters
> when they turn to prostitution,

> **nor your daughters-in-law**
> **when they commit adultery,**
> **because the men themselves consort with harlots**
> **and sacrifice with shrine prostitutes—**
> **a people without understanding will come to ruin!**

The division of verses 10 through 12, varying from one translation to another, again shows the difficulty of the Hebrew text. Yet the trend of Hosea's words is clear.

The people can gain no lasting satisfaction from the eating and wine drinking the prophet refers to, since it is a part of Baal religion. Israelite worshipers are feasting, sacrificing to idols in the pleasant shade under the trees at the Canaanite high places, and having intercourse with prostitutes to make their crops, flocks, and families increase. Such conduct is an abomination to the all-powerful, creating Lord God, the giver of every good gift. He will surely not send his blessings in response to Israel's prayers and sacrifices at the Baal shrines.

How senseless idol worshipers become when they are led astray by their own lustful appetites! The Israelites have become so foolish that they worship a wooden idol and use a divining rod, perhaps throwing a special stick on the ground and carefully observing how it falls to determine the will of their gods. Like a wife unfaithful to her true husband, Israel abandons the almighty, living Lord to commit physical and spiritual adultery in the worship of lifeless, powerless idols.

Idol worship is leading to sad experiences in Israelite families. Daughters and daughters-in-law are following their fathers to the Baal shrines and becoming cult prostitutes. Thus the fathers, by their bad example, are bringing judgment not only on themselves but also on their children. Their immoral conduct is destroying their families and ruining their nation. As the children follow their fathers' sinful example, the Lord will show that he means what he said: "I, the LORD your God, am a jealous God, punishing the children for the sin of the fathers to the third and fourth generation of those who hate me" (Exodus 20:5). Children and grandchildren will have to follow their parents and grandparents into exile.

Adultery and fornication are not generally disguised under the outward forms of divine worship in the world today. It seems to be one of the marks of our time, however, to let sexual desires have their way without concern for the will of God. Our reproductive powers, including sexual desire, were implanted in us by our Maker when he created the human race male and female and said, "Be fruitful and increase in number; fill the earth and subdue it" (Genesis 1:28). He made us sexual beings so that we may enjoy his gifts of marriage and children. But since man's fall, we sinners are constantly tempted to serve a *created* power such as sex rather than the *Creator himself* (Romans 1:25). Led by blind lust, fornicators even disregard the earthly consequences of their sin, disease and death. Children still learn the most by their parents' example, and they easily follow their fathers and mothers in immorality. Unreined sexual indulgence destroys both families and nations. "A people without understanding will come to ruin" both in this world and eternally.

Let not Judah become guilty

> [15] "Though you commit adultery, O Israel,
>   let not Judah become guilty.
>
> "Do not go to Gilgal;
>   do not go up to Beth Aven.
>   And do not swear, 'As surely as the LORD lives!'
> [16] The Israelites are stubborn,
>   like a stubborn heifer.

> How then can the LORD pasture them
>   like lambs in a meadow?
> [17] Ephraim is joined to idols;
>   leave him alone!
> [18] Even when their drinks are gone,
>   they continue their prostitution;
>   their rulers dearly love shameful ways.
> [19] A whirlwind will sweep them away,
>   and their sacrifices will bring them shame.

Hosea is prophesying in Israel, the Northern Kingdom, but his message is also meant for the kingdom of Judah. The Israelites are already far gone into idolatry, and the Lord holds up their sad example of disobedience to warn the Jews in Jerusalem against following the same way to ruin.

Evidently Gilgal, where the people observed the rite of circumcision and first celebrated the Passover in the Promised Land (Joshua 5), has become an Israelite place of worship. Hosea later speaks of "their wickedness in Gilgal" (9:15; see also Amos 5:5). Bethel, meaning "house of God," where the Lord appeared to Jacob (Genesis 28:10-22), was the place chosen by Jeroboam I for one of his calf-shrines. Therefore, Hosea mockingly calls it Beth Aven, meaning "house of wickedness."

The prophet warns the people of both Israel and Judah against going up to the shrines where false worship is practiced. In his law the Lord permitted his people to swear necessary oaths by his name (Deuteronomy 6:13), but when the Israelites of Hosea's time take an oath, the prophet says, they have no right to use the oath terminology "as surely as the LORD lives" (verse 15). They have no right to use his name, because they no longer fear the Lord as their God. They have mixed his worship with the worship of Baal.

Hosea's adulterous wife, Gomer, presents just one striking picture of the persistent unfaithfulness of God's people.

Another comparison the prophet uses in verse 16 will be easily understood by the peasants of Israel. Israelite farmers used cattle to pull their plows. If the people in their attitude toward the Lord and his law act like a young, unbroken heifer, stubbornly resisting the yoke, how can he tenderly care for them the way a shepherd tends young lambs?

Idol festivals and ritual prostitution do not accomplish their intended purpose of producing larger supplies of grain and wine. Yet Ephraim (another name for the Northern Kingdom) and its rulers stubbornly continue their shameful idolatry. "Leave him alone!" the Lord says (verse 17), because his patience has come to an end. How can he help his people if they will not listen to him? The Lord will bring shame, not salvation, upon the Israelites because of their sacrifices to Baal. Assyrian armies will sweep the nation away into captivity, as if all Israel were being wrapped in the wings of a whirlwind.

Judah will not learn a lesson from the judgment that overtakes Israel in 722 B.C. Later the Lord complains through the prophet Jeremiah: "I gave faithless Israel her certificate of divorce and sent her away because of all her adulteries. Yet I saw that her unfaithful sister Judah had no fear; she also went out and committed adultery" (Jeremiah 3:8). The same worship practices that bring shame and death to the Northern Kingdom are invading the South. Therefore, a little more than a century after the fall of Samaria, the Lord will send the Babylonian armies to carry out his judgment upon Judah, and many of the Jews will follow Israel into captivity.

It is said that those who will not learn from history are condemned to repeat it. That has been true in the history of the kingdom of God. In the Bible the Lord records the story both of his faithful grace and of his people's stubborn unbelief.

We who enjoy his gracious favor today need to learn from the history he has recorded for us. Will we Christians turn away from our Savior-God to worship the idols of our time, pleasure, and material success, or will we take a lesson from Israel's sad history and trustingly follow the Word of Jesus? Are we permitting the moral indifference of today's world to invade the church, as Israel and Judah adopted the immorality of the Canaanites, or will we, with the promised help of the Holy Spirit, live our lives according to the Word of the Lord who saved us from our sins? When the Israelites committed spiritual adultery with their idols, the Lord warned through his prophet, "Let not Judah become guilty" (verse 15). Yet Judah foolishly followed Israel's example. Today the Lord is warning us through the examples of both Israel and Judah. May we Christians heed that warning!

Judgment on Israel and its princes

5 "Hear this, you priests!
　　Pay attention, you Israelites!
　Listen, O royal house!
　　This judgment is against you:
　You have been a snare at Mizpah,
　　a net spread out on Tabor.
² The rebels are deep in slaughter.
　　I will discipline all of them.
³ I know all about Ephraim;
　　Israel is not hidden from me.
　Ephraim, you have now turned to prostitution;
　　Israel is corrupt.

⁴ "Their deeds do not permit them
　　to return to their God.
　A spirit of prostitution is in their heart;
　　they do not acknowledge the LORD.

⁵ Israel's arrogance testifies against them;
  the Israelites, even Ephraim, stumble in their sin;
  Judah also stumbles with them.
⁶ When they go with their flocks and herds
    to seek the LORD,
  they will not find him;
    he has withdrawn himself from them.
⁷ They are unfaithful to the LORD;
  they give birth to illegitimate children.
Now their New Moon festivals
  will devour them and their fields.

In chapter 4 Hosea admonished all Israel and then especially the priests. In chapter 5 he adds a judgment from the Lord against the royal house of the Northern Kingdom. Like the priests, the civil leaders of the nation bear a heavier responsibility than ordinary citizens. Since the Israelite people are God's chosen nation, his law revealed through Moses is their nation's basic law, or constitution. Civil officials in Israel are to be guided by the word of the Lord.

Yet now the kings, beginning with Jeroboam I, have entrapped their fellow Israelites in idolatry and sin the way a hunter catches birds in a net or small animals in a snare. Hosea mentions incidents of this kind, not known to us in detail, that occurred at Mizpah, just south of Bethel on the border between the Northern and Southern Kingdoms, and at Mount Tabor, north of the Valley of Jezreel.

In Hosea's time the last royal houses of Israel are being founded by "rebels . . . deep in slaughter" (verse 2). Zechariah, the son of Jeroboam II, rules for only six months before Shallum forms a conspiracy and assassinates him in 752 B.C. Shallum is in turn murdered by Menahem only a month later. After Menahem's ten-year reign, his son Pekahiah reigns only two years before dying a violent death at the hands of his officer Pekah about 740 B.C. Pekah has a longer term on the throne, but about 732 B.C. he is assassinated by Hoshea, the last ruler of the Northern Kingdom (2 Kings 15:8-30). The rebels plot against their royal masters in secret corners, but they cannot hide their treacherous, corrupt hearts from the Lord.

Israel is following a course familiar to many sinners. "Everyone who sins is a slave to sin" (John 8:34). People and princes have become addicted to immoral Canaanite ways. The Israelites no longer even desire to turn back to the Lord and to acknowledge him as their God. Instead of being ashamed, they are proud of what they have become. Therefore, they continue to stumble about in dark ignorance of the Lord's will. Nor does the Southern Kingdom learn anything from the sad example of Israel. Judah stumbles with her sister-kingdom.

Perhaps even while they worship Baal and Ashtoreth on one day, the people hedge their bets a day later by going "with their flocks and herds to seek the LORD" (verse 6), bringing sacrifices to be offered on his altar. Through Hosea, God lets them know that he is not pleased with divided, half-hearted service. Elijah, in disgust, asked the Israelites a century earlier: "How long will you waver between two opinions? If the LORD is God, follow him; but if Baal is God, follow him" (1 Kings 18:21). Even if the idol-serving Israelites take whole flocks and herds of animals to be sacrificed to the Lord, "they will not find him; he has withdrawn himself from them" (verse 6).

The mention of illegitimate children in verse 7 recalls the history of Hosea's own marriage. The Israelites have joined themselves to Baal by participating in the fertility cult at the idol shrines. Thus they have borne "children of unfaithfulness," as Gomer did (1:2).

The inhabitants of the land probably celebrate New Moon festivals on their high places, just as the beginning of each month was an occasion for special sacrifices in the Lord's temple (Numbers 10:10; 28:11-15). Instead of enjoying the fruits of the land as a reward for their Canaanite worship, as Baal's priests are promising, the Israelites will finally lose the land itself to the Assyrian armies. The sin that first charms God's people then entraps them, devours them and robs them of the blessings they have received from the Lord.

It is a story that has been repeated many times. Children of God begin to play with the sins they see around them. They think they can return to the Lord any time. But sin is a power that finally does not permit the sinner to escape. Not only drunkenness and drug abuse but all sin is addictive. Persistent disobedience hardens the heart, until finally sinners discover that the Lord has "withdrawn himself from them" (verse 6), and only the unavoidable judgment remains. May our God and Savior keep our feet from the beginning of such a path! If we have already taken the first steps, may we listen to his voice today as he calls us to repent. The Father and all his angels still rejoice over every lost son who is found again (Luke 15).

The Lord will be like a lion to Ephraim

[8] **"Sound the trumpet in Gibeah,**
the horn in Ramah.
Raise the battle cry in Beth Aven;
lead on, O Benjamin.
[9] **Ephraim will be laid waste**
on the day of reckoning.
Among the tribes of Israel
I proclaim what is certain.
[10] **Judah's leaders are like those**
who move boundary stones.

I will pour out my wrath on them
like a flood of water.
[11] Ephraim is oppressed,
trampled in judgment,
intent on pursuing idols.
[12] I am like a moth to Ephraim,
like rot to the people of Judah.

[13] "When Ephraim saw his sickness,
and Judah his sores,
then Ephraim turned to Assyria,
and sent to the great king for help.
But he is not able to cure you,
not able to heal your sores.
[14] For I will be like a lion to Ephraim,
like a great lion to Judah.
I will tear them to pieces and go away;
I will carry them off, with no one to rescue them.
[15] Then I will go back to my place
until they admit their guilt.
And they will seek my face;
in their misery they will earnestly seek me."

The time is about 735 B.C. Rezin, king of the Arameans in Damascus, and Pekah, king of Israel, have decided to rebel against the powerful and active Assyrian king, Tiglath-Pileser III, because he has bled their countries dry by the high tribute he is exacting (2 Kings 15:19,20). The only way the Israelites and Arameans can possibly succeed is to enlist all the minor kings of Syria-Palestine in their cause.

King Ahaz of Judah will not join their rebellion, and so Pekah and Rezin decide to attack Jerusalem and replace Ahaz on the throne. (2 Kings 16:5,6). (In Isaiah chapter 7, we hear the story from the viewpoint of Isaiah, the Lord's prophet in Jerusalem.) The Arameans and Israelites inflict heavy casualties on the Southern Kingdom and take many Jewish prisoners (2 Chronicles 28:5-8).

Ahaz, refusing to trust in the Lord's deliverance, sends messengers to say to Tiglath-Pileser, king of Assyria: "I am your servant and vassal. Come up and save me out of the hand of the king of Aram and of the king of Israel, who are attacking me" (2 Kings 16:7). Tiglath-Pileser responds with three campaigns into Syria and Palestine in 734, 733, and 732 B.C. He captures Damascus, kills King Rezin and strips away northern, eastern, and western territories from the kingdom of Israel, leaving King Hoshea to rule only a few square miles around Samaria.

From the prophet's words in verse 8 and following, it seems that King Ahaz also leads a Judean army north to join his overlord Tiglath-Pileser in punishing Israel. The Judean army moves north to Gibeah, a fortress about four miles from Jerusalem, and then to Ramah a little farther north, near the border of the two kingdoms. The next target will be Beth Aven ("house of wickedness"), Hosea's scornful name for Bethel ("house of God"), the calf-shrine just north of the Judean-Israelite border. The soldiers from Benjamin mentioned in verse 8 would be one element in the Judean army, invading their sister-kingdom Israel from the south, while the north is laid waste by the Assyrians.

This is Israel's day of reckoning with the Lord, who is carrying out his judgment in history through the Assyrian and Judean armies. Yet Judah also incurs guilt by trampling the territories of her sister-kingdom. The Judeans are acting like a man who enlarges his own land holdings by moving the stones that mark the borders of his neighbor's field (see Deuteronomy 27:17). Therefore the Lord will also pour out his anger on Judah like a destructive flood. It is his loving will to help and save his people in every trouble, but because of their unbelief, he becomes "like a moth to Ephraim, like rot to the people of Judah" (verse 12). He sends the Assyrians to gnaw away at Israelite territories like a moth in wool or rot in an old building. Isaiah describes the Assyrian invasion of Judah in 700 B.C. with a picture of the mighty Euphrates River in flood: "It will overflow all its channels, run over all its banks and sweep on into Judah, swirling over it, passing through it and reaching up to the neck" (Isaiah 8:7,8).

When the Lord's people forget him, they look for salvation elsewhere. During this period in their history, both Judah and Israel frequently turn to Egypt and Assyria for help. King Menahem of Israel, about a decade before the war, gave Tiglath-Pileser III a thousand talents (about 37 tons!) of silver "to gain his support and strengthen his own hold on the kingdom" (2 Kings 15:19). Now Judah is turning in the same direction for help against Israel and Syria. Hosea compares his people to a hopelessly sick man looking for a new doctor to heal him. The people's real sickness is an idolatrous trust in Baal and in various human helpers. Because of their unbelief, the Lord is bringing his judgment upon them. What remedy can "Dr. Tiglath-Pileser" apply to heal such an infection?

The Assyrians may think they are forming their own battle plans, but without their knowledge they and their armies are serving as the paw of a "great lion" (verse 14), the Lord himself. The Lord is carrying out his judgment against the people he loves and desires to save. Within about ten years, in 722 B.C., he will let the Assyrians, like a lion snatching a lamb away, capture Samaria and carry Israel off into exile. Later he will send Assyrian armies pouring over Judah, as if the lion were coming down a second time on the same flock of sheep. Only by the Lord's miraculous answer to King Hezekiah's prayer will Jerusalem be spared from destruction for another century (2 Kings 19; Isaiah 37).

Samaria's destruction and the exile of Israel are a well-deserved judgment following a long history of idolatry and disobedience. But destruction and captivity are also a final piercing call from their physician-Father who wants his children to admit their guilt so that he can heal them. In prosperity they forgot him and pursued idolatrous pleasures; in adversity they turned to earthly helpers; perhaps in their miserable captivity, they will remember the Lord, admit their guilt, and "seek [his] face" (verse 15), that is, beg for his undeserved favor.

When Israel and Judah faced adversity, they frantically searched for earthly helpers. They forgot that they were the Lord's holy nation, chosen for his special purpose of sending salvation to all mankind. They acted as though they were earthly nations no different from all the rest around them.

"My kingdom is not of this world," Jesus told Pilate. "For this reason I was born, and for this I came into the world, to testify to the truth. Everyone on the side of truth listens to me" (John 18:36,37). Jesus fights his battles with spiritual weapons. The church of Jesus Christ is called to represent him on earth. The church is here to testify to the good news of the forgiveness of sins. This message has the power to change hearts and to create faith, so that men hear the voice of Jesus.

When the church forgets its special purpose on earth and makes of itself just one more human organization among others on earth, it is falling into the same trap that destroyed Israel and Judah. If the church neglects the gospel and trusts in other means, such as the power of the state, to force people into membership, if it depends on social programs rather than the preaching of the Word to attract a following, or if it tries to coax people into worshiping and giving their support because of the charm of some leader's personality, then the church is acting like just one more earthly organization among others. A church that does not trust the power of the Word of God will look for help elsewhere. As Judah and Israel learned, to their sorrow, such "help" in the end will be as destructive as moths and rot.

If we are accomplishing less and less in the Lord's service, we easily turn to other helpers. Instead, we need to examine our relationship to him. Does he own our hearts, or have we given them to other gods? Are we depending on the power of the Lord as his Spirit works through Word and sacraments? When teaching the Word does not seem to have spectacular results, let us not turn away from our God to other helpers, as Israel and Judah did. "You do not want to leave too, do you?" Jesus asks us (John 6:67). By being faithful witnesses to his whole Word, let us answer with Simon Peter: "Lord, to whom shall we go? You have the words of eternal life. We believe and know that you are the Holy One of God" (John 6:68,69).

What can be done with impenitent Israel?

6 "Come, let us return to the LORD.
He has torn us to pieces
   but he will heal us;
he has injured us
   but he will bind up our wounds.
² After two days he will revive us;
   on the third day he will restore us,
   that we may live in his presence.
³ Let us acknowledge the LORD;
   let us press on to acknowledge him.
As surely as the sun rises,
   he will appear;
he will come to us like the winter rains,
   like the spring rains that water the earth."

⁴ "What can I do with you, Ephraim?
  What can I do with you, Judah?
 Your love is like the morning mist,
   like the early dew that disappears.
⁵ Therefore I cut you in pieces with my prophets,
   I killed you with the words of my mouth;
   my judgments flashed like lightning upon you.
⁶ For I desire mercy, not sacrifice,
   and acknowledgment of God rather than burnt offerings.

Frequently in Hebrew poetry, the speaker changes without any advance indication. (There are no quotation marks in the original text.) In verses 1 through 3 Israel is speaking. The Lord responds in verses 4 through 6.

Why do we call Israel impenitent in the heading of this section? The Lord is waiting "until they admit their guilt" (5:15), but as the Israelites exhort each other to "return to the LORD" in the first three verses of this chapter, their words do not include even the hint of a confession of sin. When they say that the Lord "has torn us to pieces" and "has injured us," they refer to the military defeats they have suffered and the tribute they must pay, not to the painful knowledge of their own guilt. The "healing" and "binding up" they look for are victory in war and deliverance from oppression. Judging by the Lord's response in verse 6, we see that Israel plans to "press on to acknowledge the LORD" (verse 3) by appearing in his sanctuary loaded down with offerings. Such an expression of devotion, Israel thinks, should bring the nation's troubles to an end. We hear not one word confessing the sin of idolatry.

Certainly the people give a beautiful description of the patience of the Lord. If his people return to him, will he not appear and pour out a blessing on them? His past favor has been like the fall rain that softens the earth for plowing. Will his mercies not come down again, like the abundant winter and spring rains that water the fields and produce a harvest? Aren't his blessings available to Israel at any time?

The Lord has heard this song before. Israel has abused his patience. He does not intend to let his people manipulate him, as if they could sing a repentance song or bring a sacrifice and then he must respond with his favor, as if he were a god like Baal. He has seen often enough how Ephraim—Israel, the Northern Kingdom—and Judah profess love for him and then run after their idols again. (Remember Hosea's wife, Gomer!) They turn to him for an hour, but the next hour their faith and love have disappeared, as the dew or the morning mist are burned off by the sun. He has sent his prophets to cut their stubborn hearts to pieces, to kill their self-righteous old Adam, to shatter their pride with the lightning bolts of his law. Do they think that they can satisfy the holy Lord God and escape the pain of saying "I have sinned, Father" just by singing a lovely bit of liturgy and by piling sacrificial animals on his altar?

What, then, does the Lord want? "I desire mercy, not sacrifice, and acknowledgment of God rather than burnt offerings" (verse 6). The word translated *mercy* means "faithful love." The Lord has shown his own faithful love to his people by making and keeping his covenant with them. He has proved true to all his promises in the past and has revealed the further promise of a Savior, who will bless all nations. He seeks faithful love from his people in return. All the animal sacrifices required in the law mean nothing if they are not brought as an expression of Israel's trust in the Lord and his promises. He wants his people to acknowledge God, that is, to trust in him alone as their Savior and Lord. All the burnt offerings described in Leviticus are worthless if Israel does not bring them in faithful love for the God who is his people's only deliverer and King.

What will be the proof of such faithful love and loyalty to the Lord? A penitent Israel will change the situation Hosea described in 4:1,2: "There is no faithfulness, no love, no acknowledgment of God in the land. There is only cursing, lying and murder, stealing and adultery . . . and bloodshed follows bloodshed." It will be as Jesus describes when he quotes Hosea 6:6 in Matthew 9:13 and 12:7: his people will show their loyalty to Israel's faithful God by worshiping him in their daily lives. They will look out for the spiritual and physical needs of their fellow Israelites. In their love for their fellowmen, they will reflect the love of their own forgiving God. They will defend the powerless, clothe the naked, and feed the hungry, showing mercy to others as their God has shown mercy to them.

The Lord leads us through Hosea's words to reexamine our own worship life. He kills us with the words of his mouth (verse 5) to lead us to acknowledge our sins and repent. He also chastises us with failure and hardship to call us back to him, our only helper. In his words and promises concerning Jesus Christ, he displays his faithful love to us, so that we will trust in him alone as our Savior. He looks for thankful fruits of repentance and faith in our lives. Such fruits appear when we worship the Lord in our workaday world by daily showing his mercy to our neighbors in all their needs. He is also pleased as we express our love for him in formal public worship with our hymns, prayers, and offerings.

Examples of unfaithfulness among God's people

> [7] "Like Adam, they have broken the covenant—
>   they were unfaithful to me there.
> [8] Gilead is a city of wicked men,
>   stained with footprints of blood.

> ⁹ As marauders lie in ambush for a man,
>   so do bands of priests;
> they murder on the road to Shechem,
>   committing shameful crimes.
> ¹⁰ I have seen a horrible thing
>   in the house of Israel.
> There Ephraim is given to prostitution
>   and Israel is defiled.
>
> ¹¹ "Also for you, Judah,
>   a harvest is appointed.

In this last part of chapter 6 and the beginning of chapter 7, the Lord indicts Israel for particular offenses. "Adam" in verse 7 could be the first human being, or it could be the name of a city on the Jordan (Joshua 3:16), where the Israelites had in some outrageous way exhibited their unfaithfulness to the Lord's covenant. Then we would translate "As at Adam, they have broken the covenant." The Hebrew text need not express the word *at*. The word *there* in the parallel half of the verse makes the city name the more likely explanation. Hosea's first listeners and readers would recognize the incident he refers to, but we have no further record of it.

The city of Gilead (see also 12:11), otherwise unknown to us, may be either in the hill country of Gilead east of the Jordan or near Mount Gilead on the edge of the Valley of Jezreel (Judges 7:3). The crime of Gilead, a city "stained with footprints of blood" (verse 8), sounds like an offense for which the whole city is somehow responsible. Perhaps notorious killers have remained unpunished by the city elders. On the road to Shechem, gangs of priests ambush a man and murder him. When such crimes are tolerated among the Israelites, their whole land is defiled. The Northern Kingdom is the first target of Hosea's words, but Judah cannot point the finger at her sister Israel. Judah also has sown adulterous disobedience to the Lord, and he has therefore appointed a harvest of judgment (verse 11).

Israel's indifference to public sin means disregard for the Lord and for his law. The same sickness of moral indifference is infecting our communities today. If open sin remains unreproved, the whole community—church or state—becomes guilty. Government, according to Scripture, is "God's servant, an agent of wrath to bring punishment on the wrongdoer" (Romans 13:4). If the state fails to punish crime, it encourages criminals to break the law more boldly.

When the apostle Paul hears of open sexual immorality within a Christian congregation, he expects that the church will deal with the impenitent sinner and excommunicate him so that he may repent (1 Corinthians 6; see also Matthew 18:15-18). Willful, unrepented breaking of God's commandments leads to the sinner's everlasting death. If the sin is public and unreproved, the moral rot spreads to other lives as well. One openly impenitent sinner who remains unreproved can lead many other souls to hell with him.

Israel does not return to the Lord

7 ¹ Whenever I would restore the fortunes of my people,
** **whenever I would heal Israel,
the sins of Ephraim are exposed
**   and the crimes of Samaria revealed.**
They practice deceit,
**   thieves break into houses,**
**   bandits rob in the streets;**
² **but they do not realize**
**   that I remember all their evil deeds.**
Their sins engulf them;
**   they are always before me.**

³ "They delight the king with their wickedness,
    the princes with their lies.
⁴ They are all adulterers,
    burning like an oven
  whose fire the baker need not stir
    from the kneading of the dough till it rises.
⁵ On the day of the festival of our king
    the princes become inflamed with wine,
    and he joins hands with the mockers.
⁶ Their hearts are like an oven;
    they approach him with intrigue.
  Their passion smolders all night;
    in the morning it blazes like a flaming fire.
⁷ All of them are hot as an oven;
    they devour their rulers.
  All their kings fall,
    and none of them calls on me.

The Lord still has one purpose for his people: to restore their fortunes (6:11). Through his chastisement he wants to heal Israel spiritually, so that he may pour out on his people the full abundance of his earthly and eternal blessings. Israel, however, reveals its stubborn sin-sickness by turning away from its physician. The Israelites deceive themselves when they take no notice of such open sins as housebreaking and banditry in the streets. Their holy God remembers all the evil deeds that surround them on every side. As long as they do not turn to him in faith, their sins constantly testify against them in his court.

At the beginning of chapter 7, Hosea particularly mentions the crimes of Samaria, the capital of the Northern Kingdom. Kings and princes, the nation's guardians of justice, do not reprove and punish their people's crimes. Instead, they take pleasure in Israel's deceitful wickedness. Hosea describes their hearts as being like a baker's oven. An ancient oven would usually be a clay structure 2 or 3 feet in diameter. A fire would be built on the pebbles that formed the oven floor. When the oven was hot enough, the baker would scoop out the embers and stick flat cakes of dough to the inside of the oven or lay them on the pebbles to bake. Thus he would be heating up the oven while he prepared the dough. The hearts of the Israelite people and princes are hot with lust for idol worship and wickedness, hot as a baker's fire that needs no stirring up the whole time he is mixing and kneading the bread.

A baker would remove the fire from the oven and let the embers burn out, but that is not how sin works. Sinful desires smoldering in the heart do not burn themselves out but blaze up in sinful deeds. The prophet cites a specific example that takes place "on the day of the festival of our king" (7:5), perhaps the festival instituted by King Jeroboam I (1 Kings 12:32). It seems that the king joins in the scornful mockery with which his drunken princes offend Israel's God. Their sin devours the king himself, as the Lord allows the princes' rebellion to punish the guilt of the king. In a dozen years of Hosea's ministry, three men become kings of Israel by assassinating their predecessors on the throne (2 Kings 15:10,14,25). In deep sadness the Lord describes the spiritual state of Israel's princes, the victims as well as their murderers: "None of them calls on me" (verse 7).

Hosea has violently condemned the sins of Israel's people, priests, false prophets, courtiers, and kings. Perhaps after several chapters of such condemnation, his preaching sounds almost monotonously negative to us. Yet we must never overlook the positive purpose of the Lord: to bring his people to repentance, so that they will call on him for forgiveness and peace. He wants to heal, bind up, revive and restore them, so that they may live in his presence now and be with him in heaven forever (6:1,2).

His purpose for us is the same. Perhaps we sometimes become tired of hearing the word *sin* in liturgies and sermons. But we need to recognize our sin-sickness before we are willing to turn to Christ for healing. Not that sorrow over our sins saves us. Salvation is God's free gift through faith alone. Yet both the Lord's law and his gospel have their purposes in his way of salvation. God's law leads us to know our sins so that we will gladly hear and believe the good news that he has justified us through Christ's redemption and now accepts us as his own. "If we claim to be without sin, we deceive ourselves and the truth is not in us. If we confess our sins, he is faithful and just and will forgive us our sins and purify us from all unrighteousness" (1 John 1:8,9).

Ephraim has strayed from the Lord

⁸ "Ephraim mixes with the nations;
   Ephraim is a flat cake not turned over.
⁹ Foreigners sap his strength,
   but he does not realize it.
His hair is sprinkled with gray,
   but he does not notice.
¹⁰ Israel's arrogance testifies against him,
   but despite all this
he does not return to the LORD his God
   or search for him.

¹¹ "Ephraim is like a dove,
   easily deceived and senseless—
now calling to Egypt,
   now turning to Assyria.
¹² When they go, I will throw my net over them;
   I will pull them down like birds of the air.
When I hear them flocking together,
   I will catch them.

¹³ Woe to them,
    because they have strayed from me!
  Destruction to them,
    because they have rebelled against me!
  I long to redeem them
    but they speak lies against me.
¹⁴ They do not cry out to me from their hearts
    but wail upon their beds.
  They gather together for grain and new wine
    but turn away from me.
¹⁵ I trained them and strengthened them,
    but they plot evil against me.
¹⁶ They do not turn to the Most High;
    they are like a faulty bow.
  Their leaders will fall by the sword
    because of their insolent words.
  For this they will be ridiculed
    in the land of Egypt.

The kingdom of Israel in Hosea's time is like an unturned, flat cake of bread on the hot surface of an oven. Such an unturned cake burns on the bottom, where the damage is unseen. Israel looks and acts like a nation among other nations. Yet thereby she destroys herself, because she forgets her calling as the Lord's chosen people. She makes alliances with Egypt to save herself from Assyria. Then she makes alliances with Assyria to save herself from other nations. In all of this, she forgets her one and only almighty Savior.

Foreign overlords sap Israel's strength by requiring the payment of murderous amounts of tribute, such as the thousand talents (37 tons) of silver King Menahem paid Tiglath-Pileser III (2 Kings 15:19,20). Israel is like a man getting old and gray but becoming no wiser in the process. Even when experiments with foreign alliances repeatedly fail, the

Israelites continue on their own arrogant way. They will not return to the Lord their God for help. In fact, they do not even "search for him" (verse 10).

The mournful cry of the dove sounds like a plea for help (Isaiah 38:14). But the dove is a simple, mindless bird. Israel, like a silly pigeon, first flutters and coos in the direction of Assyria, as in King Menahem's time, and then turns to Egypt. Tiglath-Pileser III punishes rebellious Israel by stripping away some of its territories and a part of its population (2 Kings 15:29). But the foolish pigeon does not learn and soon goes fluttering off again in another direction.

Sometime after Hoshea, the last ruler of the Northern Kingdom, comes to the throne, he sends envoys to So, king of Egypt, and withholds tribute that has been promised and annually paid to the king of Assyria. "Therefore Shalmaneser [the Assyrian king who succeeded Tiglath-Pileser] seized him and put him in prison. The king of Assyria invaded the entire land, marched against Samaria and laid siege to it for three years. In the ninth year of Hoshea, the king of Assyria captured Samaria and deported the Israelites to Assyria" (2 Kings 17:4-6). The Lord finally destroys Israel because of the very alliances that the Israelites hope will save them. He pulls them down like an ancient fowler catching a flock of foolish pigeons in his net. "Woe to them," he says, "because they have strayed from me" (verse 13).

Behind the failure of Israel's foreign policy lies a loss of faith. The Lord longs to redeem his people, to make them his own again, to hear them cry out to him from their hearts in sincere repentance. Instead, they speak lies against him by naming idols "master"—the meaning of the name Baal—and "god." They may wail on their beds because of their national misfortunes, but their mind is not on the sins that have separated them from the Lord. Instead, their bellies

are growling for grain and new wine, the rewards promised by the idol priests in exchange for Baal worship.

In verse 14 an uncommon verb form is translated "they
gather together." Perhaps the Hebrew letter *r* has been
exchanged twice for the very similar Hebrew letter *d* as
scribes recopied the text, and the translation should read
"they slash themselves." The Baal priests described in
1 Kings 18:28 cut themselves with knives in order to waken
their god's pity and to coax him to answer their prayer. Perhaps the desperate Israelites are praying to Baal in the same
way during Hosea's time.

It was the Lord who trained his people the Israelites in
Egypt during the nation's childhood (11:1-4) and who has
continued to strengthen them from their youth on. How do
they repay his faithfulness? They turn away from him and
plot evil against him by planning to persist in their idolatry
and to seek help from heathen kings. They act like a carefully crafted bow that cracks and makes the bowstring go
slack when the archer tries to shoot with it. The Lord cannot
depend on his people to be faithful. He will surely punish
the Israelites' insolent unbelief. Their leaders will die in battle. Once the Lord brought Israel out of Egypt with his
mighty arm, but now the Egyptians will laugh at these
Israelites who foolishly rebel against Assyria.

The Lord our God did not *need* Israel's worship, and he
does not *need* ours. Heaven is his throne and the earth his
footstool (Isaiah 66:1), and so he has no need for men's
praises and gifts. He invites sinners to return to him and to
trust in him for two reasons. (1) He alone deserves all the
glory for saving mankind. "I am the LORD; that is my name!"
he says. "I will not give my glory to another or my praise
to idols" (Isaiah 42:8). (2) It is especially for his people's
own sake that he calls them back to him. Israel had no

other Savior, and neither do we. That is why he warns our proud hearts against entanglements with all other helpers: idols cannot save. The Lord is considering our need when he looks for worshipers who are humble and contrite in spirit and who tremble at his word (Isaiah 66:2).

The Lord's anger burns against Israel

8 "Put the trumpet to your lips!
 An eagle is over the house of the LORD
 because the people have broken my covenant
 and rebelled against my law.
² Israel cries out to me,
 'O our God, we acknowledge you!'
³ But Israel has rejected what is good;
 an enemy will pursue him.
⁴ They set up kings without my consent;
 they choose princes without my approval.
With their silver and gold
 they make idols for themselves
 to their own destruction.
⁵ Throw out your calf-idol, O Samaria!
 My anger burns against them.
How long will they be incapable of purity?
⁶   They are from Israel!
This calf—a craftsman has made it;
 it is not God.
It will be broken in pieces,
 that calf of Samaria.

With increasing clarity Hosea describes the punishment that God will send upon the idolatry and disobedience of Israel. The Lord summons the prophet to warn Israel of his approaching judgment the way a watchman on the city walls sounds the alarm with a ram's horn when an enemy approaches. The eagle soaring over the Lord's house is a

Idolaters worship a calf-god

bird of prey. "Eagle" is the same word translated "vulture" in Habakkuk 1:8 to describe enemy cavalry swooping down: "Their horses are swifter than leopards, fiercer than wolves at dusk. Their cavalry gallops headlong; their horsemen come from afar. They fly like a vulture swooping to devour." Now the eagle or vulture is soaring over "the house of the LORD," here meaning not the temple but the Israelite nation.

The Lord leaves no doubt about the reason for his judgment: even while the Israelites claim that the Lord is still their God, they have broken their covenant with him by rejecting "what is good" (verse 3). They are saying "Lord, Lord," but then paying no attention to the will of their Father in heaven (Matthew 7:21-23). In verse 4 the prophet cites two examples of Israel's rebellion. First, the people of the Northern Kingdom have rejected the Davidic royal house to set up their own kings. In the last decades of the kingdom of Israel, the palace in Samaria almost seems to be built with a revolving door, as one king after another usurps the throne without consulting the will of the Lord.

The second evidence of covenant breaking is idolatry. The Israelite metalworkers make silver and gold images of the fertility deities. Further, the people continue to flock to Bethel and Dan to worship at the shrines of the calf-idols set up by Jeroboam I. Such images are receiving the worship that belongs only to the invisible almighty God, the Lord of Israel. The calf-idols of Samaria, worshiped at Bethel and Dan, deserve to be thrown out. The Lord's burning anger will send an enemy, "the mighty king" of Assyria (verse 10), to humble an impure, rebellious people. Samaria's man-made golden calf will be smashed to smithereens.

If we think that our hearts are free from idolatry because we do not pray to a golden calf, we need to hear Luther explain the Lord's First Commandment: "That to which your heart clings and entrusts itself is, I say, really your god." It is as if the Lord—Israel's Lord and ours—were saying to us, "See to it that you let me alone be your God, and never seek another. Whatever good things you lack, look to me for it and seek it from me, and whenever you suffer misfortune and distress, come and cling to me. I am the one who will satisfy you and help you out of every need. Only let your heart cling to no one else" (Large Catechism, page 9). Our mouths say, "Lord, Lord," but in bad times all of us are tempted to turn to other helpers first. We call ourselves his chosen people, but in good times we credit *ourselves* with our prosperity. Are we all that different from the Israelites?

Israel will reap the whirlwind

⁷ "They sow the wind
    and reap the whirlwind.
The stalk has no head;
    it will produce no flour.
Were it to yield grain,
    foreigners would swallow it up.
⁸ Israel is swallowed up;
    now she is among the nations
    like a worthless thing.
⁹ For they have gone up to Assyria
    like a wild donkey wandering alone.
    Ephraim has sold herself to lovers.
¹⁰ Although they have sold themselves among the nations,
    I will now gather them together.
They will begin to waste away
    under the oppression of the mighty king.

The Lord, through Hosea, again condemns Israel's faithless foreign policy of alliances with heathen nations. To "sow the wind" means to act in a foolish way that can produce no good result. Planting wind does not produce a crop. No shoots will sprout; no grain will be harvested to be ground into flour; if by chance a stalk should happen to grow, it will do Israel no good. The Assyrians will gain any benefit that may come of Israel's alliances with them.

In fact, the Israelites will "reap the whirlwind": their Assyrian allies will destroy them. Tiglath-Pileser III chews up and swallows most of Gilead and Galilee already during King Pekah's reign, and some of Israel's citizens are exiled among foreign nations (2 Kings 15:29). Yet again Israel angles for alliances with Assyria like an unbroken wild donkey running its willful way. She persistently follows the direction of the Baal priests like a prostitute returning to the street to sell herself to lovers. Instead of receiving payment, Israel will waste away, first under a ruinous burden of tribute imposed by the king of Assyria and then from the conquests of his armies.

Not only the Israelites' Baal worship but also their search for heathen allies was a kind of idolatry. The Lord wanted to be his people's helper in every trouble. Israel turned instead to a mighty earthly king. If "that to which your heart clings and entrusts itself is . . . really your god," as Luther explains, Israel's god was the king of Assyria.

The test of true faith often comes when we are in trouble. If our nation is in danger, is our first thought for adequate weapons and armed forces? If the trouble involves our property, do we ask first whether we have enough money to see us through? If the problem concerns our health, do we first seek help from the best medical or surgical specialist we can afford? Earthly resources like the strength of our nation or the size of our fortune and earthly helpers like our physicians and surgeons are gifts of God. Yet if the gifts take the giver's place in our hearts, they have become false gods. Like Israel, we destroy ourselves if we depend on helpers that can fail and cling to comforts that can flee. Our God invites us to turn to him and his unchanging mercy first and above all and to trust him for whatever we need in every trouble. Then we may also freely and gratefully use whatever earthly resources he provides to help us.

The Lord will send fire upon their cities

¹¹ "Though Ephraim built many altars for sin offerings,
    these have become altars for sinning.
¹² I wrote for them the many things of my law,
    but they regarded them as something alien.
¹³ They offer sacrifices given to me
    and they eat the meat,
    but the LORD is not pleased with them.
Now he will remember their wickedness
    and punish their sins:
    They will return to Egypt.
¹⁴ Israel has forgotten his Maker
    and built palaces;
    Judah has fortified many towns.
But I will send fire upon their cities
    that will consume their fortresses."

In verses 11 and 13, Hosea speaks of two kinds of sacrifices, examples of Israel's worship: sin offerings and fellowship offerings. The blood of the sin offering (Leviticus 4:1–5:13; 6:24-30) was sprinkled before the Lord, and the internal fat was burned. In some cases the priest, representing the Lord, received the meat of the sin offering for food; in other cases the meat was burned outside the camp. This sacrifice pointed to and promised the forgiveness of sins to be won by the death of the coming Savior.

But in Ephraim, the kingdom of Israel, the very altars built for sin offerings have become "altars for sinning"

73

(verse 11). Here the people bring their sacrificial bulls, goats, lambs, and pigeons, but they offer their sacrifices without faith in the Lord and his promise of forgiveness. The animals are also being offered at the Baal altars, through the Baal priests, in order to win Baal's blessing for the crops in the fields and the animals in the pastures. The Israelites are very religious, but how can their offerings please the Lord when they are disregarding his First Commandment?

Hosea reminds the people that the Lord is looking for faith that trusts his promises and brings sacrifices out of love for him. Such faith worships especially by hearing and keeping the word of God. Moses wrote the law for Israel by the Lord's inspiration (note God's expression "I wrote for them the many things of my law"), but the Israelites are acting as if the Lord had given his commandments to some other, foreign nation. Therefore none of their sacrifices can please him. King Saul once failed to kill some captured animals according to the Lord's command because he wanted to offer them as sacrifices to the Lord. But Samuel told him, "Does the LORD delight in burnt offerings and sacrifices as much as in obeying the voice of the LORD? To obey is better than sacrifice, and to heed is better than the fat of rams" (1 Samuel 15:22). Hosea is saying the same.

In the fellowship offering, sometimes called the peace offering, the animal's blood was also sprinkled against the altar. As in the sin offering, fat from the animal was burned. But the worshiper ate a part of the meat of the fellowship offering, and the priest, representing the Lord, also ate a portion (Leviticus 3; 7:11-27). The Israelite worshipers are bringing their fellowship offerings and eating their portion of the meat, but the Lord says that he has no fellowship with them. They are not members of his family.

Instead of forgiving the Israelites' sins, he will remember their wickedness and punish them by sending them back to "Egypt" (verse 13): that is, they will become slaves in a foreign country, just as their ancestors were seven centuries ago, before the Lord delivered them through Moses. This time Assyria will be the land of their captivity. See 9:3, where the word *Egypt* in the first half of the verse is explained in the second half with the parallel *Assyria*, the foreign land where the Israelites will become slaves again.

Besides their idolatry and their sacrifices offered without faith in the Lord, the Israelites display other signs of godlessness. Rich men are building luxurious palaces: Amos tells us that they adorn the walls with ivory panels. They may erect one house for a summer residence and another for the winter (Amos 3:15). God's people are becoming "complacent in Zion . . . secure on Mount Samaria" (Amos 6:1). The prosperous citizens of both Israel and Judah live for their luxuries and trust in the fortifications they have built to protect their proud cities from foreign enemies. They have forgotten who their Creator and protector is. Baal is just one of their many gods. Wealth is another.

Therefore the Assyrian armies will carry out the Lord's judgment by burning Israel's cities and fortresses. Layers of burnt rubble on the city-mounds of Israel will testify to all ages that the Lord is in earnest when he adds a threat as well as a promise to his First Commandment: "I am the LORD your God, who brought you out of Egypt, out of the land of slavery. You shall have no other gods before me. . . . for I, the LORD your God, am a jealous God, punishing the children for the sin of the fathers to the third and fourth generation of those who hate me, but showing love to a thousand generations of those who love me and keep my commandments" (Exodus 20:2-6).

Is it possible for Christians to choose death rather than life and to lose faith and salvation, as Israel did? Paul writes in the New Testament about Hymenaeus and Alexander, who rejected faith and a good conscience "and so have shipwrecked their faith" (1 Timothy 1:19). Many Israelites under the influence of Canaanite religion also "shipwrecked their faith" in the Lord and his promised Savior. As a result, their nation was destroyed and the individuals in it who did not repent were lost eternally.

Speaking of the Lord's judgment upon Israel's unbelief, Paul says: "These things happened to them as examples and were written down as warnings for us, on whom the fulfillment of the ages has come. So, if you think you are standing firm, be careful that you don't fall!" (1 Corinthians 10:11,12). God does not write down warnings against unreal dangers. It is possible for Christians to fall from faith. Satan still tempts God's people to serve false gods. He wants to trick us into adopting the morality of the society around us. He tries to persuade us to depend on earthly helpers with the trust that belongs to the Lord alone.

But believers lose their faith only if they trust in themselves and so choose death rather than life. The same merciful God and Savior who creates faith in our hearts also *keeps us* in faith by means of his Word and sacraments. We are "shielded by God's power until the coming of the salvation that is ready to be revealed in the last time" (1 Peter 1:5). As Paul tells us: "God is faithful; he will not let you be tempted beyond what you can bear. But when you are tempted, he will also provide a way out so that you can stand up under it" (1 Corinthians 10:13). May every Christian hear the Apostle's earnest warning and avoid the path that led Israel to destruction: "My dear friends, flee from idolatry" (1 Corinthians 10:14).

Exile for idolatrous Israel

9 Do not rejoice, O Israel;
　　do not be jubilant like the other nations.
　For you have been unfaithful to your God;
　　you love the wages of a prostitute
　　at every threshing floor.
² Threshing floors and winepresses will not feed the people;
　　the new wine will fail them.
³ They will not remain in the LORD's land;
　　Ephraim will return to Egypt
　　and eat unclean food in Assyria.
⁴ They will not pour out wine offerings to the LORD,
　　nor will their sacrifices please him.
　Such sacrifices will be to them like the bread of mourners;
　　all who eat them will be unclean.
　This food will be for themselves;
　　it will not come into the temple of the LORD.

The harvest season is a happy time for any agricultural people. Perhaps Hosea is preaching this sermon during an Israelite harvest festival. If the Lord, the maker and ruler of heaven and earth, has chosen the people of Israel over all the other nations to be his treasured possession and has given a bountiful harvest besides, one would think that Israel should be happy, even happier than all the other nations.

But idolatrous, adulterous Israel has been unfaithful to the Lord, her loving husband, who gave her the land and all its fruits. She has prostituted herself to the Canaanite deities, accepting bountiful harvests and overflowing winepresses as if they were a harlot's hire from her lover Baal. The Lord who owns the land and provides every grain of wheat and every drop of wine informs his unfaithful people that their threshing floors and winepresses cannot "feed" or tend them (verse 2) the way their almighty Shepherd fed them in the wilderness and in Canaan. Now he will take away their prosperity, not by locust, plague, or drought but by uprooting the Israelites and sending them off to be captives in a foreign land, as they once lived in Egypt (verse 3). In their Assyrian exile, they will have to eat food that Hosea calls ceremonially unclean, because their crops will be produced by the fields of a pagan people and cannot be consecrated to the Lord in the prescribed firstfruits offering (Leviticus 23:9-14; Deuteronomy 26:1-11). (See also Amos 7:17, where Assyria, the land of Israel's captivity, is called an unclean land.)

When Israel is exiled to Assyria, the temple offerings prescribed by the law will be impossible. There will be none of the libations of wine that accompanied the morning and evening sacrifices at the Lord's altar (Exodus 29:38-40), none of the fellowship offerings to be consumed by the worshipers in the presence of their God, with the priests eating their share as the Lord's representatives (Leviticus 7:11-36). The Israelites will have to eat their food alone in a foreign land, far from the Lord's temple. They will be like mourners, ceremonially unclean because they have touched a corpse. Unable to participate in the fellowship feasts at the Lord's temple (Leviticus 7:19-21), they will sadly eat their bread alone.

Canaanite worship was a religion in which the worshipers did their part—bringing offerings, participating in the fertility rituals at the shrines—in order to induce the god to do his part—filling the worshipers' threshing floors and winepresses with abundance. The blessings of harvest were considered payment for services rendered to Baal. That is why Hosea calls Israel's harvests the wages of a prostitute. The true religion of Israel described by Moses and the prophets was faith in the covenant promise of the Lord, to be joyfully confessed by the worship he specified in his law. The harvests of grain and wine, like every other blessing, were to be received with thanksgiving as gifts of the Lord's unmerited grace.

Do we think of going to church, supporting the Lord's work, and being Christ's witnesses in the world as acts we perform to gain our God's favor? When we receive blessings from the Lord, do we think he is paying us for the services we render him? Then, even though we call our God "the Lord" and not "Baal," we are worshiping with the Canaanites and with unfaithful Israel. Such worship cannot please God. Let us rather trust in his gracious New Covenant promise of the forgiveness of sins, guaranteed in the death of his Son, Jesus. Then we will joyfully offer him our hymns and prayers, our offerings of money, and our Christian witness as fruits of faith in our Savior. Such worship is acceptable to our God.

The days of reckoning are at hand

⁵ What will you do on the day of your appointed feasts,
   on the festival days of the LORD?
⁶ Even if they escape from destruction,
   Egypt will gather them,
   and Memphis will bury them.
  Their treasures of silver will be taken over by briers,
   and thorns will overrun their tents.
⁷ The days of punishment are coming,
   the days of reckoning are at hand.
   Let Israel know this.
  Because your sins are so many
   and your hostility so great,
  the prophet is considered a fool,
   the inspired man a maniac.

> **8 The prophet, along with my God,**
>   **is the watchman over Ephraim,**
> **yet snares await him on all his paths,**
>   **and hostility in the house of his God.**
> **9 They have sunk deep into corruption,**
>   **as in the days of Gibeah.**
> **God will remember their wickedness**
>   **and punish them for their sins.**

Three times a year, at the Feasts of Unleavened Bread, Harvest, and Ingathering, all Israelite males were to appear at the temple according to the law of Moses (Exodus 23:14-17). What will the Lord's people do for such festivals when the exile has taken them far from Canaan? The worship prescribed in the law will be impossible.

Perhaps a few of the Israelites will flee to northern Egypt to escape the Assyrian armies, just as some residents of the Southern Kingdom will do later (see Jeremiah 44:1). They will die and be buried in cities such as Memphis, south of the Nile delta, far from the Promised Land. (Another interpretation of verse 6 would say that "Egypt" and "Memphis" are metaphors for Assyria, the land of Israel's exile, as in verse 3.) All the Israelites' wealth will disappear. Thistles and briers will take over their abandoned fields. Israel should know that "the days of reckoning are at hand" (verse 7). An impenitent people will pay the penalty for years of idolatry with years of exile.

The Israelites' hostility toward the Lord shows itself in their rejection of his messengers the prophets. It seems that Hosea is being received in his homeland, Israel, with the same hostility Amos experienced when he came from Judah to preach at Bethel (Amos 7:10-17). The Israelites consider the prophet a fool and a madman because the Spirit of God has inspired him to prophesy defeat and exile. His message is out of tune with their Canaanite harvest festivals. The prophet serves his people as the Lord's own "watchman for the house of Israel" (Ezekiel 3:17), pointing out present spiritual dangers and warning about the coming judgment. Yet his guilty people hate him as an enemy. They try to lay traps for him wherever he goes and even show their "hostility in the house of his God" (verse 8).

The treatment Hosea and Amos receive in Israel reminds us of the words of Jesus: "I am sending you prophets and wise men and teachers. Some of them you will kill and crucify; others you will flog in your synagogues and pursue from town to town" (Matthew 23:34). Through such messengers the Lord seeks to gather and protect his people, "as a hen gathers her chicks under her wings," but again and again they refuse to return to him. "You were not willing," he must sadly conclude (Matthew 23:37). When the Lord God himself finally comes in the flesh to save his people, they shout "Crucify him!" (Matthew 27:22).

Hosea compares his times with the days of the Judges, when Israel had no king and "everyone did as he saw fit" (Judges 21:25). Sodomites in Gibeah abused a woman until she died, and then the men of Benjamin, rather than punishing such an outrage, went to war against their fellow Israelites to defend the criminals (Judges 19-21). The Lord does not overlook such flagrant sinning. Rather, "God will remember their wickedness and punish them for their sins" (verse 9).

When a prophet such as Hosea faithfully repeats the message he is called to proclaim, God himself is speaking through him. This is also true of our pastors and teachers today, as long as they teach according to the inspired Scriptures. When he sent his disciples out to preach, the Lord Jesus said, "He who listens to you listens to me; he who rejects you rejects me; but he who rejects me rejects him who sent me" (Luke 10:16). Our pastors, who "keep watch over [us]," (Hebrews 13:17), must speak God's law to us, put the finger on our sins, and warn us of sin's consequences. God exposes our sin through the law in order to tell us the good news about Jesus Christ, the Savior of sinners. Then, through his messengers, God himself speaks to us from heaven to forgive our sins and to promise us eternal life. Prophets and apostles, pastors and teachers deserve to be heard with respect, because of the Lord who sends them and for the sake of the precious good news they bring.

Beloved Israel is now rejected

¹⁰ "When I found Israel,
　　it was like finding grapes in the desert;
　when I saw your fathers,
　　it was like seeing the early fruit on the fig tree.
　But when they came to Baal Peor,
　　they consecrated themselves to that shameful idol
　　and became as vile as the thing they loved.
¹¹ Ephraim's glory will fly away like a bird—
　　no birth, no pregnancy, no conception.
¹² Even if they rear children,
　　I will bereave them of every one.
　Woe to them when I turn away from them!
¹³ I have seen Ephraim, like Tyre,
　　planted in a pleasant place.
　But Ephraim will bring out
　　their children to the slayer."

¹⁴ Give them, O Lord—
　　what will you give them?
　Give them wombs that miscarry
　　and breasts that are dry.

¹⁵ "Because of all their wickedness in Gilgal,
　　I hated them there.

> Because of their sinful deeds,
>> I will drive them out of my house.
> I will no longer love them;
>> all their leaders are rebellious.
> ¹⁶ Ephraim is blighted,
>> their root is withered,
>> they yield no fruit.
> Even if they bear children,
>> I will slay their cherished offspring."
>
> ¹⁷ My God will reject them
>> because they have not obeyed him;
>> they will be wanderers among the nations.

Twice in this section of text, the prophet speaks in the first person for the Lord (verses 10-13; 15,16), and then he expresses his own concurrence with God's just judgment (verses 14 and 17).

The Lord recalls the days when he chose Israel to be his people, the days of their first love. The lover wants to praise his beloved. We could imagine Hosea saying such tender words to his dear Gomer: "When I first found you it was like finding grapes in a desert oasis or like seeing the sweet early fruit on the fig tree."

But already on the way out of Egypt, when Israel was camping in Moab, "the men began to indulge in sexual immorality with Moabite women, who invited them to the sacrifices to their gods. The people ate and bowed down before these gods. So Israel joined in worshiping the Baal of Peor," the Moabite god named for a mountain in the wilderness (Numbers 25:1-3). Israel, the Lord's new bride, dedicated itself to the shameful rituals of Moabite religion, which must have resembled the fertility cult of the Canaanites. The Lord's own chosen people became as detestable as their idol.

Even in the last decades of Israel's national life, the Lord is permitting the nation to enjoy a measure of prosperity. Israel has enjoyed being planted like a tree in a pleasant meadow. God's people enjoy a favored place, like powerful Tyre on the coast of Phoenicia. Yet the people attribute their prosperity to Baal and Ashtoreth. Giving the best they have to the Canaanite fertility deities, they even sacrifice their sons and daughters in the fire (2 Kings 17:17).

The Lord will punish Israel's devotion to the Canaanite gods with barren wombs instead of fertility. Perhaps Hosea is describing a time of war when all the young men eligible for marriage are being killed in battle, so that no husbands remain. In such a time, there will be "no birth, no pregnancy, no conception" (verse 11). The few women who are able to raise children will be forced to bring them out of their captured cities to be massacred by enemy soldiers.

Hosea assents to the Lord's judgment with his prayer, one of the Bible's most chilling words of judgment: "Give them wombs that miscarry and breasts that are dry" (verse 14). Not enjoying the blessing of children at all would be better for the Israelites than to see their babies helpless in the hands of cruel Assyrian soldiers. It reminds us of what Jesus said when women wailed for him on his way to the cross. "Daughters of Jerusalem, do not weep for me; weep for yourselves and for your children. For the time will come when you will say, 'Blessed are the barren women, the wombs that never bore and the breasts that never nursed!'" (Luke 23:28,29). Better to not bring children into the world at all than to see them consumed in the Lord's terrible judgment!

Israel has become totally devoted to the worship of other gods at such shrines as Bethel, Beersheba, and Gilgal (see also 4:15; Amos 5:5). The Lord speaks strong language:

"I hated them there. . . . I will drive them out of my house" (verse 15), that is, out of the Promised Land. Because they have followed their rebellious kings and priests into idolatry, the people of Israel have forfeited the love of the Lord. Like a blighted plant with withered roots, the nation will have no fruit. The Lord himself will kill his people's few remaining children with the swords of the Assyrian soldiers: "I will slay their cherished offspring" (verse 16).

Again in the last verse of the chapter, Hosea expresses his assent to the Lord's judgment. God is not fickle in his love. He turns away from his people, hates them, no longer loves them, and rejects them because of the unbelief in their hearts, evidenced by their persistent idolatry. The people to whom he once said, "Out of all nations you will be my treasured possession" (Exodus 19:5), will be a nation no longer. The Israelites will be "wanderers among the nations" (verse 17), scattered "from one end of the earth to the other," as the Lord threatened long ago when he made his covenant with them (Deuteronomy 28:64).

How holy our God is! How his anger flames and smokes, flashes and thunders against man's disobedience! Israel's exile from Canaan, like the flood or the destruction of Sodom and Gomorrah, testifies to the Lord's holy hatred of sin. Yet it is not on account of sin that Israel perishes as a nation. The people the Lord loves destroy themselves by unbelief. The persistent idolatry of God's chosen people is the evidence that they do not trust in him and in his promise of salvation. Rejecting his promised deliverance from every evil, the Israelites place themselves under his wrathful judgment.

Yet the exile will not be the end of the story. Again we are reminded of Gomer, Hosea's adulterous wife. She certainly did not deserve a place in his house. Yet in spite of all her harlotries, the Lord still said to the prophet, "Go, show your love to your wife again, though she is loved by another and is an adulteress. Love her as the LORD loves the Israelites" (3:1). Even after all these threats of punishment, which will be carried out, the Lord will look beyond the exile and make a promise concerning his people in the last chapter of this book: "I will heal their waywardness and love them freely" (14:4).

The New Testament bears witness to the continuing love and concern of the Lord for the "lost sheep of Israel" (Matthew 10:6). Jesus even began his ministry in "Galilee of the Gentiles," the very land that was once a part of the Northern Kingdom until the Assyrians stripped it away (Matthew 4:13-16; Isaiah 9:1,2). His first disciples were Galileans, perhaps descended from some of the Israelites who remained in the land during the exile. As the apostles of Jesus preached the good news of his death and resurrection, they went to the Jews first (Acts 13:46). Like a faithful husband going after his adulterous wife once more, the Lord invited the people of Israel to return to him again.

Remembering how often we have rebelled against our God, we realize that Hosea is picturing our life history as God's people too. "He saved us, not because of righteous things we had done, but because of his mercy" (Titus 3:5). We also have often repaid his love with unfaithfulness. Again and again we have turned back to our favorite sins. Yet because of his mercy, he has kept us his own. Although we have deserved his judgment, he has repeatedly come after us and welcomed us home again with a word of forgiveness and peace, for the sake of Jesus. "How great is the love the Father has lavished on us [even us!], that we [even we!] should be called children of God!" (1 John 3:1).

Israel must bear its guilt

10 Israel was a spreading vine;
    he brought forth fruit for himself.
As his fruit increased,
    he built more altars;
as his land prospered,
    he adorned his sacred stones.
² Their heart is deceitful,
    and now they must bear their guilt.
The LORD will demolish their altars
    and destroy their sacred stones.

By picturing Israel as a spreading grapevine, Hosea reminds his people that the Lord has planted them in a "good and spacious land, a land flowing with milk and honey" (Exodus 3:8). Ephraim, the name the prophet often uses for Israel, means "double fruitfulness," and the Lord should have received abundant fruits of grateful faith from Israel. But prosperity can also lead to forgetfulness and ingratitude. Moses warned the people already before they entered the Promised Land: "When you eat and are satisfied, be careful that you do not forget the Lord, who brought you out of Egypt" (Deuteronomy 6:11,12).

That is just what is happening with Israel. Particularly in the recent times of national prosperity, "religion" has flourished, but it is not the worship of a grateful people serving the Lord. Israel has multiplied its idol altars and decorated the standing stones that represent the presence of Baal at the Canaanite sanctuaries. The Israelites' slippery hearts are not firmly established in faith. Having rejected the Lord's love and forgiveness, they now "must bear their guilt" (verse 2). The Baal altars will be demolished—the derogatory term Hosea uses means "to break an animal's neck"—and the sacred stones that Israel has decorated will be smashed.

When Hosea calls the Israelites' hearts slippery—that is, deceitful—he is not accusing his people of insincerity. Israel is deceitful because the people, after promising to serve the Lord and him alone, have abandoned and denied their faith in his promises. Now the people sincerely expect greater prosperity from Baal than from the Lord.

But sincere trust in a false god never saved anyone. We need to remember that fact as we live in a world that tolerates any and all kinds of worship, as long as people are sincere about it. "I am the LORD," our God says; "that is my name! I will not give my glory to another or my praise to idols" (Isaiah 42:8). Doesn't our God care about us at least as much as a faithful husband cares about his wife? When a husband truly loves his wife, doesn't it break his heart if she leaves him for another man? How can the God who loves his people look on indifferently when they abandon him to fear, love, and trust in things that are false gods?

Ephraim will be disgraced

³ Then they will say, "We have no king
    because we did not revere the LORD.
But even if we had a king,
    what could he do for us?"
⁴ They make many promises,
    take false oaths
    and make agreements;
therefore lawsuits spring up
    like poisonous weeds in a plowed field.
⁵ The people who live in Samaria fear
    for the calf-idol of Beth Aven.
Its people will mourn over it,
    and so will its idolatrous priests,
those who had rejoiced over its splendor,
    because it is taken from them into exile.

⁶ It will be carried to Assyria
   as tribute for the great king.
Ephraim will be disgraced;
   Israel will be ashamed of its wooden idols.
⁷ Samaria and its king will float away
   like a twig on the surface of the waters.
⁸ The high places of wickedness will be destroyed—
   it is the sin of Israel.
Thorns and thistles will grow up
   and cover their altars.
Then they will say to the mountains, "Cover us!"
   and to the hills, "Fall on us!"

The brief reigns of Zechariah son of Jeroboam II (six months) and Shallum (one month) on the throne of the Northern Kingdom after the death of Jeroboam II leave the people's heads spinning. The Northern monarchy has never been called legitimate by the Lord, and now it seems as if Israel has no king at all. In such unstable times, legal institutions break down. Hosea speaks of broken promises and false oaths in Israelite courts, leading to an abundance of lawsuits springing up "like poisonous weeds in a plowed field" (verse 4). Hosea's fellow prophet Amos describes the perversion of the legal system already in the days of Jeroboam II: "You hate the one who reproves in court and despise him who tells the truth. . . . You oppress the righteous and take bribes and you deprive the poor of justice in the courts" (5:10,12). "You have turned justice into poison" (6:12).

More and more in these chapters of his book, Hosea speaks of the coming judgment that Israel's sins deserve: exile in Assyria. Hoshea, the last king of Israel, will be carried off with his people and will die in far-off Mesopotamia. Then his people may finally realize the reason for their national disaster, which some are now beginning to see: "We did not revere the LORD" (verse 3). Not only the king but his royal stronghold, Samaria, will be cut off and disappear "like a twig on the surface of the waters" (verse 7).

The same judgment will befall the Israelite gods, the calf-idol, for example, in the shrine at Bethel (meaning "house of God"), which Hosea ironically calls Beth Aven ("house of wickedness"). The great king—a title for the ruler of Assyria—will consider his gods to be more powerful than the Israelite gods. After all, hasn't he captured their capital city? Therefore, he will cart off the golden calf of Bethel to his homeland. Priests and people who would not revere the Lord must now fear and mourn for the fate of their idol. (Hosea 8:6 says that the "calf of Samaria" will be broken to pieces. Jeroboam I made calf images for shrines at both Bethel and Dan, and it would be surprising if the Israelites made no more than two.)

When they have seen the powerlessness of the Baals, the people will be ashamed of the advice they accepted from the priests of such non-existent deities. The Hebrew words for *advice* and *wood* (verse 6) are similar; according to the NIV translation, the destitute Israelites who remain in the land will be ashamed of the poor wooden images left to them, since their golden calf will be carted off to Assyria. The conquerors will desecrate the "high places of wickedness" (verse 8)—again a reference to Bethel, "house of God," which Hosea often calls "house of wickedness." Thorns and thistles will grow over the neglected altars where Israel offered sacrifices to idols.

With their nation defeated, many of their people languishing in exile, their king gone, their Canaanite gods shown to be powerless nothings, their impoverished land going to ruin, their people dying out (9:11), how can the Israelites face the future with anything in their hearts but despair? "Then they will say to the mountains, 'Cover us!' and to the hills, 'Fall on us!'" (verse 8).

Jesus quoted these words on his way to the cross when women of Jerusalem were mourning and wailing for him. He suggested that they rather weep for themselves and for their children: "For if men do these things when the tree is green, what will happen when it is dry?" (Luke 23:28-31). If the punishment that befell righteous Jesus brought tears to the women's eyes, how would they react when the Lord's flaming judgment would overtake the whole people of Israel, spiritually dead in unbelief? Better to die than to see their nation suffer such a horrible end.

In fact, the Bible pictures the world's kings, princes, generals, the rich, and the mighty saying the same words on judgment day: "They called to the mountains and the rocks, 'Fall on us and hide us from the face of him who sits on the throne and from the wrath of the Lamb!'" (Revelation 6:15,16). When the Lord, through his Scriptures, predicts his coming judgment, it is not as if he is eagerly anticipating the fireworks. Since he warns about punishment to come, sinners will have no excuse when his anger bursts upon them. The Lord's specific purpose in foretelling his judgment is that sinners may hear him, take warning now, and be saved.

This is the appeal that his prophets presented to Israel and Judah: "Repent! Turn away from all your offenses; then sin will not be your downfall. Rid yourselves of all the offenses you have committed, and get a new heart and a new spirit. Why will you die, O house of Israel? For I take no pleasure in the death of anyone, declares the Sovereign LORD. Repent and live!" (Ezekiel 18:30-32). When we tell our unbelieving friends about the coming judgment, we do so in order to address the same appeal to them: "God takes no pleasure in your death. He sacrificed his Lamb for the sins of the world and also for your sins. Repent, trust Jesus Christ and live—forever!"

The Lord will punish evildoers

⁹ "Since the days of Gibeah, you have sinned, O Israel,
  and there you have remained.
Did not war overtake
  the evildoers in Gibeah?
¹⁰ When I please, I will punish them;
  nations will be gathered against them
  to put them in bonds for their double sin.
¹¹ Ephraim is a trained heifer
  that loves to thresh;
so I will put a yoke
  on her fair neck.
I will drive Ephraim,
  Judah must plow,
  and Jacob must break up the ground.
¹² Sow for yourselves righteousness,
  reap the fruit of unfailing love,
and break up your unplowed ground;
  for it is time to seek the LORD,
until he comes
  and showers righteousness on you.
¹³ But you have planted wickedness,
  you have reaped evil,
  you have eaten the fruit of deception.
Because you have depended on your own strength
  and on your many warriors,
¹⁴ the roar of battle will rise against your people,
  so that all your fortresses will be devastated—
as Shalman devastated Beth Arbel on the day of battle,
  when mothers were dashed to the ground with their
    children.

¹⁵ Thus will it happen to you, O Bethel,
   because your wickedness is great.
When that day dawns,
   the king of Israel will be completely destroyed.

For an example of evildoing to compare with Israel's conduct in his own times, Hosea thinks far back in history to an incident in the days of the judges (Judges 19-21). The Sodomites of Gibeah in Benjamin, foiled in their desire to rape a visiting Levite, abused the man's concubine all night until she fell down dead at the door of the house where the Levite was staying. He cut up her body into 12 pieces and sent it to all the tribes as a demand for punishment, because the men of Gibeah "committed this lewd and disgraceful act in Israel" (Judges 20:6). All the rest of Israel went to war with Benjamin when the Benjamites would not deliver the criminals to be put to death. The final result was the death of 25 thousand Benjamites and the destruction of their towns and families.

Hosea's point is that the Israelites in his day have sunk just as deep into corruption as the city of Gibeah. They have not turned back to the Lord but have remained in their sin. Israel waged war against the Benjamites and the evil men of Gibeah; now it is the will of God to have other nations punish Israel, because the whole nation has become tolerant of idolatry and immorality. Perhaps Hosea speaks of Israel's "double sin" (verse 10), to play on the name Ephraim, that is, the Northern Kingdom, because Ephraim means "twice fruitful" (Genesis 41:52). Heaping guilt on guilt, "twice-fruitful" has become "doubly-sinful" and well deserves captivity.

After the Israelites had reaped and dried their grain, they would spread it on a hard-packed threshing floor, yoke up their cattle, and drive the animals over the grain to tread the kernels out of the husks. Israel, and Judah also, have not been willing to bear the easy yoke of the Lord's covenant. Instead, they have submitted to training in Canaan to be driven around and around by other masters, the Canaanite gods.

Now the Lord will send them into captivity to pull his plow and harrow. He directs them to "sow righteousness" and to "reap the fruit of unfailing love" (verse 12). Like John the Baptist, the prophet urges God's people to "produce fruit in keeping with repentance" (Luke 3:8). His purpose in the exile of Israel will be to break up the ground that has lain fallow and barren: to soften the hard hearts of his people and to lead them to repentance. The Lord summons Israel in its time of exile to seek him in faith. Then he will come to his people and rain down his righteousness, like showers falling on the newly planted crops of Canaan.

The Lord's people are living their life in the Promised Land without any such repentance, faith, or fruits of faith. "You have planted wickedness, you have reaped evil, you have eaten the fruit of deception," Hosea tells the Israelites (verse 13). Again he reminds them that, like an unfaithful wife, they have lied to the Lord, Israel's faithful husband. What passes for worship in the Canaanite religion, the Lord calls wickedness in his law.

Israel's trust in false gods has also led to a foreign policy that denies the Lord. Instead of trusting him to guard and protect them, his people have put their trust in their own warriors (see Amos 6:13) and even in the armies of heathen allies like Assyria and Egypt (7:11). "Shalman" in verse 14 may be Shalmaneser V of Assyria, who began the siege of Samaria about 725 B.C. (2 Kings 17:3-5) or some other enemy of Israel. When he captured Beth Arbel, a city in Galilee or Gilead out on the fringes of the kingdom, he let his soldiers massacre Israelite women and children. The same fate will befall the people of Bethel, the very center of Israel's religion. Israel's king, who worshiped the calf god there, will be annihilated.

In the sheer number of Hosea's words, God's condemnation of Israel's sin and the threats of his judgment far outweigh the prophet's gospel message. And yet above the voice of the law, roaring like a lion (5:14), and above the threatening crash of Assyrian weapons (10:14), the prophet lets us hear the quiet voice of the gospel. Israel's exile in Assyria will be a well-deserved punishment for sin, but the Lord will use the same experience to invite his people to come back to him: "It is time to seek the LORD, until he comes and showers righteousness on you" (verse 12).

The coming judgment is real, but so is the invitation to receive the Lord's own righteousness. "This righteousness from God comes through faith in Jesus Christ to all who believe. There is no difference, for all have sinned and fall short of the glory of God, and are justified freely by his grace through the redemption that came by Christ Jesus" (Romans 3:22-24). God's righteousness is his own answer to what his law demands. The righteousness of Christ silences every threat of punishment for those who trust in him. When we hear the good news of the forgiveness of all our sins through the sufferings and death of God's Son, the Lord's own righteousness rains down on us from heaven, like showers on parched ground.

God's love for Israel

11 "When Israel was a child, I loved him,
    and out of Egypt I called my son.
² But the more I called Israel,
    the further they went from me.

They sacrificed to the Baals
and they burned incense to images.
³ **It was I who taught Ephraim to walk,**
taking them by the arms;
but they did not realize
it was I who healed them.
⁴ **I led them with cords of human kindness,**
with ties of love;
I lifted the yoke from their neck
and bent down to feed them.

In this chapter the Lord allows us to look right into his heart, to experience his feelings for his child Israel. In the tender language of a father remembering his son's childhood, the Lord reflects on how he loved his people during their young years as a nation. His voice, speaking through his prophet Moses, called them out of slavery in Egypt to go to the land he prepared for them.

The Lord preserved Israel, his Old Testament child, from death in a famine through a flight into Egypt at the time of Joseph, Jacob's son. Then the Lord called the nation back to the Promised Land to carry out his plan of salvation. The New Testament tells us that Hosea 11:1 was fulfilled in the life of Jesus (Matthew 2:15). Israel was a type, or picture, of Christ. When God's "time had fully come" (Galatians 4:4), he led Joseph and Mary to Egypt to protect his one and only incarnate Son from the hands of murderous King Herod. After Herod's death the Father called his Son back out of Egypt to live, suffer, die, and rise again for our redemption.

The Lord's remembrance of his love for youthful Israel is now mixed with the bitter memory of Israel's Baal worship in Canaan. (Verse 2 is a place where the NIV translators used the text of the Septuagint, the Greek translation of the Old Testament made before the time of Christ, because the

Hebrew text is too hard to understand.) But then the Father's thoughts go back again to the old days, when he leaned down and held his little one's arms to teach him how to walk. It was love, the tender love of a father for his child, that delivered Israel from slavery in Egypt ("I lifted the yoke from their neck"), brought them through all their wanderings ("I led them with cords of human kindness"), gave them manna in the wilderness ("[I] bent down to feed them"). Yet the Israelites have gone their own heedless way without remembering who trained, protected, and fed them.

Often we repeat the national history of Israel in our personal lives. The Lord made many of us his own sons and daughters through Baptism so early in our lives that we have no memory of the event. Yet even then he loved us and freed us from the yoke of slavery to sin and Satan. His care and protection have gone with us from our youngest years, through the love of our Christian parents and teachers. Yet many days of our lives, we totally forget that it is the Lord who fed, protected, trained, and healed us. How can we forget to thank him for all the goodness and mercy we have experienced from little on?

Assyria will rule over Israel

[5] "Will they not return to Egypt
and will not Assyria rule over them
because they refuse to repent?
[6] Swords will flash in their cities,
will destroy the bars of their gates
and put an end to their plans.
[7] My people are determined to turn from me.
Even if they call to the Most High,
he will by no means exalt them.

To impress his lesson, the Lord uses the word *return* in two different ways. His people will not "return" to him, that is, they refuse to repent of their unfaithfulness and will not trust in him (verses 5 and 7). Therefore, they will "return to Egypt," that is, they will be prisoners in the future Assyrian exile just as once they slaved for Pharaoh in Egypt. Assyrian soldiers will whirl their swords in Israelite cities and break the "bars of their gates" to let the conquering armies in. Then this people will see their proud plans finished by the sword of the Assyrians. The Lord will refuse to hear the Israelites when they call from the pit into which they fall. He will not lift them up but will let the Assyrians humble them.

Will that be the end of the Lord's people? Is nothing left for them but the judgment of an angry God? At the end of chapter 11, the Lord shares with us the innermost thoughts of his heart about the future of his people.

The Lord will come again in compassion

⁸ "How can I give you up, Ephraim?
    How can I hand you over, Israel?
How can I treat you like Admah?
    How can I make you like Zeboiim?
My heart is changed within me;
    all my compassion is aroused.
⁹ I will not carry out my fierce anger,
    nor will I turn and devastate Ephraim.
For I am God, and not man—
    the Holy One among you.
I will not come in wrath.
¹⁰ They will follow the LORD;
    he will roar like a lion.
When he roars,
    his children will come trembling from the west.

¹¹ **They will come trembling
like birds from Egypt,
like doves from Assyria.
I will settle them in their homes,"
declares the LORD.**

We remember Hosea's words to his children about
Gomer, his unfaithful wife: "Rebuke your mother, rebuke
her, for she is not my wife, and I am not her husband. . . . I
will punish her for the days she burned incense to the
Baals; she decked herself with rings and jewelry, and went
after her lovers, but me she forgot" (2:2,13). Yet the Lord
said to the prophet once more: "Go, show your love to your
wife again, though she is loved by another and is an adulteress. Love her as the LORD loves the Israelites" (3:1).

The love of God for his son Israel speaks once more in
these last verses of chapter 11. As the Lord deliberates with
himself, his undying love for his people defends them from
the holy justice that has spoken in verses 5 to 7. The father's
heart yearns for his lost son and will not give him up.
Admah and Zeboiim were cities near Sodom and Gomorrah
(Genesis 14:8), cities "which the LORD overthrew in fierce
anger" (Deuteronomy 29:23; see also Genesis 19:24,25). The
Lord asks himself how he can treat his son Israel like
Admah and Zeboiim.

His heart is changed—the Hebrew word actually
means "overturned" (verse 8). His compassion will not let
him carry through to the end the penalty that Israel's
unfaithfulness deserves, at least not yet. Israel will have
another chance. If reason asks how the Lord's perfect
love can stand in the way of his perfect justice, he
answers, "I am God, and not man" (verse 9): his unspeak-
able love simply surpasses all human understanding. He
remains "the Holy one," and yet he will not come to his
unworthy people only in wrath.

The Lord will send Israel into exile in Assyria after the fall of Samaria in 722 B.C. The Babylonian king Nebuchadnezzar will attack Judah in 605 B.C. and, in several deportations, will also carry off many of the Jews to Babylon. The lion roars in earnest, and his punishment is real. Yet the lion's roar will also call his trembling people back to him from far away. The exile itself will lead some of the people of Israel to repent and trust the Lord's promises again. These Ephraimites have been like doves, "easily deceived and senseless—now calling to Egypt, now turning to Assyria" (7:11) for help instead of trusting in the Lord, who promised to deliver them. Now "'they will come trembling like birds from Egypt, like doves from Assyria. I will settle them in their homes,' declares the LORD" (verse 11).

Isaiah, who prophesied in Judah shortly after Hosea's ministry in Israel, taught the same truth: "In that day the remnant of Israel, the survivors of the house of Jacob, will no longer rely on him who struck them down [i.e., a heathen king with whom Israel made alliances] but will truly rely on the LORD, the Holy One of Israel. A remnant will return, a remnant of Jacob will return to the Mighty God" (Isaiah 10:20,21). In order to keep his promises, the Lord will restore a believing remnant of his people to the Promised Land after the exile. There believers such as Simeon and Anna will be "waiting for the consolation of Israel" (Luke 2:25) when God's hour strikes and his Messiah comes.

In this single chapter of Hosea, the Lord has described his innermost thoughts to us: his tender remembrance of how he raised and trained his son Israel, who has now turned disobedient; his threat, soon to be carried out, that Assyrian swords will flash in Israelite cities; and his turbulent emotions as his heart is "overturned" and he decides not to annihilate his people. The prophet teaches us to know our

God close up. The Lord is the stern judge who punishes sin but also the Father who loves sinners beyond human understanding and therefore saves his children who have deserved nothing but punishment.

Only at the cross of Jesus Christ will the Father allow us to look so deeply into his heart again. There his holiness will exact the full penalty for sin, but through the sacrifice of Christ, his love will prepare an eternal home for all sinners, Jews and Gentiles. "God in his holiness will not destroy; neither can His love merely overlook and tolerate man's rebellion. His love will deal effectively with man's sin. With the *roar of a lion* the Lord will declare both his inexorable wrath against sin and his inextinguishable love for His children; and at that roar his wayward children will at last *come trembling* home to Him (10-11). That roar was ultimately heard at Calvary, and all history since then is the history of the homecoming of mankind."*

Israel's sin requires repentance

¹² Ephraim has surrounded me with lies,
    the house of Israel with deceit.
And Judah is unruly against God,
    even against the faithful Holy One.

12 ¹Ephraim feeds on the wind;
    he pursues the east wind all day
    and multiplies lies and violence.
He makes a treaty with Assyria
    and sends olive oil to Egypt.
² The LORD has a charge to bring against Judah;
    he will punish Jacob according to his ways
    and repay him according to his deeds.

---

*M. Franzmann, *Concordia Self-Study Commentary* (St. Louis: Concordia, 1971), 597.

³ In the womb he grasped his brother's heel;
   as a man he struggled with God.
⁴ He struggled with the angel and overcame him;
   he wept and begged for his favor.
 He found him at Bethel
   and talked with him there—
⁵ the LORD God Almighty,
   the LORD is his name of renown!
⁶ But you must return to your God;
   maintain love and justice,
   and wait for your God always.

The Lord wants to dwell among his people, but Ephraim—Hosea's name for the kingdom of Israel—has surrounded him with false gods. Hosea calls them lies (11:12) because they are really not gods at all. Before the people of Judah can point fingers at the idolatry of the Northern Kingdom, Hosea reminds them that they also have wandered away from a loyal trust in their faithful and holy Lord. Instead of seeking the Lord and feeding on the pastures to which he would lead them, the Israelites pursue and feed on "wind," the worthless spiritual food that idol worship supplies.

In their religious life, Israel "multiplies lies" (12:1), that is, worships many false gods. In their social life, the nation "multiplies violence": see 4:2, for example, or the words of Amos, who says that even the Israelite women "oppress the poor and crush the needy" (4:1). The kings of Israel show their lack of trust in Israel's Lord by making mutual defense treaties with heathen nations such as Assyria and Egypt and sending them tribute in kind such as olive oil, a product of the land.

The Lord summons the whole nation, including Judah, to hear his accusation and to be sentenced for its wrongdoing. Here God refers to the nation as "Jacob," and he uses incidents from the life of Jacob as a pattern to describe Israel first as it is and then as he wants it to become in Hosea's time. In the womb Jacob grasped the heel of Esau, his twin brother; the name Jacob means "tripper" or "supplanter" (Genesis 25:26). The name recalls how Jacob later stole first his brother's birthright (Genesis 25:29-34) and then the blessing their father intended for Esau (Genesis 27). Because Jacob did not fully trust the promises of God, he thought he had to arrange for his own future prosperity.

Many years later Jacob returned to Canaan a changed man. The Angel of the LORD—God's Son himself in human form—met him and wrestled with him at the Jabbok River (Genesis 32). Jacob, now trusting in the Lord's covenant promises, would not let the Angel go and begged for the blessing that God had promised him. That was the occasion when the Lord changed the patriarch's name from Jacob, "supplanter," to Israel, "one who struggles with God" (Genesis 32:28) to show how he had changed the man's heart and strengthened his faith. Later the almighty Lord God of hosts appeared to Jacob again at Bethel, reminded him of the change in his name, and impressed the covenant promises on his memory once more (Genesis 35:6-15).

Hosea shows the people of Israel that the Lord wants to repeat the patriarch's history in them. They have failed to keep their covenant with the Lord and have shown injustice to each other. They have gone chasing after the Canaanite Baals. They think they must assure their future prosperity by what they do instead of waiting in faith to receive a blessing from the Lord. Therefore, Hosea says, "you must return to your God": repentance is necessary. Sincere repentance and true faith will bear fruit: "maintain love and justice, and wait for your God always" (12:6).

The Lord calls not only Israel but also us to return to him every day and to "wait for [our] God always." Whenever we sin, he looks for repentance. The Lord himself gives us faith, so that we trustfully look up to him and wait for his forgiveness and every blessing. The proof of our repentance and faith should not be lacking in our lives: that we faithfully keep the promises we make to God and to each other, that we deal fairly with all our fellowmen, and that we look up to the Lord in childlike confidence, waiting for his blessing. His faithful love deserves such a response.

Israel's response

⁷ The merchant uses dishonest scales;
    he loves to defraud.
⁸ Ephraim boasts,
    "I am very rich; I have become wealthy.
   With all my wealth they will not find in me
       any iniquity or sin."

⁹ "I am the LORD your God,
    who brought you out of Egypt;
   I will make you live in tents again,
    as in the days of your appointed feasts.
¹⁰ I spoke to the prophets,
    gave them many visions
    and told parables through them."

¹¹ Is Gilead wicked?
    Its people are worthless!
   Do they sacrifice bulls in Gilgal?
    Their altars will be like piles of stones
    on a plowed field.
¹² Jacob fled to the country of Aram;
    Israel served to get a wife,
    and to pay for her he tended sheep.
¹³ The LORD used a prophet to bring Israel up from Egypt,
    by a prophet he cared for him.

¹⁴ **But Ephraim has bitterly provoked him to anger;**
his Lord will leave upon him the guilt of his bloodshed
and will repay him for his contempt.

How does Israel answer the Lord's call to repentance?
Merchants selling grain and other products in the marketplaces practice dishonesty and fraud, "skimping the measure, boosting the price and cheating with dishonest scales"
(Amos 8:5). Then they act as if they themselves have created
their own wealth from nothing. They think that their riches
excuse them from all accountability to God.

The Lord sends his prophets to call Israel to account
and to announce the coming loss of all the nation's
wealth. During the "appointed feasts" of tabernacles
(verse 9) every year, the Israelites live in booths to
remind them of their wandering in the wilderness (Leviticus 23:33-43). On the way out of Egypt, they were
nomads, living in tents. Now they will have to go tenting
again on their way to exile in Mesopotamia.

Israel does not want to hear the message of defeat
and exile that prophets such as Hosea and Amos are
preaching, but the Lord reminds his people that the
words, visions, and parables of the prophets come from
him. The judgment the prophets announce is the judgment of the Lord: "I spoke to the prophets," the Lord says
(verse 10).

Israel takes great pride in Gilead, the fine cattle country
Jeroboam's armies recovered for the Northern Kingdom
(Amos 6:13). Gilgal is another prominent place for the
Israelites, a center of their religious life, where they offer
bulls to Baal. The Lord looks at the spiritual and moral con-
dition, not the outward importance and prosperity of such
places (Hosea 4:15; 6:8; 9:15). He declares the people of
Gilead worthless because of their wickedness. The altars of

Gilgal are destined to become like the jumbled heaps of stones a farmer piles up on the borders of his plowed fields.

In the last three verses of chapter 12, Hosea returns to three themes he has mentioned in earlier verses. (1) According to verse 12, Jacob's life is a pattern for the life of the people of Israel. Jacob did not make himself rich. In fact, he owned nothing but the staff in his hand when he fled to Haran in Northern Aram (Syria), and he had to pay the bride-price for his wives, Rachel and Leah, with years of labor tending flocks for their father, Laban (Genesis 29:14-30). Penniless Jacob, the Israelites' ancestor, received all his blessings from the Lord. So his Israelite descendants have no reason to boast about their wealth as if they had created it themselves (see verse 8).

(2) According to verse 13, the Lord used his prophet Moses to lead Israel up from Egypt to the Promised Land. Through Moses he gave his people water and food in the wilderness and led them all the way to the border of Canaan. Thus the prophets, God's spokesmen, have an important part to play in the Lord's plans for his people. The Lord cares for his people through the word of his prophets (see verse 10). Therefore the Israelites must listen when the prophets summon them to confess their sins and to trust in the Lord.

(3) Finally the Lord speaks another word of judgment in verse 14. Israel has angered the Lord by treating with contempt his invitations to return, his condemnations of the nation's sin, his warnings of judgment to come. Therefore the Israelites will bear the guilt for their own blood that the Assyrians will shed. They have shown contempt for the Lord; he will return upon their heads the shame of defeat and exile. This sentence of national death will be the just outcome of the Lord's legal charge against Israel. Israel will be repaid according to its own deeds (see verse 2).

How can anyone escape that judgment? Scripture teaches us to pray: "If you, O LORD, kept a record of sins, O Lord, who could stand?" (Psalm 130:3). All of us deserve to be repaid according to our own selfish and sinful deeds. But the Lord's very purpose in calling his people to return to him is to forgive and restore them. "With you there is forgiveness; therefore you are feared," we pray (Psalm 130:4). That forgiveness is there for us because the heavenly Father laid on Jesus the iniquity of us all. After generations of worshiping Baal and Ashtoreth, Israel learned via the hard way of defeat and exile that no god except the Lord provides forgiveness. Have we learned that? Our hearts should wait for his salvation always, trusting in him above all things. Such hearts pray: "I wait for the LORD, my soul waits, and in his word I put my hope. . . . For with the LORD is unfailing love and with him is full redemption" (Psalm 130:5,7).

The Lord's anger against Israel

13 **When Ephraim spoke, men trembled;**
he was exalted in Israel.
But he became guilty of Baal worship and died.
² Now they sin more and more;
they make idols for themselves from their silver,
cleverly fashioned images,
all of them the work of craftsmen.
It is said of these people,
"They offer human sacrifice
and kiss the calf-idols."
³ Therefore they will be like the morning mist,
like the early dew that disappears,
like chaff swirling from a threshing floor,
like smoke escaping through a window.

Hosea mentions Ephraim as the outstanding tribe in the kingdom of Israel. Often, in fact, the prophet has used the name Ephraim to stand for the whole nation in the north. Descendants of Joseph's second son, Ephraim became prominent among the 12 tribes especially because of two individuals. Israel's great leader Joshua was an Ephraimite (Numbers 13:8) and received his family inheritance in the hill country of Ephraim (Joshua 19:50). The notorious Jeroboam I, who led the revolt of the northern ten tribes, came from the same tribe (1 Kings 11:26). Jeroboam, however, was not a leader in the tradition of faithful Joshua. By erecting the golden calves in Bethel and Dan, Jeroboam set the course that mired the Northern Kingdom deeper and deeper in Baal worship and led to the spiritual death of his people. Israel abandoned the Lord, the source of all spiritual life. Like the prodigal son, as long as he remained far from home (Luke 15:24), Israel was as good as dead, "dead in . . . transgressions and sins" (Ephesians 2:1).

The calves that Jeroboam erected are not the only images the Israelites are worshiping. The people fashion their own household gods of silver. (Every important archeological dig in Israel has turned up samples of such fertility images. They are usually female figures, often with exaggerated sexual features, fashioned of precious metals or of humbler material such as clay.) These deities, Hosea says contemptuously, are all "the work of craftsmen" (verse 2), created by human hands and so not to be compared with the Lord, man's Maker, the Creator of the world.

Israel has adopted not only such Canaanite gods as Baal, Asherah, and Ashtoreth but also the Canaanite worship ceremonies: "They offer human sacrifice and kiss the calf-idols" (verse 2). The biblical writers describe such worship by saying that they "sacrificed their sons and daughters in the fire" (2 Kings 17:17). The Lord's law expressly forbade such sacrifices: "You must not worship the LORD your God in their way, because in worshiping their gods, they do all kinds of detestable things the LORD hates. They even burn their sons and daughters in the fire as sacrifices to their gods" (Deuteronomy 12:31). Kissing an image of Baal was another way of expressing devotion to the Canaanite god (1 Kings 19:18).

Hosea describes the Lord's judgment upon such idol worship with four comparisons. Like mist or early dew burning off in the morning sun, like chaff driven by a windstorm from the threshing floor, or like smoke escaping from a house through a latticed hole in the wall, the Israelites will simply disappear from the stage of history. By the exile in Mesopotamia, the Lord will "remove them from his presence," as he warned through all his servants the prophets (2 Kings 17:23).

Before Israel entered the land, the Lord described his disgust with the sins of the Canaanites, especially their perversion of his gift of sex. It was as if the land of Canaan had become sick to its stomach because of the sins of its inhabitants. "Even the land was defiled; so I punished it for its sin, and the land vomited out its inhabitants" (Leviticus 18:25). The Lord warned the Israelites before they entered Canaan: "If you defile the land, it will vomit you out as it vomited out the nations that were before you" (Leviticus 18:28).

Today most people would be horrified to hear that human sacrifice is a common practice in their countries. Yet in most of the "civilized" nations of the world, uncounted thousands of mothers and fathers kill their children before they are born. They do so to maintain a high standard of living, to avoid the inconvenience of a family, or just to enjoy the pleasure of sexual intercourse without the responsibility of providing for a child. If what we love above all things is our god, then the gods named comfort, convenience, and pleasure are receiving an abundance of human sacrifices every day from those who worship them. "In worshiping their gods, they do all kinds of detestable things the LORD hates" (Deuteronomy 12:31). Can we Christians remain silent as such sins pollute our land or will we testify against them, as God's law and prophets do?

Deliverance, ingratitude, judgment

> 4 "But I am the LORD your God,
>   who brought you out of Egypt.
>   You shall acknowledge no God but me,
>   no Savior except me.
> 5 I cared for you in the desert,
>   in the land of burning heat.
> 6 When I fed them, they were satisfied;
>   when they were satisfied, they became proud;
>   then they forgot me.
> 7 So I will come upon them like a lion,
>   like a leopard I will lurk by the path.
> 8 Like a bear robbed of her cubs,
>   I will attack them and rip them open.
>   Like a lion I will devour them;
>   a wild animal will tear them apart.

Here is Israel's whole history summed up in just a few verses, describing first the Lord's deliverance, then his people's ingratitude, and finally the Lord's judgment. When the Lord calls himself Israel's God "of Egypt" (verse 4) he recalls how he created this nation in Egypt and then delivered them from their Egyptian slavery. How can they acknowledge any other god except the Lord? Did he not care for them—the Hebrew says "I knew you"—in the desert, that is, did he not make his covenant with them in the burning wilderness of Sinai? Then he kept his promise and shepherded his people into Canaan, "a good and spacious land, a land flowing with milk and honey" (Exodus 3:8).

Satisfied with all the riches of the Promised Land, the Israelites are exalting themselves against their God and forgetting him, as Moses warned in some of his last words: "Jeshurun"—that is, the upright one, Israel—"grew fat and kicked; filled with food, he became heavy and sleek. He abandoned the God who made him and rejected the Rock his Savior" (Deuteronomy 32:15).

To describe his judgment upon his people's forgetfulness, the Lord pictures himself with some of the fiercest similes in the whole Bible. Can we picture the Lord our God as being like a devouring lion, a lurking leopard, a female bear robbed of her cubs and ready to rip someone open, a wild animal tearing its victim's body apart? Those are the comparisons he himself uses in verses 7 and 8 to describe his anger when his love is spurned!

Are we Christians ever tempted to despise the blood of Christ and to insult God's gracious Spirit by stifling the voice of conscience and turning back to unbelief and sin? Then we need to hear law warnings such as this. The New Testament repeats the same truth: "It is a dreadful thing to fall into the hands of the living God" (Hebrews 10:31). His consuming anger is just as real as his boundless love. When we hear God's law, do we think that he is just pretending to be angry before announcing his forgiveness? God is no play actor. If we cannot think of our God in the terms that Hosea uses, we underestimate his holy anger against sin. This was the anger Christ bore when he took our place under the just wrath of his holy Father: the rage of a devouring lion, a fierce leopard, a bear robbed of her cubs. It was no make-believe curse our Savior redeemed us from when he became a curse for us (Galatians 3:13).

The Lord will destroy Israel

⁹ "You are destroyed, O Israel,
　　because you are against me, against your helper.
¹⁰ Where is your king, that he may save you?
　　Where are your rulers in all your towns,
　of whom you said,
　　'Give me a king and princes'?
¹¹ So in my anger I gave you a king,
　　and in my wrath I took him away.
¹² The guilt of Ephraim is stored up,
　　his sins are kept on record.
¹³ Pains as of a woman in childbirth come to him,
　　but he is a child without wisdom;
　when the time arrives,
　　he does not come to the opening of the womb."

The Lord is resolved to carry out his judgment, since Israel has turned against him. Verse 9 illustrates the difficulty of some parts of the book of Hosea. Translated word for word, it says, "He has destroyed you, Israel, for in (or against) me, in (or against) your helper." Many translators have changed the person of the verb at the beginning, reading "I have destroyed" or "you have destroyed" to fit the thought of the last part of the verse. All English translations must add some supplementary words. Faced with difficulties in this verse, we try to translate in keeping with the verses before and after it. The King James Version has "O Israel, thou hast destroyed thyself; but in me is thine help," in agreement with such passages as Isaiah 3:9 and Jeremiah 2:17.

"Where is your king? Where are your rulers?" the Lord asks (verse 10). Perhaps by this time, Shalmaneser V has already seized and imprisoned Hoshea, the last king of Israel, and the capture of Samaria is near. God is reminding the Israelites that the request they brought to Samuel over three centuries ago, "Appoint a king to lead us, such as all the other nations have," already showed a lack of faith in him and aroused his anger. The Lord told Samuel, "It is not you they have rejected, but they have rejected me as their king" (1 Samuel 8:7).

Now in his anger against the Israelites' rebellious idolatry, the Lord has taken away their king and banished him to Assyria. God will no longer forgive the guilt of his backsliding people: their iniquity is bound to them, like the guilt of the impenitent sinners mentioned by Jesus in Matthew 16:19 and 18:18. Their sin is "kept on record" (verse 12) to accuse them in the judgment. The Lord would like to call Israel his dear son again, but this people is like a child misplaced in the womb, an "unwise" child that does not know how to be born when the mother's time comes and the birth pains begin. By despising its opportunity to repent, Israel refuses to be reborn as God's child.

Very early in the book of Hosea, we observed the prophet's sudden alternations of threat and promise, law and gospel (1:10; 2:14). The most striking example of all occurs in 13:14, a promise of the resurrection, followed immediately by a further threat of judgment for Samaria, the capital of the Northern Kingdom.

Victory over death

> ¹⁴ "I will ransom them from the power of the grave;
> I will redeem them from death.
> Where, O death, are your plagues?
> Where, O grave, is your destruction?"

The Lord's will is to save his people, not to destroy them. Every word of judgment for Israel is put aside for a moment as the Lord describes a great victory over an enemy that has dominated all mankind ever since the Fall of man. Death is the enemy that entered the world and oppresses all mankind as a result of sin. Using Hebrew parallelism, the Lord designates death with two words: the first, Hebrew *Sheol,* usually translated "the grave," a term reaching beyond temporal death to describe God's judgment upon sin; the second, the simple word *death,* which ever since the fall, man has shared with the animals, as God said, "Dust you are and to dust you will return" (Genesis 3:19).

The Lord will pay whatever price is necessary to ransom his people from death for himself. He will act like the Israelite kinsman-redeemer who buys back family property to keep it from passing into the possession of another (see Ruth 3:12; 4:1-10). Even though Israel as a nation will die, the Lord has his chosen remnant of believers in Israel, and for them death in an Assyrian siege or exile in Mesopotamia will not mean the end of life with God. He will buy them for himself even from the power of death and the grave.

When Paul quotes this passage in 1 Corinthians 15:55, he also cites Isaiah 25:8: "He will swallow up death forever." The ransom price is paid in the death of God's Son, Jesus. He guarantees the victory over death by his bodily resurrection from the grave. The Lord's prophecy in Hosea 13:14 will be fulfilled, and the final victory celebration will begin when "the trumpet will sound, the dead will be raised imperishable, and we will be changed. For the perishable must clothe itself with the imperishable, and the mortal with immortality" (1 Corinthians 15:52,53).

Then the "plagues" and "destruction" that death imposes on our bodies in the grave will be undone in a moment. Both believing Old Testament Israel and the New Testament Christian church enjoy victory over death already now by faith. Therefore, an Old Testament believer could confidently say, "God will redeem my life from the grave; he will surely take me to himself" (Psalm 49:15), and even in the face of our own and our believing dear ones' deaths, we Christians thank God, because "he gives us the victory through our Lord Jesus Christ" (1 Corinthians 15:57).

The people of Samaria must bear their guilt

> "I will have no compassion,
> ¹⁵ even though he thrives among his brothers.
> An east wind from the LORD will come,
> blowing in from the desert;
> his spring will fail
> and his well dry up.
> His storehouse will be plundered
> of all its treasures.
> ¹⁶ The people of Samaria must bear their guilt,
> because they have rebelled against their God.
> They will fall by the sword;
> their little ones will be dashed to the ground,
> their pregnant women ripped open."

The word translated "compassion" in the last line of verse 14 could mean "repentance" in the sense of a change of mind (Psalm 110:4). In that case, this line concludes the prophecy of the resurrection: the Lord will not change his mind about his promise. If the end of verse 14 introduces the final verses of chapter 13, the Lord is saying that he will not change his mind about Israel's doom. The trial is over, the sentence is spoken, and there can be no appeal to the mercy of the court.

The hot wind blowing in from the eastern desert, drying up every spring and well, pictures the Assyrian armies wreaking destruction as they burn the Israelite cities and lay siege to Samaria. Israel has paid tribute to Assyria for decades, and now the Assyrian armies will seize whatever precious things remain.

Hosea, the other prophets, and even the historical writers of the Bible are not primarily interested in giving us a blow-by-blow description of the war in the style of a daily newspaper. They concentrate instead on the power and purpose behind Israel's defeat. The withering blast from the east, representing the Assyrians, is referred to as "the wind of the LORD." The underlying reason for the end of the Northern Kingdom is not unpreparedness in Israel's armed forces or a lack of wisdom in the nation's foreign office but rebellion against the Lord: "The people of Samaria must bear their guilt, because they have rebelled against their God" (verse 16).

Hosea has documented the spiritual and moral failure of the Israelites as a nation earlier in his book. The last verse of chapter 13 describes in three stark sentences the end of the history of the Northern Kingdom. When the Assyrians take Samaria in 722 B.C., many inhabitants of the city will die by the sword. Enemy soldiers will dash out the brains of little children on the stones. They will even rip open pregnant mothers to destroy their babies in the womb. Through such enemy atrocities, the Lord will cut off the nation's future.

The history of the Northern Kingdom began when Jeroboam I led the ten northern tribes away from the Lord's chosen king of the house of David in Jerusalem. It ended when the Assyrians captured Samaria in 722 B.C. and exiled Israel to Mesopotamia. "The Israelites persisted in all the sins of Jeroboam and did not turn away from them until the LORD removed them from his presence, as he had warned through all his servants the prophets" (2 Kings 17:22,23). The Lord carried out the judgment he described through Moses at Mount Sinai: "If you reject my decrees and abhor my laws and fail to carry out all my commands and so violate my covenant. . . . Your land will be laid waste, and your cities will lie in ruins. . . . You will perish among the nations; the land of your enemies will devour you. Those of you who are left will waste away in the lands of their enemies because of their sins; also because of their fathers' sins they will waste away" (Leviticus 26:15,33,38,39).

Israel called to repentance

14 Return, O Israel, to the LORD your God.
> Your sins have been your downfall!
> ² Take words with you
> > and return to the LORD.
> Say to him:
> > "Forgive all our sins
> and receive us graciously,
> > that we may offer the fruit of our lips.
> ³ Assyria cannot save us;
> > we will not mount war-horses.
> We will never again say 'Our gods'
> > to what our own hands have made,
> > for in you the fatherless find compassion."

Hosea addresses these verses to those Israelites who take the Lord's warning of judgment to heart, including the people in exile who recognize, "[Our] sins have been [our] downfall" (verse 1). The Lord's tender appeal to return to him recalls the plan Hosea proposed concerning his adulterous wife, Gomer, in 2:14: "Therefore I am now going to allure her; I will lead her into the desert and speak tenderly to her." The exile itself, the fulfillment of the Lord's threatened judgment upon Israel's idolatry, becomes an occasion for him to call his people all the long way back to him.

When the Israelites prayed in 6:1-3, they expected healing and life from the Lord even while they refused to acknowledge their guilt. Hosea urges them to confess their sin, to bring to the Lord the sacrifice of "a broken and contrite heart" (Psalm 51:17). Penitent sinners will pray "Forgive all our sins and receive us graciously" (verse 2). Repentance is what the Lord is looking for. He longs to hear his beloved people bring the "fruit of their lips"—another translation would be "their lips as bulls," that is, sincere words of repentance and faith, the humble praises that please him more than all the sacrificial animals on the temple altar.

Returning to the Lord means turning way from all false gods. Here is the new life that springs from repentance and faith. Idolatrous Israel made alliances with heathen nations, trusting in Assyrian swords or Egyptian horses and chariots (Ezekiel 17:15). Penitent hearts will say "Assyria cannot save us; we will not mount war-horses" (verse 3), because "the Lord is my helper; I will not be afraid. What can man do to me?" (Hebrews 13:6). Idolatrous Israel worshiped false gods such as Baal and Asherah, idols fashioned by human hands. Believing hearts will say "We will never again say 'Our gods' to what our own hands have made" (verse 3). Rather they confess, "My soul finds rest in God alone; my salvation comes from him" (Psalm 62:1).

Orphans, that is, those who have no earthly helper to protect and provide for them, find compassion in the Lord. The "fatherless" mentioned in Israel's penitent prayer recalls the name given to Hosea's second son, Lo-Ammi, "Not my people." The Lord promised, "I will say to those called 'Not my people,' 'You are my people'; and they will say, 'You are my God'" (2:23). When orphaned Israel repents, it will find a compassionate helper in the Lord.

How could dead Israel (13:1) possibly return to the Lord? Jeremiah has these same Israelites speak a confession: "Restore me [Hebrew: "turn me"], and I will return, because you are the LORD my God" (Jeremiah 31:18). It is God himself who, through his law, leads sinners to confess, "[My] sins have been [my] downfall" (verse 1). It is God himself who turns runaway sinners around by means of his gospel promises and leads them home to himself again. It is all his doing when they trust in him to forgive their sins and he accepts them again as his people.

A penitent remnant of God's people will return from the Babylonian captivity almost two centuries after Hosea concludes his book. They will acknowledge their own and their fathers' sin. "In all that has happened to us," they will pray, "you have been just; you have acted faithfully, while we did wrong. Our kings, our leaders, our priests and our fathers did not follow your law; they did not pay attention to your commands or the warnings you gave them. Even while they were in their kingdom, enjoying your great goodness to them in the spacious and fertile land you gave them, they did not serve you or turn from their evil ways" (Nehemiah 9:33-35). Works of penitent faith in the Lord will be evident as his restored people rebuild the temple and the walls of Jerusalem.

Israel's restoration

4 **"I will heal their waywardness**
and love them freely,
for my anger has turned away from them.
5 **I will be like the dew to Israel;**
he will blossom like a lily.
Like a cedar of Lebanon
he will send down his roots;
6 **his young shoots will grow.**
His splendor will be like an olive tree,
his fragrance like a cedar of Lebanon.
7 **Men will dwell again in his shade.**
He will flourish like the grain.
He will blossom like a vine,
and his fame will be like the wine from Lebanon.

⁸ O Ephraim, what more have I to do with idols?
I will answer him and care for him.
I am like a green pine tree;
your fruitfulness comes from me."

The Lord speaks an unconditional promise of new spiritual life, entirely his gift. He will heal their "waywardness"—the word actually means their "turning [away]." His anger "turns [aside]" from Israel, and he loves them generously, with no holding back. He compares his healing love with the gently falling dew. In Israel from April to October, little rain falls, and plants would dry up in late summer if it were not for the abundant dew. As the dew preserves Canaan's vegetation, so the gracious favor of God creates and nourishes his people's spiritual life.

Verses 5 through 7 illustrate the splendid growth that results from copious dew and rain: lilies blossom, the cedars of the Lebanon mountain range strike their roots deep into the ground and send out new shoots, the foliage of the olive trees gleams silver, the cedars spread their fragrance on the wind. Great trees provide shade for men to live under. Fields of grain flourish to supply bread. Grapevines sprout and blossom, and their fruit produces famous wine. It sounds like paradise.

Hosea's poetic picture of spiritual life glows with such vivid colors that we rightly look for a fulfillment beyond the Jews' return from the Babylonian exile. Verses 4 to 8 are an unconditional promise of glorious plenty, a description of a restored paradise, like the endings of the books of both Joel and Amos. The words of Amos 9:11,12 are quoted by James in Acts 15:16,17 as a prophecy fulfilled in the everlasting kingdom of Jesus Christ. Here, near the end of his book, Hosea also illustrates the Old Testament manner of describing the New Testament kingdom of the Lord's Messiah. In concrete, earthly terms easily visualized by his Old Testament listeners, the prophet pictures the spiritual blessings Christ will bring.

Thus Hosea's words are parallel to Solomon's hymn, Psalm 72, which says of the Lord's anointed Savior: "He will judge your people in righteousness, your afflicted ones with justice. The mountains will bring prosperity to the people, the hills the fruit of righteousness. He will be like rain falling on a mown field, like showers watering the earth. In his days the righteous will flourish; prosperity will abound till the moon is no more. Let grain abound throughout the land; on the tops of the hills may it sway. Let its fruit flourish like Lebanon; let it thrive like the grass of the field. May his name endure forever; may it continue as long as the sun. All nations will be blessed through him, and they will call him blessed" (Psalm 72:2,3,6,7,16,17). When Jesus rules us by his gospel in the holy Christian church, his Spirit gives us faith and enlightens us with all spiritual gifts already in this life. On the day we die, he promises, we will pass over to eternal life with him in paradise, the restored garden of Eden (Luke 23:43).

At one time Israel said of the Canaanite gods, "[My lovers] give me my food and my water, my wool and my linen, my oil and my drink" (2:5). No more. There will be no more wavering between two opinions (1 Kings 18:21); *the LORD alone* will be his people's God. Three times in verse 8 the Lord places the pronoun first to emphasize "It is *I*": I will answer my people's prayers and will watch them closely to care for all their needs; I am like a pine tree, ever green and living; *from me* your fruitfulness comes. Spiritual life is the gift of God alone.

In Luther's explanation of the Third Article of the Apostles' Creed, we confess, "I believe that I cannot by my own thinking or choosing believe in Jesus Christ, my Lord, or come to him. But the Holy Spirit has called me by the gospel, enlightened me with his gifts, sanctified and kept me in the true faith." With that confession we are echoing what both the Old and New Testaments say about the only source of spiritual life and salvation. As dew and rain make the fields produce crops, so the message of the Lord's self-giving love creates faith and brings forth the fruits of faith. Our whole salvation is in the hands of an almighty, gracious God. This message gives all glory to God and supplies sure comfort for sinners like us. Hosea writes in Old Testament terms what Jesus plainly teaches when he calls himself the vine and describes believers as fruit-bearing branches. "If a man remains in me and I in him, he will bear much fruit; apart from me you can do nothing" (John 15:5).

True wisdom

> ⁹ Who is wise? He will realize these things.
>   Who is discerning? He will understand them.
> The ways of the LORD are right;
>   the righteous walk in them,
>   but the rebellious stumble in them.

The book of Hosea closes with a confession of faith. The wise and discerning child of God will realize that the Lord's promises proclaimed by the prophet are true. He will understand that the Lord's punishments foretold by the prophet are justified and that all the Lord's ways—his works of judgment as well as his works of grace—are straight and right. Those who, through Spirit-worked faith, are righteous trust the Lord's promises, submit to his judgments, and willingly follow the path he has marked out with his commandments. They pass through the trials of life in this world to life with God in heaven forever.

As the history of the kingdom of Israel during Hosea's ministry shows, the rebellious stumble in the ways of the Lord. He invites them to know and follow him, but they turn aside to other gods, disobey his law, refuse to hear his prophets, despise his promises, put their trust in other helpers. Therefore, the rebellious stumble: the Lord's word declares their downfall.

The end of the kingdom of Israel in 722 B.C. was the great event in the history of the kingdom of God during Hosea's ministry. Thus his book fittingly ends with a word of judgment. Yet that will not be the Lord's last word of all. Through the preceding verses, the prophet leads believers to look beyond the judgment to eternal life. The Lord promises: "I will heal their waywardness and love them freely, for my anger has turned away from them" (14:4).

In Christ that promise is fulfilled. He covers our sins with his own perfect righteousness. All the ways of the Lord are right. Let us walk in them!

A swarm of locusts approaches

Introduction to Joel

Author and date

Besides the fact that he was the "son of Pethuel" (1:1), we know nothing about the person of the prophet Joel. His name means "the LORD is God." His book speaks powerfully and often about "the day of the LORD." That day is heralded in Joel's time by a plague of locusts and a terrible drought, described in chapters 1 and 2.

Joel does not mention Israel, the Northern Kingdom, at all. In his brief prophecy, he refers to Judah, Jerusalem, Mount Zion, and the temple. Joel evidently did his prophetic work in Judah, the Southern Kingdom, perhaps in Jerusalem.

This prophet does not tell us the name of his country's king, nor does he date his book in any other way. Hosea and Amos, whose books come before and after the prophecy of Joel in the usual arrangement of the minor Prophets, ministered in Israel under King Jeroboam II (793–753 B.C.). Because Joel's book is regularly placed between theirs, we might guess that he prophesied in Judah at about the same time that Hosea and Amos preached in Israel.

Joel speaks of priests (1:9,13) and elders (1:2,14) as leaders of the land, but says nothing about a king. Jehoiada the priest took the lead in placing the Judean boy-king Joash (835–796 B.C.) on the throne. Perhaps, some say, Joel ministered during this period of priestly leadership, while King

Joash still played a minor role (2 Kings 11:4-21). In that case Joel prophesied even before Hosea and Amos.

Scholars who would date Joel much later interpret the prophet's silence about a king in a different way. Joel also does not mention Assyria or Babylon, Judah's enemies during much of its history. Did he perhaps write during the Persian period, sometime after the Jews' return from the Babylonian captivity when Assyria and Babylonia had passed from the scene? When the exiles returned under Prince Zerubbabel in 538 B.C. and with Ezra about 80 years later, no Jewish king assumed the throne. Elders and priests would have directed the affairs of city and temple under the administration of a Persian governor.

If Joel dates from this later period, why would his book be placed between the prophecies of Hosea and Amos? The position of Joel among the minor Prophets may be topical, not chronological. Both Joel and Amos proclaim "the day of the LORD" (Joel 2:1,2; Amos 5:18-20). The first part of Joel 3:16 is the same as the first part of Amos 1:2, and the beginning of Joel 3:18 matches the end of Amos 9:13. The scribes who arranged the books in order might have placed the undated, short book of Joel before the earlier and longer book of Amos, since the two prophets shared some common themes.

Thus the guesses of scholars about the date of Joel range over more than 400 years, from before 800 to after 400 B.C. Most of the reasons they give for various dates are arguments from silence. We simply cannot be certain of the date. Therefore, it seems best to explain and apply Joel's message without reference to a particular period of Old Testament history. The words that the Lord inspired the prophet to write have something to say not only to the Jews in his own time but to every age of the church.

Old Testament prophecy also speaks to New Testament Christians. When Peter preached Christ to the Jews gathered in Jerusalem on Pentecost, he announced that God was fulfilling "what was spoken by the prophet Joel: 'In the last days, God says, I will pour out my Spirit on all people. . . . And everyone who calls on the name of the LORD will be saved'" (Acts 2:16,17,21, quoting Joel 2:28-32). That gospel message is timeless.

The locust plague

An important feature of the book of Joel is a plague of locusts, insects that still periodically threaten the crops in large areas of Asia and Africa. The female desert locust lays eggs under the sand in "pods" of about one hundred. There may be as many as one hundred of such egg pods per square foot. When the insects hatch, usually after rains, they "cover the face of the ground so that it cannot be seen" (Exodus 10:5). Hatching may continue for several days, with young hoppers numbering up to one thousand per square foot at any one time. The young insects, each about one-half inch long, immediately get on the move, looking for green plants to eat.

Over a period varying from weeks to months, locusts shed their skins five times, gradually growing wings, until they mature into hard-shelled flying grasshoppers about three inches long with a four-inch wingspread. If only a few are hatched in the same place, they may remain solitary and be greenish in color. Others, colored yellow or tan and black, hatch and move in swarms. In all their phases, locusts eat all kinds of plants, not only the leaves but even tender branches and bark.

"The potential for destruction is appalling. A locust weighing 3.5 grams will eat its own weight each day. . . . A swarm may number a billion insects and 100 swarms may be on the move during a plague. . . . They are prodigious travelers; a swarm may cover 200 miles a day while moving 2000 miles."*

An observer described a swarm of locusts in a field of millet in Sudan, Africa, in the late 1960s: "A hint of grayness slid along the sand, vague as a touch of smoke. Then, as we watched, it gathered into a wisp and began to spill over the dune slopes. . . . The wisp quickened and spread in the wind until it became a cloud of locusts three miles wide that swept straight toward us. . . . Flying locusts the size of index fingers bounced off my face, tangled in my hair, and grabbed at my shirt with twitchy legs. . . . All around us locusts struggled for room on the plants; they pushed, kicked, and shoved each other, semaphoring furiously with excited antennae. They ravaged the ears on top. They tugged at the leaves. They gnawed at the stems with such

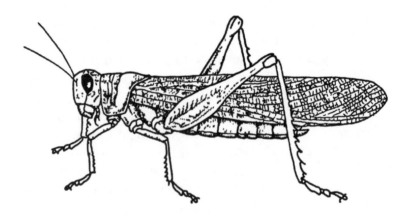

Swarming locust

---

* "Going with the Wind," *Science,* October 1986, 18.

frenzy that we could hear the faint sound of thousands of tiny jaws grinding and chewing, as if someone were scraping a carrot. . . . In 1958 Ethiopia alone lost 167,000 tons of grain, enough to feed more than a million of her people for a year."*

The occasion for the book of Joel was a terrible plague of such desert locusts and then a drought, devastating the land of Judah.

Outline of Joel

   I. The prophet summons his people to mourning and repentance in view of the Lord's judgment (1:1–2:17).

     A. A summons to mourning and repentance because of a locust plague and drought (1:1-20).

     B. The announcement of the Lord's coming judgment, foreshadowed by the locust plague (2:1-17).

  II. The Lord promises to avert judgment and to bestow a blessing (2:18–3:21).

     A. The end of the locusts' destruction (2:18-27).

     B. The outpouring of the Spirit (2:28-32).

     C. Condemnation of Israel's enemies (3:1-16a).

     D. Everlasting blessing for Zion, where the Lord dwells (3:16b-21).

---

* Conley, Robert, "Locusts: Teeth of the Wind," *National Geographic*, August 1969, 202-206.

PART ONE

A Call to Mourning and Repentance
(1:1–2:17)

A summons to witness the locust plague

1 The word of the LORD that came to Joel son of Pethuel.

² Hear this, you elders;
    listen, all who live in the land.
Has anything like this ever happened in your days
    or in the days of your forefathers?
³ Tell it to your children,
    and let your children tell it to their children,
    and their children to the next generation.
⁴ What the locust swarm has left
    the great locusts have eaten;
what the great locusts have left
    the young locusts have eaten;
what the young locusts have left
    other locusts have eaten.

Usually the prophets indicate at the beginning of their books the times in which they are prophesying, since God gives us his revelation within history. Some books, like Nahum or Malachi, let us infer their dates from their contents. Joel gives us no such clues. He only tells us that he is "the son of Pethuel," a name that does not occur elsewhere in the Bible, and that his words are "the word of the LORD." Our God no doubt has his reasons for giving us no further information about Joel than his father's name and for not describing how or when the prophet received this revelation. We need to hear the Lord's message. The person of the messenger and, in this case, even the time when he received the message from God are not our concerns.

In this chapter of his book, Joel first addresses the elders (verse 2). Then he tells the drunkards to wake up and weep (verse 5), the people in general to mourn (verse 8), the farmers to be ashamed or downcast ("despair," verse 11), and the priests to put on sackcloth, that is, mourning dress (verse 13). He is summoning the whole community of God's people to join in a lament.

The elders not only serve as the people's judges and local administrators of the land, but they also preserve the nation's historical memory. Locusts must have been a fairly common agricultural pest in Canaan. Yet none of the elders can remember and none has even heard about a plague in the land like the one in Joel's time. No disaster like this has struck since the Lord plagued the Egyptians with locusts just before the exodus (Exodus 10:13-20). Nor will there be a plague such as this in the days of the children, grandchildren, or great-grandchildren of Joel's generation. The word must be passed on to the coming generations, because the message of this plague also concerns them. This disaster needs to be understood in view of "the day of the LORD" (1:15).

Joel uses four different words for locusts. The KJV translates "palmerworm," "locust," "cankerworm," and "caterpillar." Rather than being four different insects, however, the four words describe different aspects of the same insect, the desert locust. Since the same four words are found in different order in 2:25, it seems unlikely that they are technical terms for phases of the insect as it grows. We might translate with words such as *cutter, swarmer, hopper,* and *jumper.* The repetition "what [some] have left, [the others] have eaten" emphasizes the number of locusts and the total destruction they leave behind.

It is difficult for us today to imagine the horror experienced by an ancient Jewish farmer as a locust swarm descended to feed on fields and orchards. The swarms fly hundreds and even thousands of miles on the wings of the wind, and in an age that knew no insecticides, there was little the people could do to protect their crops. A swarm can do its work so thoroughly that crops of more than one year are affected (2:25). If the locusts almost totally consume one year's crop, little seed remains for the following year. Vines and fruit trees stripped of their leaves and tender bark take some time to recover. The locust plague means empty barns and starving people in Judah and Jerusalem.

The drunkards summoned to mourn

> 5 Wake up, you drunkards, and weep!
>> Wail, all you drinkers of wine;
> wail because of the new wine,
>> for it has been snatched from your lips.
> 6 A nation has invaded my land,
>> powerful and without number;
> it has the teeth of a lion,
>> the fangs of a lioness.
> 7 It has laid waste my vines
>> and ruined my fig trees.
> It has stripped off their bark
>> and thrown it away,
>> leaving their branches white.

Joel is calling all the people to lament. Having summoned the respectable elders to observe the devastation caused by the locusts, he turns to some of those who least deserve honor. He summons the most conspicuous consumers of the fruit of the vine, those who habitually drink too much, to wake up from their stupor and weep. Not only will their excess be cut off. The locusts chew up everything green with the fierceness of lions tearing their prey. The destruction of grapes, vine leaves, young branches, and tender bark, leaving the branches stripped bare, will mean no wine at all this year. (The Lord speaks of *my* vines, *my* fig trees: the land is really his.) Perhaps Joel especially summons the drunkards to mourn because they represent the people's tendency to live only for the here and now. They carelessly grab all the enjoyment they can and take no thought for the coming day of the Lord.

All the people summoned to mourn

> [8] Mourn like a virgin in sackcloth
> grieving for the husband of her youth.
> [9] Grain offerings and drink offerings
> are cut off from the house of the Lord.
> The priests are in mourning,
> those who minister before the Lord.
> [10] The fields are ruined,
> the ground is dried up;
> the grain is destroyed,
> the new wine is dried up,
> the oil fails.

Having called elders and drunkards, the top and bottom of the social scale, to lament, Joel now summons all the people. Elsewhere in the Scriptures, the Israelites are compared to a young virgin (e.g. Amos 5:2), since the Lord illustrates his people as his own promised bride. Here this thought may be in the background. The prophet's main purpose is to call up a picture of the deepest grief. The locusts have so devastated the land as to break the heart of anyone who loves it. Because of the loss of Canaan's riches, all the Israelites will mourn. Their sorrow will be like the grief of a young virgin ready for marriage who must put on rough sackcloth instead of her wedding dress because the husband to whom she is promised is taken from her.

The lack of crops will mean no grain or drink offerings for the temple of the Lord. According to the law, grain offerings in the form of fine flour mixed with oil and incense, or bread baked without yeast, or crushed and roasted heads of new grain were to be salted and offered on the altar. In some cases a portion was set aside for the priests. (See Leviticus 2; 6:14-23.) Fine flour also served as the sin offering of Israelites too poor to bring two doves (Leviticus 5:11-13). A grain offering and a quart or more of wine as a drink offering were to accompany all burnt offerings (Numbers 15:1-12).

Such sacrifices testified that the Lord was giving the people of Israel the land of Canaan itself, as well as all the fruits of the ground. But the locusts will leave no grain to offer, no olives to make oil for mixing with the meal offerings, no grapes to press out into wine for the drink offering. From verses 10 and 12, as well as 17 through 20, it appears that a severe drought follows the locust swarms. (Drought is the only factor in nature that ordinarily ends a locust plague, since the females cannot lay their eggs in sand that is totally dry.) The Israelites and their priests are unable to show their gratitude and love to the Lord by bringing the offerings ordained in his law. They are cut off from expressing their fellowship with God through their prescribed worship in the temple.

The farmers summoned to mourn

¹¹ **Despair, you farmers,**
  wail, you vine growers;
 grieve for the wheat and the barley,
  because the harvest of the field is destroyed.

¹² The vine is dried up
  and the fig tree is withered;
the pomegranate, the palm and the apple tree—
  all the trees of the field—are dried up.
Surely the joy of mankind
  is withered away.

Joel summons the farmers to lament. They are the first people to see and feel the effects of the locust plague and drought. The word translated *despair* actually means "be ashamed." When the time comes to offer their first-fruits, the farmers will have to appear before the Lord empty handed. In speaking to the men who work the ground, the prophet fittingly gives the fullest listing of crops destroyed by the locusts and the drought: wheat, the finest grain; barley to make coarse bread for the poor; grape vines and fruit trees, including fig, pomegranate, date and apple. A good harvest brings rejoicing to the people who work the fields, vineyards, and orchards, but if locusts and drought destroy the crops, the farmers' joy "is withered away."

The priests summoned to mourn

¹³ Put on sackcloth, O priests, and mourn;
  wail, you who minister before the altar.
Come, spend the night in sackcloth,
  you who minister before my God;
for the grain offerings and drink offerings
  are withheld from the house of your God.
¹⁴ Declare a holy fast;
  call a sacred assembly.
Summon the elders
  and all who live in the land
to the house of the LORD your God,
  and cry out to the LORD.

Now Joel speaks with special urgency to the priests: "Put on sackcloth! Mourn! Wail! Come, spend the night in sackcloth! Declare a fast! Call an assembly! Summon the elders! Cry out to the LORD!" Through their worship in the temple, the people of Israel confessed the Lord as their God, acknowledged that he had kept his promise and given them the land, received the promise of his forgiveness, and enjoyed fellowship with him. Now without the ordained sacrifices, the priests cannot fulfill their functions according to the law of Moses. The signs of Israel's fellowship with the Lord are cut off. Therefore it is fitting that the priests should put on rough sackcloth, the clothing of mourners, instead of the white linen garments that express the joy of worshiping Israel's holy Lord. Instead of entering the temple at the hours of worship to offer the people's sacrifices with psalms of praise, the priests should remain in the temple day and night to lament before the Lord.

Since the priests represent all Israel at worship, it is also fitting that they should summon all the people to assemble in the temple court, to fast as a sign of national repentance, and to cry out with one voice to the Lord. The Lord placed his temple in Jerusalem so that his people could gather and pray to him there in times of need. After the temple dedication, he told Solomon, "When I shut up the heavens so that there is no rain, or command locusts to devour the land or send a plague among my people, if my people, who are called by my name, will humble themselves and pray and seek my face and turn from their wicked ways, then will I hear from heaven and will forgive their sin and will heal their land" (2 Chronicles 7:13,14).

The substance of the people's prayer is given in verses 15 through 20, which might be enclosed in quotation marks.

The prophet himself leads the prayer, but he has called all the people to join him in this lamentation. With the sad evidence of locust plague and drought all around, Joel summons the people to lift their eyes and look beyond the present calamity to "the day of the LORD."

The day of the Lord

¹⁵ **Alas for that day!**
   For the day of the LORD is near;
   it will come like destruction from the Almighty.

¹⁶ **Has not the food been cut off**
   before our very eyes—
joy and gladness
   from the house of our God?
¹⁷ **The seeds are shriveled**
   beneath the clods.
The storehouses are in ruins,
   the granaries have been broken down,
   for the grain has dried up.
¹⁸ **How the cattle moan!**
   The herds mill about
because they have no pasture;
   even the flocks of sheep are suffering.

¹⁹ **To you, O LORD, I call,**
   for fire has devoured the open pastures
   and flames have burned up all the trees of the field.
²⁰ **Even the wild animals pant for you;**
   the streams of water have dried up
   and fire has devoured the open pastures.

"Alas for that day!" the prayer begins. It is the cry of someone who is experiencing a terrible loss. Joshua begins his prayer to the Lord with the same word when his people had been defeated at Ai (Joshua 7:7), and Ezekiel says it when the Lord shows him the destruction of Jerusalem (Ezekiel 9:8).

The locusts have destroyed the people's food and made offerings impossible. Granaries are failing to ruin, since there is no harvest to store in them. The cattle bellow in distress and restlessly mill about looking for water, because the drought that follows the locust plague has dried up streams and grasslands. Even the sheep, which can graze on pasture so marginal that it will not support cattle, are suffering for lack of grass and water. The "fire" and "flames" (verses 19,20) testify to the anger of the Lord (Exodus 19:18; Deuteronomy 4:24), while they also serve as comparisons for the searing heat of the drought that parches the grasslands and dries up the watercourses. Wild animals along the dry streambeds pant for water from the Lord, while his hungry and thirsty people cry out to him.

The key words in this part of Joel's book are in verse 15: "[What a dreadful day!] For the day of the LORD is near; it will come like destruction from the Almighty." The same thought is repeated in 2:1,2 and again in 2:11. On first reading of this book, we may be mystified. What can be the connection between the plague of locusts in Joel's day and the coming "day of the LORD"?

To the farseeing and believing eye of the inspired prophet, the history of his own time is transparent and prophetic. The present day is like a window with a view of another day to come, or like the threatening shadow cast by a more terrible future day. Joel sees the effects of locusts and drought, but he is also looking through and beyond this plague to *the day when the Lord will come to his people for judgment.* That is what "the day of the LORD" means here. In fact, the locust plague itself and the drought that follows are signs of the Lord's judgment.

In his last words to the people of Israel before they entered the land of Canaan, Moses promised them blessings if they kept their law covenant with the Lord and threatened curses if they broke it. "If you do not obey the LORD your God and do not carefully follow all his commands and decrees I am giving you today, all these curses will come upon you and overtake you. . . . The LORD will strike you . . . with scorching heat and drought. . . . The sky over your head will be bronze, the ground beneath you iron. The LORD will turn the rain of your country into dust and powder" (Deuteronomy 28:15, 22-24). "You will sow much seed in the field but you will harvest little, because locusts will devour it. . . . Swarms of locusts will take over all your trees and the crops of your land" (Deuteronomy 28:38-42).

Now this threat is being carried out. According to the Lord's own revelation through Moses, the locust plague and drought mean that the people of Israel have been unfaithful to their God. They have broken their covenant with him. He is angry with his people and sends the locust plague because of their disobedience and unrepented sins.

To escape his anger, they can only flee to his mercy. The very purpose of the drought and locusts is to lead Israel to repent, to "return to the LORD" (see Leviticus 26:40-45; Amos 4:6-9). That is why Joel has called upon all the people of the land to assemble in the temple and to lament before the Lord. The thirsty cattle moan and the wild animals pant for God's gift of water without being urged, but the prophet must plead with the people of Israel to confess their sin and to cry to their Maker for mercy.

If the people do not heed the prophet's summons to repentance, then another "day of the LORD" is coming. Moses spoke of it at the conclusion of the threats connected with disobedience to the Lord's covenant: "Then the LORD will scatter you among all nations, from one end of the earth to the other. . . . Among those nations you will find no repose, no resting place for the sole of your foot" (Deuteronomy 28:64,65). That "day of the LORD" will mean the end of Israel as a nation in the Promised Land.

But the "day of the LORD" as it is described in the last chapter of Joel's book means an even more severe judgment. It will be a day when "the LORD will roar from Zion and thunder from Jerusalem" (3:16) against his enemies. The storm of judgment will descend not only on the Gentile unbelievers outside of Israel but also on impenitent Israelites who have forsaken his covenant. For impenitent sinners the day of the Lord will bring destruction, not salvation, as Amos reminded the Israelites of Samaria: "Woe to you who long for the day of the LORD! Why do you long for the day of the LORD? That day will be darkness, not light" (Amos 5:18).

If the Old Testament prophets generally paint "the day of the LORD" in dark and angry colors, it is because they are usually dealing with an impenitent people, and the impenitent can expect only God's anger when he returns for judgment. That day "will come like destruction from the Almighty" (verse 15). For the believers in Judah, Joel will also present the other side of the picture: "The LORD will be a refuge for his people, a stronghold for the people of Israel" (3:16). In the very last verse of this book, the Lord promises to pardon their guilt and to dwell among them forever (3:21).

What does this mean for God's New Testament people, the members of the Christian church? We do not live under the terms of the covenant the Lord made with Israel at Sinai. At the cross our Creator made a new covenant, sealing his promise with the blood of Christ: "I will forgive their wickedness and will remember their sins no more" (Jeremiah 31:34). In this new covenant relation with God, we also look forward to a "day of the LORD." We call it "the day of our Lord Jesus Christ" (1 Corinthians 1:8), and we anticipate it with joy. We "eagerly wait for our Lord Jesus Christ to be revealed" (1 Corinthians 1:7).

When Jesus described the signs of the end, he also made the natural phenomena and disasters of this world's history transparent and prophetic for us. We see nation rising against nation, great earthquakes, famines like the one in Joel's time, epidemics, terrifying events and great signs from heaven, persecutions of the church, nations in anguish and perplexity. Finally there will be signs in the sun, moon, and stars, "for the heavenly bodies will be shaken" (Luke 21:10-26).

The words of Jesus help us look through and beyond such events to his second coming. All these signs are like a long shadow cast by his coming at the end of time. The signs of the end bring a message from the Lord Jesus to his waiting people: "When these things begin to take place, stand up and lift up your heads, because your redemption is drawing near" (Luke 21:28).

The old covenant that the Lord made with Israel at Mount Sinai included both blessings and curses, so that Moses concluded, "See, I set before you today life and prosperity, death and destruction" (Deuteronomy 30:15). The new covenant that Jesus established at Mount Calvary promises only blessing. Yet outside of that covenant, *there is no blessing for all eternity:* "Whoever believes and is baptized will be saved, but whoever does not believe will be condemned" (Mark 16:16). Only repentant faith can look up and await the day of the Lord with hope and joy.

It was unbelief and impenitence that led the Israelites to break their agreement with a Lord who ever since Abraham had shown them only grace and mercy beyond measure. In the prophecy of Joel, we hear a solemn warning "not to receive God's grace in vain" (2 Corinthians 6:1). Whoever is tangled in impenitence and unbelief when the judgment comes—or at death, when his own time of grace is past— will have to say with the people of the prophet's generation, "What a dreadful day!" because "it will come like destruction from the Almighty" (1:15).

How blessed we are when we can look forward to that day with hope and joy, trusting in Jesus as our Lord and Savior. We know that we will all appear "before the judgment seat of Christ" (2 Corinthians 5:10). The *Lord* who died for our sins and rose to justify us will come again to be our judge. The "day of the LORD" will be his day!

The alarm announces the day of the Lord

2 **Blow the trumpet in Zion;**
sound the alarm on my holy hill.
Let all who live in the land tremble,
for the day of the LORD is coming.
It is close at hand—
² **a day of darkness and gloom,**
a day of clouds and blackness.
Like dawn spreading across the mountains
a large and mighty army comes,
such as never was of old
nor ever will be in ages to come.

A watchman on a city's walls would blow a horn to warn the people of an attack by a hostile army. Joel pictures himself as a lookout on the walls of Jerusalem catching first sight of the advancing enemy columns. He calls another watchman to sound the alarm with a ram's horn. Again the locust plague, the present event, is transparent and prophetic to Joel's eye. He speaks of the locusts and the Lord's coming day of judgment in one breath, much as Jesus mingles his warning about the fall of Jerusalem with his words about signs of the world's endtime (Luke 21:20-28).

The inhabitants of the land have broken their covenant with the Lord. Locusts are advancing to destroy their crops. Because the people will not repent, the day of the locusts serves as advance notice of a more terrible day. For the impenitent people of Israel, the day of the Lord will be "a day of darkness and gloom, a day of clouds and blackness" (verse 2). It is not a day to hope for but a day to dread (see Amos 5:20), "a day of wrath, a day of distress and anguish, a day of trouble and ruin, a day of darkness and gloom, a day of clouds and blackness" (Zephaniah 1:15).

The enemy overruns the hills around Jerusalem "like dawn spreading across the mountains" (verse 2). When Joel writes that "a large and mighty army comes," are these and the following verses a literal picture of a foreign army's invasion of Judah? Some interpreters think so. But the same sort of expressions appear in chapter 1, where Joel wrote, "A nation has invaded my land" (1:6). There he described the sharp teeth of invaders stripping off all the bark of vines and figs, clearly picturing a plague of locusts (1:6,7). When the prophet writes about this "large and mighty army" (verse 2; see also 2:25), he is picturing the swarms of insects. He writes that "they charge *like* warriors, they scale walls *like* soldiers." He is still describing the locust plague, but in terms that suggest an enemy army following a "scorched-earth" policy.

In the next verses, the prophet gives his fullest description of the locust plague. Joel was not only a prophet but also a poet with a gift for vivid description. The Lord who created Joel, gave him the gift of speech, and inspired his book also

143

uses the poet's way with words. Joel paints a picture of the locust swarms with a metaphor of plundering enemies who wreak destruction wherever they go.

The locust army

³ Before them fire devours,
   behind them a flame blazes.
Before them the land is like the garden of Eden,
   behind them, a desert waste—
   nothing escapes them.
⁴ They have the appearance of horses;
   they gallop along like cavalry.
⁵ With a noise like that of chariots
   they leap over the mountaintops,
like a crackling fire consuming stubble,
   like a mighty army drawn up for battle.

⁶ At the sight of them, nations are in anguish;
   every face turns pale.
⁷ They charge like warriors;
   they scale walls like soldiers.
They all march in line,
   not swerving from their course.
⁸ They do not jostle each other;
   each marches straight ahead.
They plunge through defenses
   without breaking ranks.
⁹ They rush upon the city;
   they run along the wall.
They climb into the houses;
   like thieves they enter through the windows.

¹⁰ Before them the earth shakes,
   the sky trembles,
the sun and moon are darkened,
   and the stars no longer shine.
¹¹ The LORD thunders
   at the head of his army;

his forces are beyond number,
and mighty are those who obey his command.
The day of the LORD is great;
it is dreadful.
Who can endure it?

Joel compares the effect of the locust army to that of a prairie fire, turning a land as lush as the Garden of Eden into a desert waste. Seen close up, a locust's long head somewhat resembles the head of a horse, and the insects are as destructive as troops of cavalry and chariots, the armored corps of ancient armies. More mobile than cavalry, the swarms of locusts can even fly over the mountains. When they land, dry stalks and young tree branches crackle under their weight. The line of advance of large swarms stretches for miles, "like a mighty army drawn up for battle" (verse 5). In a day when farmers' efforts at control could consist of no more than stamping on the locusts and burying them or beating them off the vines and trees with sticks, we do not wonder that at the sight of the swarms, "nations are in anguish" and "every face turns pale" (verse 6).

An observer describing the locust plague in Jerusalem from 1915 to 1916 wrote that they "eat up everything green that they encounter. Wild growth, grain, the leaves of fig trees, vines, even olive trees, everything disappears where they move along. They cover the walls of houses [and] penetrate to the inside through doors and windows."* The description reminds us of Joel's words: "They rush upon the city; they run along the wall. They climb into the houses; like thieves they enter through the windows" (verse 9).

---

* G. Dalman, quoted by H. W. Wolff, *Joel and Amos* (Philadelphia: Fortress, 1977), 28.

At verses 10 and 11, it seems again as if the prophet is looking through and beyond the locust plague and referring to other events. We cannot read about the locust swarms without being reminded of the hosts of Assyrians advancing on Samaria, and later the Babylonian armies and then the Roman legions besieging Jerusalem. But under the Spirit's inspiration, the prophet looks even further into the future.

Still another "day of the LORD" will come at last. As a sign of that day, the earth will shake, and sun, moon, and stars will be darkened (verse 10; compare Isaiah 13:10; 34:4; Mark 13:24,25). "At that time men will see the Son of Man coming in clouds with great power and glory. And he will send his angels and gather his elect from the four winds, from the ends of the earth to the ends of the heavens" (Mark 13:26,27).

Whether the prophets describe swarms of locusts swooping in over the Judean hills or an enemy army coining down on Jerusalem, they always make it unmistakably clear that the Lord is in command. He controls both history and nature. When he prophesies the defeat and exile of the Israelites, he says, "*I* will drive them out of my house" (Hosea 9:15). When the Assyrians attack Jerusalem in 700 B.C., the Lord says through the prophet Isaiah, "*I* send him [i.e., the Assyrian] against a godless nation, *I* dispatch him against a people who anger me, to seize loot and snatch plunder, and to trample them down like mud in the streets" (10:6).

Here as the locusts swarm over Judah, Joel writes that *"the LORD thunders at the head of his army; his forces are beyond number, and mighty are those who obey his command"* (verse 11). The front chariot may carry an Assyrian general, but it is the Lord, the commander of history, who leads the enemy army against Jerusalem. The locusts may seem to be following blind instinct as they lay their eggs in the moist sand or take flight in the direction the wind is blowing, but it is the Lord, the ruler of nature, who directs the swarms over the desert and into the Judean fields.

We easily forget God's total control over his world—it is his world, not ours—or we only apply this truth to ancient biblical history. But the Lord's prophets correct our understanding of history. It is our God who still makes all history happen. Joel describes the Lord's rule of the locust swarms so that we will confess his power over nature—wind and calm, storms and sunshine, germs and medicine, the rhythm of the waves, and the beating of human hearts.

We experience our own "locust plagues and droughts": tornadoes, hurricanes, floods, and volcanic eruptions; wars among nations and social upheavals that we experience or hear about on the TV evening news. Joel's book will accomplish its purpose in our lives if we learn to look beyond and through such present events to the day that they foreshadow. In his plan for the world, the Lord has set an end and a goal, a day that will bring all history to a close.

Joel lifts our vision beyond the swarms of locusts, beyond enemy armies besieging Jerusalem, beyond the troubles of our own lives, to the final judgment. He wants his readers to experience the locust plague and the drought in view of the day of the Lord. His purpose is to lead them to repentance, so that the Lord will acknowledge them as his people at the end of time and will gather them to himself forever.

We need to see each day and view every event in view of the end of all things. Then we are ready to hear the Lord's own answer, given through the prophet, to the question "Who can endure the day of the Lord?" We *must* know the answer to that question if we are to be gathered with the elect on the last great day of the Lord. His Word has the answer for us.

Rend your heart

> ¹² "Even now," declares the LORD,
>   "return to me with all your heart,
>   with fasting and weeping and mourning."

> ¹³ Rend your heart
>   and not your garments.
>   Return to the LORD your God,
>   for he is gracious and compassionate,
>   slow to anger and abounding in love,
>   and he relents from sending calamity.
> ¹⁴ Who knows? He may turn and have pity
>   and leave behind a blessing—
>   grain offerings and drink offerings
>   for the LORD your God.

"Return to me," the Lord invites through his prophet. The Lord gave his promise of a Savior to Adam and Eve and then repeated the promise in the covenant he made with Abraham, Isaac, Jacob, and their descendants. He delivered the people of Israel from slavery in Egypt and made his law-covenant with them at Sinai to separate them from all nations for himself, to be his holy people. They broke their covenant with him, disobeyed his commandments, and worshiped other gods. Joel's message, "Return to me"—that is, come all the way back to me—"with all your heart," fittingly sums up the preaching of all the prophets. It also answers this question: "How can we be delivered from judgment on the day of the Lord?"

Joel calls for "fasting and weeping and mourning" (verse 12). These are marks of heartfelt sorrow for sin. The only

fast-day ordained by the law of Moses was the Day of
Atonement (Leviticus 16:29,31). (In Acts 27:9 the Day of
Atonement is simply referred to as "the Fast.") The Israelites
"denied themselves" on that day to confess to God their
deep sorrow over their sins. The Lord through his prophet
calls for a sorrow that sees farther than the famine brought
on by locusts and drought. This is to be no mere complaint
about barren fields and empty stomachs. Joel is calling his
people to mourn because they have abandoned the Lord
their God.

Sinners like to build defenses against the Lord and his
call to repentance. Worldly people laugh at God's invitation
and surround themselves with "life's worries, riches and
pleasures" (Luke 8:14). But religious people have a line of
defense all their own. Religious ceremonies themselves can
become a defense against God's call to repent. People in
Joel's time might lament loudly and tear their garments as a
sign of sorrow and then think that God must hear them,
without ever letting his Word penetrate their hard hearts.

That is why Joel continues, "Rend your heart and not
your garments. Return to the LORD your God'" (verse 13).
He does not want his "religious" people just going
through the motions of repentance. In speaking to the
people of God, the prophet expects that they will let the
Word sink into their hearts and consciences. He expects
that the visible signs, fasting and weeping and mourning,
will be outward marks of an inward sorrow about past
sin. Such "godly sorrow brings repentance that leads to
salvation" (2 Corinthians 7:10).

Worldly people who laugh at God's call to repentance
will probably not buy or read books such as the one you are
reading. Commentaries on the Bible are generally used by
people who are "religious." Unfortunately, we Christians are

often not all that different from the "religious" people in Joel's time: we recite our confession of sins, sing our hymns ("Alas, my God, my sins are great, My conscience doth upbraid me"—The Lutheran Hymnal [TLH] 317:1), sit through a sermon, put our offering in the basket, and think that God must be satisfied with us. Our worship can become a mere "going-through-the-religious-motions," a defense against the Lord's call to repentance, without faith in our hearts or the fruits of faith in our lives.

Joel would tear down our "religious" defenses. Through him the Lord continues to call his wandering people home: "Return to me with all your heart. . . . Rend your heart and not your garments." Let the law of your holy God humble your pride. Let him lead you to contrition, even though your broken heart may hurt. True repentance is appalled at sin, because sin separates us from the Lord, the source of life and love. And true repentance includes faith in the promised forgiveness of sins. The repentant sinner turns back to the Lord, confident of his grace: "Have mercy on me, O God, according to your unfailing love; according to your great compassion blot out my transgressions" (Psalm 51:1).

When Joel invites the Israelites to repent, he fittingly describes Israel's God: "He is gracious and compassionate, slow to anger and abounding in love, and he relents from sending calamity" (verse 13). These are the same terms the covenant LORD used to describe himself when he passed before Moses on Mount Sinai (Exodus 34:6,7). Then also the Lord was dealing with a disobedient people. The Israelites had forgotten him and his deliverance from Egypt in favor of the pleasures of worshiping a golden calf. Yet Israel's Lord remained ready to welcome sinners home again.

He showed Moses what kind of God he is. He loves us when we do not deserve it ("gracious"). His heart is warm with mercy for sinners ("compassionate"). Even though often provoked, he does not let his wrath flame up and destroy us ("slow to anger"). He is totally faithful in keeping his covenant promise of abundant blessing ("abounding in love"). Even though his law threatens punishment, he gladly turns his judgment aside when he sees that his Word has had its intended effect ("he relents from sending calamity").

Joel does not promise that the locusts will disappear or that the drought will end. The Lord "*may* turn and have pity" (verse 14). The prophet leaves it to the Lord how he will answer his people's penitent prayer. Joel knows that any prosperity to come will be undeserved. Yet until God answers otherwise, the prophet expects that the Lord will save his people again, just because he is a gracious God.

In fact, Joel has already considered how Israel should use any crops that may be harvested after the locusts depart. If the Lord shows his people such great kindness as to end the plague and the drought, they will bring thank offerings of grain and wine to the temple. Joel is not bargaining with God; he simply is certain that God will be merciful, so certain that he already thinks in terms of thank offerings. He knows that a living faith will bear thankful fruit.

The Lord may use the bitter results of sin—perhaps a severe accident or illness—to turn sinners back in his direction, much as the locust plague and drought called forth Israel's fasting, weeping, and mourning. The message of Joel, however, sets before Israel and before us a better reason for turning away from sin and back to the Lord: "he is gracious and compassionate, slow to anger and abounding in love" (verse 13). The motive for sincere repentance, like every other good effect in our hearts and lives, is the grace and mercy of a loving God, displayed in the sacrifice of his Son for the sins of the world. It is true that our sins deserve damnation, and in fact they did bring the pains of hellfire on Jesus. But once we have recognized that, God's Word immediately draws our whole attention away from our sins to our Savior's grace, compassion, patience, and love.

A call to prayer for deliverance

> ¹⁵ **Blow the trumpet in Zion,**
> **declare a holy fast,**
> **call a sacred assembly.**
> ¹⁶ **Gather the people,**
> **consecrate the assembly;**
> **bring together the elders,**
> **gather the children,**
> **those nursing at the breast.**
> **Let the bridegroom leave his room**
> **and the bride her chamber.**
> ¹⁷ **Let the priests, who minister before the LORD,**
> **weep between the temple porch and the altar.**
> **Let them say, "Spare your people, O LORD.**
> **Do not make your inheritance an object of scorn,**
> **a byword among the nations.**
> **Why should they say among the peoples,**
> **'Where is their God?'"**

The prophet summons all the people to observe a "holy fast," to come together in a "sacred assembly," and to let the priests lead them in prayer. On the first day of the seventh month of every year and on the Day of Atonement (Yom Kippur) in the Jubilee Year, the ram's horn was to be sounded throughout the land (Leviticus 23:23; 25:9). Joel would have the people set aside a special day of repentance and prayer for the Lord, like the Day of Atonement, because of the locust plague and drought.

The prophet summons even the young children from their mothers' breasts. He calls even the bride and bridegroom, who might be expected to be thinking only about each other. In this way Joel makes it plain that *everyone* should fast and pray. Again, as in 1:13, the prophet first summons the people and then the priests. Their prayers sum up the petitions of the whole people of Israel. They must stand in the inner court of the temple before the Lord's altar empty-handed, without thank offerings. Instead of singing psalms of thanksgiving and praise, they should approach the altar to pray with tears of repentance, while all the people assembled in the outer court of the temple join in repentant prayer.

Their prayer bears a strong resemblance to the intercession of Moses at Mount Sinai when the people had set up the golden calf. God had threatened then to destroy the people of Israel, and Moses prayed, "Why should the Egyptians say, 'It was with evil intent that he brought them out, to kill them in the mountains and to wipe them off the face of the earth'? Turn from your fierce anger; relent and do not bring disaster on your people. Remember your servants Abraham, Isaac and Israel." (Exodus 32:12,13).

Joel also leads the priests to pray, "Spare *your* people, O LORD . . . *your* inheritance" (verse 17)—these descendants of Abraham, Isaac, and Jacob, with whom you made your everlasting gospel covenant. The priests' prayer, like the prayer of Moses, appeals to the honor of God, as if to say, "Don't let the heathen scorn your people and make fun of you, Israel's God. The heathen might say that you abandoned Israel or that you were too busy elsewhere to protect your chosen people. Spare us, and don't let the heathen talk that way about you."

Joel is not presumptuous: he does not dictate to the Lord what the answer to Israel's prayer should be. Yet because of the Lord's promises, he is very bold, and he encourages the priests and people to appeal boldly to the honor of God and to his covenant promises in their prayer for deliverance.

Can the prophet teach us such boldness in prayer? When the church prays—whether it is for workers in the Lord's harvest, for protection against persecutors, or for strength to confess Christ in a hostile world—we remind God that we are *his* people. We pray as children of God through faith in Christ Jesus. We bear our Father's name on earth, and his honor is at stake as we represent him.

When we as individual Christians pray for healing in sickness, for help in all our other troubles, for strength to bear hard burdens, or for joyful hearts in depressing times, we may also remind God, "Dear Father, through Jesus I am your child. Forgive me, help me, deliver me from trouble. Then I will thank and honor you. Let the deliverance you send me glorify your name before men, so that others will join me in praising you."

With the next verse, the second main part of Joel's book begins. The Lord answers his people's penitent, believing prayer.

PART TWO

A Promise to Avert Judgment and to Send a Blessing
(2:18–3:21)

The Lord's answer: an end to locusts and drought

¹⁸ Then the LORD will be jealous for his land
and take pity on his people.

¹⁹The LORD will reply to them:

"I am sending you grain, new wine and oil,
enough to satisfy you fully;
never again will I make you
an object of scorn to the nations.

²⁰ "I will drive the northern army far from you,
pushing it into a parched and barren land,
with its front columns going into the eastern sea
and those in the rear into the western sea.
And its stench will go up;
its smell will rise."

The Lord describes himself as a "jealous" God (Exodus 20:5). He is zealous to carry out his threats and his promises. Here he means that he is solicitous for his own land and his own people. He has paid close attention to their prayer. He also is concerned that the heathen should not scorn him and the people of Israel. Therefore, he answers that he will renew their supply of grain, wine, and olive oil. He will drive off the locusts and end the drought.

The locusts are called "the northern army" in verse 20, a strange title, since the swarms generally flew into Israel from the deserts in the east and south. Together with the locust plague, the prophet possibly also has in mind the Assyrian and Babylonian armies that poured into Canaan from the north (Jeremiah 1:14,15) to carry out the Lord's judgments. He may be naming the locust swarm "the northerner" after them. Or perhaps these particular swarms approached on a wind that came from the north. A witness says that in 1915 the locusts flew over Jerusalem from the northeast as well as from the south.

The Lord promises to drive the locust armies off into the desert, the barren wilderness south of the Judean Negev. One way that masses of locusts perish is by being blown out to sea. If Joel has the Negev in mind, the "eastern sea" would be the Dead Sea, and the "western sea" the Mediterranean. The stench rising when the locusts' bodies wash up and decay on the shore will show that the Lord has destroyed Israel's enemies by drowning them in the sea, just as he triumphed over the horsemen and chariots of Pharaoh during the exodus from Egypt (Exodus 15:4,5).

The Lord has assured his people of an answer to their penitent, believing prayer. His promise leads to such certainty of deliverance that Joel immediately breaks into a psalm of praise, calling the land itself, the wild animals, and the people of Zion to rejoice with him.

A psalm of thankful praise

> Surely he has done great things.
> 21   Be not afraid, O land;
>   be glad and rejoice.
> Surely the LORD has done great things.
> 22   Be not afraid, O wild animals,
>   for the open pastures are becoming green.

> The trees are bearing their fruit;
>> the fig tree and the vine yield their riches.
> ²³ Be glad, O people of Zion,
>> rejoice in the LORD your God,
> for he has given you
>> the autumn rains in righteousness.
> He sends you abundant showers,
>> both autumn and spring rains, as before.
> ²⁴ The threshing floors will be filled with grain;
>> the vats will overflow with new wine and oil.

The book of Joel beautifully illustrates how God invites us to pray, promises to hear us, and summons us to praise him: "Call upon me in the day of trouble; I will deliver you, and you will honor me" (Psalm 50:15). Israel has gone through a day, a year of trouble: the locust plague and drought. The Lord has promised deliverance, and his prophet leads the people in honoring him with this psalm. The wild animals that panted for the Lord (1:20) will be satisfied. Fig trees, vineyards, olive trees, and grainfields will yield abundant harvests again. The autumn rains, falling in October and November, will soften the ground so that the farmers can plant, and the spring rains, coming in March and April at the end of the wet winter, will ensure well-filled heads of grain. The day of trouble has led God's people to return to him. The Lord's goodness in answering their prayer now leads them to praise him.

A disagreement among translations of these verses comes in verse 23: "He has given you the autumn rains in righteousness." An earlier printing of the NIV read "He has given you a teacher of righteousness." The Hebrew word *moreh* means "teacher," but later in the verse this same word means "former rain," the autumn rain in Israel that softens the ground for planting. There it is coupled with a word that means "latter rain," the late winter and spring rains that must fall to ensure a good crop. It is a sound translation principle to render a word according to its context: thus the NIV translators now prefer "autumn rains" both times the word occurs in this verse.

If Joel had meant "teacher," this passage would be a reference to the Messiah as the final cause of God's favor and for his people's rejoicing. On the other hand, "he has given you the autumn rains in righteousness" fits the other words and verses in this part of Joel's book. God shows his righteousness by listening to his people's repentant prayer and ending the drought in time for the fall planting season.

The Lord God has given us his teacher for righteousness, our Lord Jesus Christ. He also sends the rains that make our crops grow. His gift of a Savior is the greatest gift, bearing fruit for eternity, but we confess that "every good and perfect gift is from above" (James 1:17). The fact that believing Bible translators continue to revise their translation need not disturb our faith, provided that their interpretations are faithful to the text and in agreement with other clear passages of Scripture.

After his people's thankful psalm of praise, the Lord speaks again.

A promise of plenty

> ²⁵ "I will repay you for the years the locusts have eaten—
> the great locust and the young locust,
> the other locusts and the locust swarm—
> my great army that I sent among you.
> ²⁶ You will have plenty to eat, until you are full,
> and you will praise the name of the LORD your God,
> who has worked wonders for you;
> never again will my people be shamed.

²⁷ **Then you will know that I am in Israel,**
   that I am the LORD your God,
   and that there is no other;
   never again will my people be shamed.

Just like 1:4, verse 25 has four different words for the
locust army that has ravaged the land. They probably do not
designate the different life phases of the insect but emphasize the number of swarms and the total devastation they
caused. The locusts have "eaten the years"; they have consumed whatever crops the land would have produced for
two years or more.

The Lord calls them "*my* great army that *I sent* among
you" (verse 25). He leaves no doubt that he is still in command when his people suffer drought, defeat, or disaster of
any kind. "I form the light and create darkness, I bring prosperity and create disaster; I the LORD, do all these things," he
reminds his ancient people and also us today (Isaiah 45:7).

By saying "I will repay you," the Lord tells his people
that the blessing to follow in the next years will more than
balance out the harm of "the years the locusts have eaten."
The Lord, through the prophet, has taught his people to
look beyond and through the locust plague and drought to
the "day of the LORD," when he will judge the world. In the
same way, a prophecy of coming prosperity foreshadows
and includes perfect happiness for God's people in eternity.
Then we will praise the name of the Lord forever for working the wonders of his salvation for us. Joel's promise
reminds us of Paul's words: "I consider that our present sufferings are not worth comparing with the glory that will be
revealed in us" (Romans 8:18). Then God's people will
never again be put to shame. Their enemies will never be
able to jeer at them again, because they will be delivered
from all enemies forever.

Reading about how the Lord sent the locust plague, followed by the drought, and then delivered his people in Joel's time, our initial reaction may be, "What does this have to do with me? How can it comfort me in my troubles?"

The prophet has taught us to look through and beyond the Lord's judgments in history— including the sicknesses, sorrows, and failures of our own lives—to "the day of the LORD." In view of that day, the Lord calls us to return to him with repentant hearts and to look for his mercy. Each time the Lord our God works his wonders to heal our sicknesses, comfort us in our sorrows, and pick us up after our failures, he is teaching us that we can always hope in him.

Christians can be realistic optimists. We know that "we must go through many hardships to enter the kingdom of God" (Acts 14:22), but the Lord's deliverance will come. He will show that "he is the LORD our God and there is no other" (verse 27). Then we will glorify him for the rest of our days on earth. Even if his deliverance does not come on earth, we will spend eternity praising him in heaven. If not sooner, then later, a time will come when the Lord our God will work wonders for us. Now we may feel abandoned and shamed before the world, but in the words of the promise given through Joel, the time will come when the Lord will assure us, "Never again will my people be shamed" (verse 27).

The outpouring of the Spirit

²⁸ "And afterward,
   I will pour out my Spirit on all people.
Your sons and daughters will prophesy,
   your old men will dream dreams,
   your young men will see visions.
²⁹ Even on my servants, both men and women,
   I will pour out my Spirit in those days.

³⁰ **I will show wonders in the heavens**
  and on the earth,
  blood and fire and billows of smoke.
³¹ **The sun will be turned to darkness**
  and the moon to blood
  before the coming of the great and dreadful day of the
    LORD.
³² **And everyone who calls**
  on the name of the LORD will be saved;
 for on Mount Zion and in Jerusalem
  there will be deliverance,
  as the LORD has said,
 among the survivors
  whom the LORD calls.

God revealed himself during Old Testament times by dreams and visions and through the gift of his Spirit to the prophets. When he wanted Joseph to know that he would rule over his brothers, he gave the young man a dream (Genesis 37:5-9). God wanted Jacob to know he need not fear going down to Egypt, so he spoke to the aged patriarch in a vision at night (Genesis 46:2). He wanted his people to trust in a Savior who would bear their sins, so he gave his Spirit to prophets such as Joel and Isaiah to let them see prophetic visions (Isaiah 1:1) and to inspire them to write about "a man of sorrows" on whom the Lord would lay the iniquity of us all (Isaiah 53:3-5).

These revelations through dreams and visions and prophecy by the gift of the Holy Spirit did not come to all God's people but only to those he selected. When the Lord in a special way took of the Spirit that was on Moses and inspired 70 elders who were to help Moses judge the people, Joshua did not consider it proper for two of the elders to prophesy in the Israelite camp. Moses answered, "I wish that all the LORD's people were prophets and that the

LORD would put his Spirit on them!" (Numbers 11:29) This wish expressed by Moses is to be granted "afterward," Joel says, before the last great day of the Lord. The prophet looks forward to a time when the Lord will put his Spirit on all God's people, boys and girls, men and women, old and young, even the lowliest slaves. All of them will be privileged to receive the Lord's revelation.

When all the followers of Jesus were gathered in one place 50 days after his resurrection, "suddenly a sound like the blowing of a violent wind came from heaven and filled the whole house." (In Greek, as also in Hebrew, the same word means both "spirit" and "wind.") "All of them were filled with the Holy Spirit and began to speak in other tongues as the Spirit enabled them" (Acts 2:2,4). When the people asked, "What does this mean?" Peter stood up and answered, "This is what was spoken by the prophet Joel" (Acts 2:16). Then he quoted Joel 2:28-32 as the text of his sermon. Pentecost was the visible fulfillment of Joel's prophecy.

Some people claim that Joel's promise is being fulfilled again today when they lift their hands to heaven, swing and sway, and babble words that cannot be understood. They encourage all Christians to seek such a gift of "speaking in tongues." But God used dreams, visions and the gift of his Spirit in Old Testament times to *reveal his will to men*. God reveals himself today through the words of his Old Testament prophets and his New Testament apostles in the Holy Scriptures.

All of God's people can read this revelation and teach it to others. God gives his Word to all of us, boys and girls, men and women, old and young, even the simplest, lowliest Christian. Through the Word, God pours out his Spirit on all his people, creates and strengthens their faith in Jesus, produces fruits of faith in their lives, and enables them to speak his revelation to others in the world.

In close connection with Joel's prophecy of Pentecost, the Lord describes the time before the end of the world. This word picture of the sights and sounds of battle and the signs in the heavens is similar to other prophets' descriptions of the day of the Lord (e.g. Zephaniah 1:14-16), to John's visions of the endtimes in Revelation (6:12; 8:7), and to the words of Jesus as he pictured the signs of his coming (Matthew 24:29). In his Pentecost sermon on this text, Peter clearly proclaimed the deliverance from judgment that the Lord established "on Mount Zion and in Jerusalem": "Let all Israel be assured of this: God has made this Jesus, whom you crucified, both Lord and Christ. . . . Repent and be baptized, every one of you, in the name of Jesus Christ for the forgiveness of your sins. And you will receive the gift of the Holy Spirit" (Acts 2:36-38).

When God's prophets speak of the time "afterward" or of "those days" (3:1), they do not divide the New Testament period into years, decades, or centuries. In the span of only a few verses, Joel speaks of Pentecost and of the signs that announce the second coming of Christ. He includes also the whole time of grace between these events, the entire New Testament era. This is the time in which we live, when the gospel is being proclaimed, and "everyone who calls on the name of the LORD"—that is, the Lord Jesus Christ—"will be saved" (verse 32).

We have all inherited the blessings of Pentecost and have been prepared through faith in the gospel to face and survive the final judgment. We need to remind ourselves that God's great day of grace has been extended for a reason. As Peter said, referring to the last verse of Joel chapter 2, "The promise is for you and your children and for all who are far off—for all whom the Lord our God will call" (Acts 2:39). The apostle Paul also quotes this verse in Romans 10:13. He impresses on us what the work of the church is: "'Everyone who calls on the name of the Lord will be saved.' How then, can they call on the one they have not believed in? And how can they believe in the one of whom they have not heard? And how can they hear without someone preaching to them? And how can they preach unless they are sent?" (Romans 10:13-15)

Some churches offer all kinds of social services, recreational facilities, and cultural events to their communities. Sometimes we may feel a little apologetic for our own church when all it offers to the world is the Word. But what does the world really *need* more than the Word? The good news about Jesus is God's call to sinners near and far. The Spirit works by the Word and Baptism to bring them to faith in the Savior. Through faith sinners will survive the "great and dreadful day of the LORD" and be blessed with life forever. The church is here to extend God's call to all mankind, in our homelands and everywhere in the world. God pours out his Spirit on us and on our children so that we can extend his gospel call to others. May we faithfully do that work until the final day of the Lord dawns and Jesus comes again to judge the living and the dead.

The nations judged

3 **"In those days and at that time,**
when I restore the fortunes of Judah and Jerusalem,
² I will gather all nations
and bring them down to the Valley of Jehoshaphat.
There I will enter into judgment against them
concerning my inheritance, my people Israel,
for they scattered my people among the nations
and divided up my land.

³ **They cast lots for my people**
   and traded boys for prostitutes;
 they sold girls for wine
   that they might drink.

In this chapter the Lord describes the final judgment, when all nations must gather before him. The judgment has two sides: the fortunes of Judah and Jerusalem will be restored, but the enemies who scattered God's people, divided up their land, and treated their children with contempt will be punished. The Lord begins to carry out his judgments within the world's history, but the final settling of all accounts will take place at the end of time.

In the days of King Jehoshaphat of Judah (873–848 B.C.), the Lord gave the Jews a victory over the Moabites, Ammonites, and Edomites at a gorge in the wilderness (2 Chronicles 20:1-30). The gorge was named "the Valley of Praise" (2 Chronicles 20:26), and perhaps some of the people gave it the name of Judah's victorious king. But by using the term "the Valley of Jehoshaphat" (verse 2), the prophet probably does not mean a particular geographical location in the land of Canaan. The name Jehoshaphat means "the Lord judges." The "Valley of Jehoshaphat" is simply the Lord's judgment seat (see 3:12). Later Joel calls it "the valley of decision" (3:14).

Moses said that "when the Most High gave the nations their inheritance, when he divided all mankind, he set up boundaries for the peoples according to the number of the sons of Israel. For the LORD's portion is his people, Jacob his allotted inheritance. . . . He shielded him and cared for him; he guarded him as the apple of his eye" (Deuteronomy 32:8-10). Even when the Lord's righteous punishment fell upon his people, they were still dear to him. Foreign nations might carry out his judgment upon Israel, but they themselves incurred guilt when they touched "the apple of his eye" (Zechariah 2:8). By taking Israel into exile, carving up the Promised Land for themselves, enslaving Israelite children and using them like money to buy prostitutes and wine for themselves, enemy nations were sinning against Israel's God.

The Lord who calls us "a chosen people, a royal priesthood, a holy nation, a people belonging to God" (1 Peter 2:9) protects his church today with the same watchful care. Calling us his sheep, he promises, "No one can snatch them out of my hand" (John 10:28). Jesus loves, feeds, and cares for the church as his bride, dear as his own body (Ephesians 5:22-31). He guards us as "the apple of his eye."

Judgment on Tyre, Sidon, and Philistia

⁴"Now what have you against me, O Tyre and Sidon and all you regions of Philistia? Are you repaying me for something I have done? If you are paying me back, I will swiftly and speedily return on your own heads what you have done. ⁵For you took my silver and my gold and carried off my finest treasures to your temples. ⁶You sold the people of Judah and Jerusalem to the Greeks, that you might send them far from their homeland.

⁷"See, I am going to rouse them out of the places to which you sold them, and I will return on your own heads what you have done. ⁸I will sell your sons and daughters to the people of Judah, and they will sell them to the Sabeans, a nation far away." The LORD has spoken.

From this reference we would like to establish the time when Joel prophesied to an attack by the Philistines, Israel's ancient enemies to the southwest, and the Phoenicians, northwest of Israel. The Philistines, however, were Israel's enemies from the period of the Judges until at least the time of the prophet Zechariah, who ministered about 500 B.C. Phoenicia under Hiram of Tyre was friendly to David and

Solomon. At some later time, Tyre and Sidon must have turned against Israel (see also Amos 1:9,10), but we do not know when. The references are too general to establish the date of Joel's ministry. At some time the Philistines and Phoenicians must have attacked Judah, plundered Jerusalem, and carried off Jewish slaves in their trading ships to be sold far away in Greece.

The Lord threatens to bring the Jewish captives back from their captivity and to use them as an instrument of his judgment on their enemies. They will capture Philistine and Phoenician cities and sell their inhabitants to the far-off Sabeans, the people who inhabited Sheba in southwest Arabia (present-day Yemen). We do not know when or how this prophecy was fulfilled, but it testifies that God exercises his justice in human history. The enslavers themselves may be enslaved.

The Lord at times demonstrates his justice in history, before the final judgment, but we might remind ourselves here that man dare not appoint himself to carry out God's judgments. The Lord is not addressing Israel, saying, "Treat your enemies as they have treated you." Here the words of Jesus apply, "Love your enemies" (Matthew 5:44), as well as Paul's admonition, "Do not take revenge, my friends, but leave room for God's wrath, for it is written: 'It is mine to avenge; I will repay,' says the Lord" (Romans 12:19). In this respect also the Lord has spoken.

Judgment for the nations

⁹ **Proclaim this among the nations:**
　　Prepare for war!
　Rouse the warriors!
　　Let all the fighting men draw near and attack.
¹⁰ **Beat your plowshares into swords**
　　and your pruning hooks into spears.

> Let the weakling say,
>> "I am strong!"
> Come quickly, all you nations from every side,
>> and assemble there.
>
> Bring down your warriors, O LORD!
>
> ¹² "Let the nations be roused;
>> let them advance into the Valley of Jehoshaphat,
> for there I will sit
>> to judge all the nations on every side.
> ¹³ Swing the sickle,
>> for the harvest is ripe.
> Come, trample the grapes,
>> for the winepress is full
>> and the vats overflow—
> so great is their wickedness!"

The prophet describes God's final judgment with two pictures: battle and harvest. First he compares judgment day to a final battle. On the one side are the Lord and his holy angels, the "mighty ones who do his bidding" (Psalm 103:20), "numbering thousands upon thousands, and ten thousand times ten thousand" (Revelation 5:11; also Daniel 7:10). On the other side are all the unbelieving nations of the world. They have used their power to oppress many weaker nations, including God's chosen people. Now the prophet ironically calls the warriors of the nations into a battle they are sure to lose.

To picture the peace the Lord has in store for his own battle-weary people at the end of time the prophets Isaiah and Micah say, "They will beat their swords into plowshares and their spears into pruning hooks" (Isaiah 2:4; Micah 4:3). Joel uses these same words in the opposite order. Thus the proud nations that have lived in prosperity are summoned to the final battle: "Beat your plowshares into swords and your pruning hooks into spears." No one can escape this confrontation. Even the weakling must join the battle. We are reminded of Paul's words: "We must all appear before the judgment seat of Christ, that each one may receive what is due him for the things done while in the body, whether good or bad" (2 Corinthians 5:10).

The prophet and the faithful people of God are ready: "Bring down your warriors, O LORD!" they pray (verse 11). In verse 12 the Lord himself speaks, summoning all the nations into the "Valley of Jehoshaphat," that is, before his judgment seat, as in verse 2. Here the Lord introduces a second comparison for the last judgment. That day will be like a final harvest in the grainfields and vineyards. The growing season is over and the crops are mature. The harvester swings the sickle to cut down the grain; he plucks the bunches of grapes and dumps them into the winepress, the stone pit where the juice will be trodden out.

These are pictures of God's final act of separation. His time of grace for the world will end on judgment day. He will bring the world's history to a close. John the Baptist said of Jesus, "His winnowing fork is in his hand, and he will clear his threshing floor, gathering his wheat into the barn and burning up the chaff with unquenchable fire" (Matthew 3:12). Isaiah uses the image of a winepress to picture the Messiah as the judge of the nations: "I have trodden the winepress alone; from the nations no one was with me. I trampled them in my anger and trod them down in my wrath" (Isaiah 63:3).

In this part of the chapter, the prophet is especially describing the judgment of the godless nations. Therefore he speaks of punishment for sin: "so great is their wickedness" (verse 13). For the godless nations, just as for the impenitent in Israel, the day of the Lord will be dreadful indeed, since it will be the beginning of everlasting punishment.

The day of the Lord in the valley of decision

¹⁴ Multitudes, multitudes
    in the valley of decision!
For the day of the LORD is near
    in the valley of decision.
¹⁵ The sun and moon will be darkened,
    and the stars no longer shine.
¹⁶ The LORD will roar from Zion
    and thunder from Jerusalem;
    the earth and the sky will tremble.
But the LORD will be a refuge for his people,
    a stronghold for the people of Israel.

Who are these "multitudes, multitudes"? "All the nations on every side," Joel has written (verse 12). Jesus said: "All who are in their graves will hear his voice and come out" (John 5:28,29). They will be gathered in "the Valley of Jehoshaphat," the place where the Lord judges (verses 2,12). In verse 14 it is called "the valley of decision," from a Hebrew word meaning "to cut" and then "to decide strictly." The Lord, the just judge, will make known his strictly righteous decision, which will divide all mankind for eternity into two groups. "Multitudes who sleep in the dust of the earth will awake: some to everlasting life, others to shame and everlasting contempt" (Daniel 12:2).

How can we hear Joel's description of the last judgment without hungering and thirsting for God's good news? All of us can picture ourselves among those "multitudes, multitudes in the valley of decision." But we do not need to wait for that day of the Lord before we find out what the Judge's strictly righteous decision is. "For God did not send his Son into the world to condemn the world, but to save the world through him. *Whoever believes in him is not condemned*" (John 3:17,18). The final judgment only makes known a decision of grace that God made when he chose us from eternity to be his own and then redeemed us from all sin by the blood of his Son.

We also dare not be silent about the other outcome of the final judgment. "Whoever does not believe stands condemned already because he has not believed in the name of God's one and only Son. This is the verdict: Light has come into the world, but men loved darkness instead of light because their deeds were evil" (John 3:18,19). "Then they will go away to eternal punishment, but the righteous to eternal life" (Matthew 25:46).

If the twofold outcome of the final judgment has sunk into our hearts and minds, the work of Christ's church will become very urgent for us. God's good news says that his Son died for the sins of the human race and rose again to proclaim his pardon for the whole wicked, guilty world. "Now he commands all people everywhere to repent. For he has set a day when he will judge the world with justice by the man he has appointed. He has given proof of this to all men by raising him from the dead" (Acts 17:30,31). The risen Jesus himself pointed to the judgment and its double outcome when he sent us to make disciples of all nations: "Go into all the world and preach the good news to all creation. Whoever believes and is baptized will be saved, but whoever does not believe will be condemned" (Mark 16:15,16).

Joel describes the darkening of the heavenly bodies that will introduce the last times. The Lord promised Noah that "as long as the earth endures, seedtime and harvest, cold and heat, summer and winter, day and night will never cease" (Genesis 8:22). By having sun, moon, and stars stop shining, the Lord will give final notice that the days of this world are numbered.

On that day "the LORD will roar from Zion and thunder from Jerusalem" with such force that "the earth and the sky will tremble" (verse 16). Here is one outcome of the final judgment. The Lord, Israel's God, who made himself known during Old Testament times at the temple in Jerusalem, who later chose to enter the world as a Jewish baby, will come back in glory to be the world's judge. He will send a fierce firestorm of judgment on the wicked.

Verse 16 also reveals the other outcome of the final judgment: "The LORD will be a refuge for his people, a stronghold for the people of Israel." A "refuge" and a "stronghold" are designed for protection from enemies. The Lord God himself will surround his people to keep them safe forever. God's people can meet the Last Day in the same calm confidence with which they face every other day of their lives: "God is our refuge and strength, an ever-present help in trouble. Therefore we will not fear, though the earth give way and the mountains fall into the heart of the sea" (Psalm 46:1,2).

If this were the only passage to describe the last judgment, we might think that the prophet pictures the whole nation of Israel on the judge's right hand and all the other nations on his left. Joel clarified that picture earlier in his book. The prophet's earlier words of warning were spoken and written first for the people of Israel: "The day of the LORD is great; it is dreadful. Who can endure it?" (2:11). Israelites who forsook the Lord were not ready to face him on the Last Day. God's impenitent and unbelieving enemies, whether Jews or Gentiles, must tremble when they hear their judge speaking to them with a voice as awesome as thunder, terrible as a lion's roar. For them "that day will be darkness, not light" (Amos 5:18).

On the other hand, God prepared some in advance for glory "not only from the Jews but also from the Gentiles"

(Romans 9:24). A penitent people, Jews and Gentiles who trust God's mercy will find that the Lord is their refuge from every storm, their stronghold against every enemy. They are God's true, believing Israel, Abraham's children because they are "of the faith of Abraham" (Romans 4:16; see also Galatians 3:9).

The Lord concludes the prophecy of Joel with a promise of everlasting blessing for his believing people.

> ¹⁷ "Then you will know that I, the LORD your God,
>   dwell in Zion, my holy hill.
> Jerusalem will be holy;
>   never again will foreigners invade her.
>
> ¹⁸ "In that day the mountains will drip new wine,
>   and the hills will flow with milk;
> all the ravines of Judah will run with water.
> A fountain will flow out of the LORD's house
>   and will water the valley of acacias.
> ¹⁹ But Egypt will be desolate,
>   Edom a desert waste,
> because of violence done to the people of Judah,
>   in whose land they shed innocent blood.
> ²⁰ Judah will be inhabited forever
>   and Jerusalem through all generations.
> ²¹ Their bloodguilt, which I have not pardoned,
>   I will pardon."

The LORD dwells in Zion!

The Lord promises to live among his people in Zion. South of the temple mount is Mount Zion on which the ancient city of David was built. Mount Zion or "Zion" stands for the city of Jerusalem, the location of the temple, where the holy Lord placed his name among the people of Israel. His holy people who live with him there need never fear an invasion by any foreign army.

What does this promise mean? Is it fulfilled in the present-day state of Israel? Hardly. Neither that nation nor any other nation on earth enjoys perfect security from every enemy. Is the Lord giving Mount Zion and Jerusalem a special part to play in the history of the last days before his coming in glory? Some Christians think so, expecting that Jesus will establish a thousand-year kingdom on earth with his headquarters in Jerusalem immediately before or after his visible coming in glory. But he himself testified, "My kingdom is not of this world" (John 18:36).

The Lord is prophesying *New Testament truth* in the terms of *Old Testament history*. He is speaking not about the present earthly city of Jerusalem but about what the apostle Paul calls "Jerusalem that is above" (Galatians 4:26), the holy Christian church. As the temple, the place where God was pleased to place his name in Old Testament times, was in Jerusalem, the city built on Mount Zion, so the Lord himself lives now among his people in the person of Jesus Christ to deliver us from every enemy, even from the devil and death.

When our God is with us, we have every blessing. The gifts that God gives us by the means of grace through faith in Christ are poetically pictured here in vivid earthly terms: new wine, dripping down the mountains from vineyards on the terraces; milk flowing down from the hills where the goats and cattle are pastured; water constantly filling the Judean wadis, which usually stood dry for most of the year; and even a spring pouring water out of the temple, enough to water "the valley of acacias."

Acacia trees grow in the wilderness. They provided much of the wood from which parts of the tabernacle were constructed (Exodus 35:24; 36:20; 37:1, etc.). The Hebrew word for acacias is *shittim*. This is the name of the place where

Israel camped on the east side of the Jordan (Numbers 25:1). Since acacias grow in the wilderness, the Lord may be using "the valley of acacias" to describe the wilderness in general.

In a dry land like Canaan, and for a people who once wandered through the even more arid wilderness, there is no more precious earthly blessing than water. Like Joel, Ezekiel also pictures a river running out of the temple in the last times, growing deeper and deeper as it runs, turning salt water fresh, carrying large numbers of fish, and watering fruit trees of all kinds (Ezekiel 47:1-12).

In such Old Testament terms, the prophets present the blessings that Christ provides for his people in the New Testament. Even now, believers enjoy the forgiveness of sins, life with God, his help in every trouble. We Christians now live "in that day" (verse 18) and enjoy these blessings even while we still inhabit a world suffering from the pain, trouble, toil, and tears that have followed the fall into sin.

At the same time, the Lord is painting a picture for us of the blessings of eternal life in heaven, using the scenery, colors, and shapes of our life on earth. In the Bible's last chapter, John sees "the river of the water of life, as clear as crystal, flowing from the throne of God and of the Lamb down the middle of the great street of the city [i.e., the new Jerusalem]" (Revelation 22:1,2). Everlasting life with God is pictured as the fruit of the tree of life, produced every month throughout the year, "and the leaves of the tree are for the healing of the nations. No longer will there be any curse" (Revelation 22:2,3). Heavenly blessings shine through these earthly pictures.

This is the kind of language Joel and other Old Testament prophets use to describe the blessings of the New Testament church. Their words mingle the earthly and the heavenly, time and eternity together, describing the entire life of the

Lord's church from here to eternity. The prophets deliver all God's gifts, so to speak, wrapped up in one box.

Once more in verses 19 through 21, the Lord describes the double outcome of the judgment. Egypt and Edom shed the blood of God's people. The Egyptians, for example, killed good King Josiah (2 Kings 23:29); the Edomites cut down fugitives fleeing from Judah (Obadiah 14,15). Because Egypt and Edom were the enemies of Israel, they represent all the enemies of the Lord. Their lands will be a desert wasteland forever—a picture of the desolation of damnation. Judah and Jerusalem, on the other hand, "will be inhabited forever" (verse 20)—again a reference in Old Testament terms to the everlasting reign of Christ among his believing people, the holy Christian church.

There was a time when God did not pardon the guilt of the people of Israel. Not forgiveness but judgment—exile in Assyria and Babylon—followed upon the "bloodguilt" of the impenitent Israelites who sacrificed their children to idols (2 Kings 17:17). Manasseh, a wicked king of Judah, "shed so much innocent blood that he filled Jerusalem from end to end" (2 Kings 21:16). The Lord was angry with Jerusalem and Judah, "and in the end he thrust them from his presence" (2 Kings 24:20).

But the Lord's promised Savior will carry man's bloodguilt away. Inhabitants of the "new Jerusalem," Jews and Gentiles, look in faith to this Savior from sin. Under his new covenant, the Lord "will forgive their wickedness and will remember their sins no more" (Jeremiah 31:34). Jesus will shed his "blood of the covenant . . . for many for the forgiveness of sins" (Matthew 26:28).

To conclude his prophecy, Joel praises God with a thankful confession: "The LORD dwells in Zion!" (verse 21). The prophet Ezekiel ends his book on a similar note, giving the "new Jerusalem" the new name "THE LORD IS THERE" (Ezekiel 48:35). The Lord was with his people in Joel's days to deliver them from the scourges of locust plague and drought. The Lord lived visibly among his people in the person of his Son Jesus. Before being taken from the sight of his believers, Jesus promised them, "Surely I am with you always, to the very end of the age" (Matthew 28:20). He continues to assure us of his presence when he speaks to us in his gospel and gives us his own body and blood in the Sacrament.

Yet it is also true that we New Testament believers still live in hope. We already live in the day of the Lord, but we also "eagerly wait for our Lord Jesus Christ to be revealed" (1 Corinthians 1:7). Then in a new way, far better than our poor human words can describe or our poor human minds can imagine, all God's people gathered from every nation and from all the centuries will clearly see and fully know what it means that "the LORD dwells in Zion!"

In the very last chapter of the Bible, John tells us what we are hoping and waiting for: "Now the dwelling of God is with men, and he will live with them. They will be his people, and God himself will be with them and be their God. He will wipe every tear from their eyes. There will be no more death or mourning or crying or pain, for the old order of things has passed away" (Revelation 21:3,4).

Waiting in hope for that day of the Lord, we pray, "Come, Lord Jesus" (Revelation 22:20)!

Amos tends his flock

INTRODUCTION TO AMOS

The life of Amos

Many of the prophets chosen by the Lord to be his spokesmen did not put their messages into writing. Moses wrote the law for Israel's instruction (Exodus 24:12; Joshua 1:8), and perhaps Joshua and Samuel wrote the books that bear their names, but prophets such as Nathan (2 Samuel 7:2-17), Elijah (1 Kings 17:1-4), and Elisha (1 Kings 19:15-18) preached their messages orally, and their own records are not preserved for us in writing. (But see 1 Chronicles 29:29.) We have their words only from the inspired accounts about them and their times in the books of Samuel, Kings, and Chronicles. Amos, on the other hand, like Hosea and Joel, left us the whole message of his ministry in the book he wrote. His name does not occur elsewhere in the Old Testament.

What resources do we have for learning about the prophet's life and times? (1) Amos himself tells us how the Lord called him to be a prophet (1:1; 7:14-16). His preaching also reflects the conditions of the times in which he worked. We might compare, for example, how much we can learn about the American Civil War period from the speeches of President Lincoln. (2) According to the first verse of his book, Amos prophesied during the reigns of Uzziah—also called Azariah—king of Judah (792–740 B.C.). and Jeroboam II king of Israel (793–753 B.C.). The Bible gives us the history of this period in 2 Kings chapters 14 and 15 and in

179

2 Chronicles chapter 26. (3) Contemporaries of Amos were the prophets Hosea and Jonah in the Northern Kingdom, Israel. In Judah, the Southern Kingdom, Isaiah and Micah prophesied at about the same time. The books of these other prophets help to illuminate the period of Amos. (4) Archeology has uncovered evidence of the earthquake mentioned in Amos 1:1 and has also revealed some details of life in Israel during the eighth century B.C.

Amos himself tells us that by occupation he was not a professional prophet but a shepherd (7:14). He came from Tekoa (1:1), a fortified town six miles south of Bethlehem in Judah. Besides herding sheep, he also took care of sycamore fig trees (7:14). One day while Amos was tending his flock, the Lord said to him, "Go, prophesy to my people Israel" (7:15). God was sending the prophet on a difficult mission. He was calling Amos to leave his home in Judah and to take a message to Israel, the land of King Jeroboam II.

The times of Amos

Jeroboam II "did evil in the eyes of the Lord and did not turn away from any of the sins of Jeroboam [I] son of Nebat, which he had caused Israel to commit" (2 Kings 14:24). What were these sins?

Jeroboam I rebelled against Solomon's son Rehoboam and was proclaimed king of the northern ten tribes about 930 B.C. The usurper also tried to make sure that his subjects would not return to Rehoboam's capital, Jerusalem, to worship at the Lord's temple. At Bethel on his southern border and at Dan in the north, Jeroboam I set up golden calf images and proclaimed, "Here are your gods, O Israel, who brought you up out of Egypt" (1 Kings 12:28). Although he still claimed to be worshiping the Lord, Jeroboam I established a worship that was contrary to the

Lord's First Commandment: "You shall not make for yourself an idol" (Exodus 20:4).

Following the pattern of Canaanite worship, Jeroboam I also erected idol shrines on "high places" at other locations in his kingdom and encouraged his people to worship there. Israelites apparently made pilgrimages to such sanctuaries at Gilgal and Beersheba (Amos 5:5). Jeroboam I appointed priests who did not belong to the tribe of Levi (1 Kings 12:31; 13:33), even though the Lord had designated the Levites to serve him in the Temple. The king even instituted his own festival and sacrifices (1 Kings 12:32,33) to replace those established by the law of Moses.

Jeroboam I intended his calf images at Bethel and Dan to represent the Lord. The bull calf, however, also represented the fertility god Baal in Canaanite ritual, and so even more easily than before, the Israelites slipped into the worship practices of their heathen neighbors. On their high places, God's chosen people worshiped sacred stones and poles that represented the goddess Asherah. To promote the fertility of their flocks and fields, worshipers had sexual intercourse with prostitutes devoted to the fertility deities. (See the book of Hosea.) They might also offer grain, oil, and animals or even their own children as sacrifices (2 Kings 17:17). These were some of the "sins of Jeroboam [I] son of Nebat," the founding father of the Northern Kingdom.

In Amos's time, about a century and a half later, Jeroboam II "did not turn away from any of the sins of Jeroboam son of Nebat" (2 Kings 14:24). Israelites living in that time, however, would rather have pointed out the considerable prosperity they enjoyed as Jeroboam II enlarged the territory of the Northern Kingdom.

No strong king ruled Assyria, the great world power to the northeast of Israel, and the Assyrians temporarily showed no interest in Canaan. The absence of the Assyrians left Jeroboam II a free hand to deal with his nearer neighbors to the north, the Arameans (Syrians) of Damascus. The Arameans had annexed Israelite territories some decades before Jeroboam II's reign. Joash, Jeroboam II's father, began to recover these lands, and by his own military successes against his enemies, Jeroboam II restored the boundaries of Israel from the territory of Hamath, almost 200 miles north of Samaria, to the Dead Sea in the south (2 Kings 14:25). He also reconquered the land of Gilead, east of the Jordan (Amos 6:13). Thus the spiritual corruption of Jeroboam's kingdom was accompanied by military victories, expanded territories, and a renewed national pride.

The victories of Jeroboam II, Israel's most successful king, meant a brief period of peace and prosperity for the Northern Kingdom. With new opportunities for international trade, the nation prospered, and wealthy merchants inhabited the cities. Such people lived in "stone mansions" (5:11), their inner walls adorned with ivory (3:15); rich Israelite families might even have separate winter and summer residences (3:15). From all outward appearances during Jeroboam's reign, a "silver age" had dawned for Israel, rivaling the "golden age" of the united kingdom under David and Solomon.

Modern archeology provides a sidelight on life in an Israelite town. In one excavated city, there was a wealthy quarter, with houses built of stone that had been dressed smooth on both sides. The poor, on the other hand, lived on the other side of town in small, crowded makeshift dwellings, separated from the rich quarter by a long wall.

From Amos's own writings, we gain a clear picture of conditions in Israelite society during the reign of Jeroboam II. The rich lived high at the expense of those who had less: "They trample on the heads of the poor as upon the dust of the ground" (2:7). The courts that should have dispensed justice without regard for a man's wealth and social standing became instruments for turning the screws of oppression tighter: "You oppress the righteous and take bribes and you deprive the poor of justice in the courts" (5:12). Merchants looked out only for their own profit, "skimping the measure, boosting the price and cheating with dishonest scales" (8:5). Religion flourished at the Israelite shrines, but ceremony and sacrifice were not accompanied by godly living (4:4,5; 5:21-24).

Judgment upon Israel

Through the preaching of Amos, the Lord thundered, "I hate, I despise your religious feasts; I cannot stand your assemblies. . . . Away with the noise of your songs! I will not listen to the music of your harps. But let justice roll on like a river, righteousness like a never-failing stream" (5:21-24). The Lord sent the prophet to announce judgment upon the house of Jeroboam II (7:9) and the coming end of the kingdom of Israel (8:2). These prophecies of doom were fulfilled within one generation. Zechariah, the son of Jeroboam II and his successor on the Israelite throne, was assassinated after a six-month reign. In 722 B.C., about 40 years after the ministry of Amos, Assyrian armies captured Samaria and deported many citizens of Israel to Assyria, never to return.

Scripture makes it clear that the end of the kingdom of Israel took place "because the Israelites had sinned against the LORD their God, who had brought them up out of Egypt from under the power of Pharaoh king of Egypt. They worshiped other gods and followed the practices of the nations the LORD had driven out before them, as well as the practices that the kings of Israel had introduced. . . . The LORD warned Israel and Judah through all his prophets and seers. . . . But they would not listen and were as stiff-necked as their fathers, who did not trust in the LORD their God. . . . They forsook all the commands of the LORD their God and made for themselves two idols cast in the shape of calves, and an Asherah pole. They bowed down to all the starry hosts, and they worshiped Baal. They sacrificed their sons and daughters in the fire. They practiced divination and sorcery and sold themselves to do evil in the eyes of the LORD, provoking him to anger. So the LORD was very angry with Israel and removed them from his presence" (2 Kings 17:7-18). Only the kingdom of Judah was left as a visible remnant of God's people in the land of Canaan. Through Judah and a descendant of the royal house of David, the Lord would bless all nations, as he promised in his covenant with Abraham, Isaac, and Jacob.

Applying the message of Amos

We can see many parallels between the times of Amos and our own. But before we seek to apply the preaching of the prophets to our own times, we need to have a clear understanding of the audience to whom the Lord addressed these messages. It is true that Israel was a nation among the other nations of the world. The opening chapters of Amos make it very clear that the Lord is King and judge of all the nations under the sun, whether they acknowledge him as their God or not. The Creator implanted conscience and a natural knowledge of right and wrong in the hearts of all people, including the heathen who do not have the revealed knowledge of his law and gospel. "Righteousness exalts a nation, but sin is a disgrace to any people" (Proverbs 14:34).

Yet the entire Old Testament testifies that the descendants of Abraham were a unique people. To no other nation in history did God ever say as he said to Israel, "The LORD your God has chosen you out of all the peoples on the face of the earth to be his people, his treasured possession" (Deuteronomy 7:6). "You only have I chosen of all the families of the earth," he reminded them through Amos (3:2). The population of the whole earth enjoys sunshine and rain, food, clothing, and shelter by the blessing of the almighty Creator. Yet only to his people Israel did God send his special messengers, Moses and the prophets. Israel was "entrusted with the very words of God" (Romans 3:2). Whenever we read the books of Amos and the other Old Testament prophets, we must remember that these books were first addressed to God's chosen people, the visible church of the Old Testament.

Whom does the Lord honor as "his people, his treasured possession" today? Not our land or any earthly nation, but his church, the Israel of the New Testament. To his church, the believers in Jesus Christ, he says, "You are a chosen people, a royal priesthood, a holy nation, a people belonging to God" (1 Peter 2:9). In Baptism God makes a covenant of grace with every Christian, so that all believers together make up his covenant people today. Wherever the gospel is proclaimed and the sacraments are administered, the Holy Spirit gathers the church. Christians form visible assemblies—churches—to hear the Word, to receive the Sacrament, and to share their faith with other sinners who do not yet know Jesus. Such churches form the New Testament equivalent of God's Old Testament nations, Israel and Judah.

Although God expects justice and righteousness of every nation, since he has written his law in every human heart, any application of Amos's words that simply applies them to our nation or to other nations of the world today is seriously misleading. The boundaries of the church are not the boundaries of any present-day nation. As we strive to learn what the words of God's prophet mean for us today, we must constantly remember that they are addressed to us as people who confess, "I believe in God, the Father Almighty . . . and in Jesus Christ, his only Son our Lord. . . . I believe in the Holy Spirit, the holy Christian church, the communion of saints, the forgiveness of sins. . . ." We must remain aware that Amos is addressing us as God's people, whom the Holy Spirit has called by the gospel and enlightened with his gifts. The Lord has every right to expect much more of us than of others, as Jesus teaches: "From everyone who has been given much,

much will be demanded; and from the one who has been entrusted with much, much more will be asked" (Luke 12:48).

How have we responded to the abundance of the Lord's blessings? Doesn't God have good reason to include us as he reproves his Old Testament people: "What more could have been done for my vineyard than I have done for it? When I looked for good grapes, why did it yield only bad?" (Isaiah 5:4). The Old Testament prophets also summon God's New Testament people to repent of their sins. Amos calls us to live our faith as we work and do business in our daily lives. He invites us to worship the Lord our God in spirit and in truth. He demands that we serve no other gods. He looks for fruits of faith. He warns especially against the temptations that come with power and wealth. In prosperous times the lure of luxury can tempt us to exploit those weaker and poorer than ourselves.

Hearing the judgment of God on his unfaithful Old Testament people, we cannot take grace for granted. We, like Israel, were chosen by the undeserved mercy of God. Israel blindly forfeited his grace. "These things occurred as examples to keep us from setting our hearts on evil things as they did" (1 Corinthians 10:6). Together with the whole history of God's Old Testament people, the words of Amos "were written down as warnings for us, on whom the fulfillment of the ages has come. So, if you think you are standing firm, be careful that you don't fall!" (1 Corinthians 10:11,12).

Judgment seems to outweigh mercy in this book, but we will constantly sense in the words of Amos the fiery zeal of our God for the salvation of his people. Only unbelief, the willful rejection of his love, can replace his gospel invitation with the threat of the fiery flames of judgment. "Seek me and live," he invites (5:4); "seek good, not evil, that you may live" (5:14). When that tender invitation is rejected, nothing but judgment remains, and then "the LORD roars from Zion and thunders from Jerusalem" (1:2).

Yet even while the lion roars and the storm thunders, we are assured that Israel's Lord does not forget his mercy. He promised that he would not totally destroy the house of Jacob but that a believing remnant would remain (9:8). The book of Amos closes with a radiant picture of the blessings that David's Son, the Messiah, has in store for all his subjects, both Jews and Gentiles, in his everlasting kingdom (9:11-15).

Outline of Amos

The book of Amos has three main parts and a conclusion.

I. Announcement of judgment on the nations—and on Israel (1,2).

II. Further proclamations of judgment (3–6).

    A. Judgment on the whole house of Israel (3).

    B. Judgment on the women of Samaria (4).

    C. A lamentation for virgin Israel (5).

    D. Woe to the complacent lovers of luxury (6).

III. Five visions and messages of judgment (7:1–9:10).

    A. A vision of locusts (7:1-3).

    B. A vision of fire (7:4-6).

    C. A vision of a plumb line (7:7-9), and the story of how the Lord called Amos (7:10-15).

    D. A vision of summer fruit (8:1-3), and a message of judgment (8:4-15).

    E. A vision of the Lord standing at the altar (9:1-4), and a message of judgment (9:5-10).

Conclusion: A message of hope for God's believing people (9:11-15).

PART ONE

Judgment on the Nations— and on Israel

(1:1–2:16)

The approaching judgment

1 The words of Amos, one of the shepherds of Tekoa—what he saw concerning Israel two years before the earthquake, when Uzziah was king of Judah and Jeroboam son of Jehoash was king of Israel. ²He said:

> "The LORD roars from Zion
>   and thunders from Jerusalem;
> the pastures of the shepherds dry up,
>   and the top of Carmel withers."

Like the apostles of Jesus, Amos is not a spokesman for the Lord by his own choice or training. He is not a priest, nor has he studied at the feet of a senior prophet (7:14). Amos cares for some of the flocks that graze on the hillsides near Tekoa. Perhaps he also owns and breeds larger numbers of sheep: the word *shepherd* with which he describes himself in 7:14 is also used for Mesha, king of Moab, in 2 Kings 3:4. By choosing a shepherd to carry his message to the Northern Kingdom, the Lord makes it clear that the power of the prophet's word is not a matter of personal gifts or skillful oratory. The power lies in the words themselves, because they are the words of God. Amos "saw" these words. At least a part of God's revelation comes to him in visions, as he reports in chapters 7 through 9.

God still chooses his spokesmen today from all sorts of backgrounds and occupations. Christian pastors and teachers grow up in the homes of farmers, office workers, factory laborers. The LORD does not even require that those who speak his Word must have professional training. The church today carefully trains its full-time workers, but the Word spoken by lay Christians works with the same power of God in the hearts of those who hear it.

The name Amos, from a word that means "to load, carry a load," occurs only here in the Old Testament. Amos tended his flocks in the harsh and rugged wilderness that slopes from Jerusalem southeastward toward the Dead Sea. About 6 miles south of Bethlehem, 12 miles from Jerusalem, the ruins of Tekoa still stand on top of a hill, occupying an area of 4 or 5 acres. King Rehoboam fortified Tekoa and garrisoned troops there as part of his chain of defenses around Jerusalem (2 Chronicles 11:6). The top of the hill is high enough so that the inhabitants could see the Mount of Olives to the north and the Jordan Valley off to the northeast.

Amos dates his book with the names of Uzziah, king of Judah, and Jeroboam [II], king of Israel. Uzziah, also called Azariah, became king of Judah about the year 792 B.C. "He did what was right in the eyes of the LORD. . . . The high places, however, were not removed; the people continued to offer sacrifices and burn incense there" (2 Kings 15:3,4). Judah was blessed with a number of military successes during Uzziah's 52-year reign, described in 2 Chronicles chapter 26. It may seem strange that Amos, who served as a prophet in the Northern Kingdom, mentions the name of a king who rules in Jerusalem when he dates his prophecy. The Judean kings, as members of the house of David, were the legitimate rulers of all 12 tribes and the ancestors of the Messiah. That may be the reason why Amos mentions King Uzziah in the heading of his book.

The ruler of the Northern Kingdom at this time is Jeroboam II (793–753 B.C.). The prosperous conditions of his reign have been described in the introduction. Sometime during the latter part of Uzziah's and Jeroboam's reigns, the land experienced a severe earthquake, such a terrifying experience that the Jews still remembered it more than two centuries later (Zechariah 14:5). Amos especially mentions that he delivered his prophecy "two years before the earthquake." That earthquake was no chance shifting of the earth's surface layers. Amos predicted it as a message of warning from the Lord to his disobedient people (8:7,8). The fact that the prophet's prediction came true should make every believer pay attention to all the words of his book (Deuteronomy 18:21,22).

The book of Amos is primarily a message of judgment. The Lord's word speaks like the roar of a lion devouring his prey, like the thunder that accompanies a violent storm. Because his earthly temple was on Mount Zion in Jerusalem, the Lord's voice comes from there in the prophecy. The most devastating experience for people dependent on raising animals and crops is drought. Therefore Amos pictures the Lord's voice of judgment as drying up the pastures on which the shepherds depend and blasting even the luxuriant green foliage that covers Mount Carmel.

Judgment on Israel's heathen neighbors

³**This is what the LORD says:**

"For three sins of Damascus,
 even for four, I will not turn back my wrath.
Because she threshed Gilead
 with sledges having iron teeth,

⁴ I will send fire upon the house of Hazael
    that will consume the fortresses of Ben-Hadad.
⁵ I will break down the gate of Damascus;
    I will destroy the king who is in the Valley of Aven
and the one who holds the scepter in Beth Eden.
    The people of Aram will go into exile to Kir,"
                                    says the LORD.

⁶This is what the Lord says:

"For three sins of Gaza,
    even for four, I will not turn back my wrath.
Because she took captive whole communities
    and sold them to Edom,
⁷ I will send fire upon the walls of Gaza
    that will consume her fortresses.
⁸ I will destroy the king of Ashdod
    and the one who holds the scepter in Ashkelon.
I will turn my hand against Ekron,
    till the last of the Philistines is dead,"
                                says the Sovereign LORD.

⁹This is what the LORD says:

"For three sins of Tyre,
    even for four, I will not turn back my wrath.
Because she sold whole communities
    of captives to Edom,
    disregarding a treaty of brotherhood,
¹⁰ I will send fire upon the walls of Tyre
    that will consume her fortresses."

Following the Lord's call, Amos puts down his shepherd's staff and leaves his home in Tekoa to do his work as a prophet in Israel, the Northern Kingdom. Although he begins by condemning the sins of three foreign enemies of God's people, his eye never leaves his Israelite audience.

Each of the following prophecies of the Lord's judgment begins, "For three sins of [a nation], even for four, I

191

will not turn back my wrath." This use of one number and then the next higher one also occurs in other passages of the Bible, especially in the book of Proverbs (e.g. 30:29-31). The writer may name three comparable things, and then he particularly emphasizes the fourth. Amos does not mention the first three sins of the nations. They have actually sinned many more times than that. By repeatedly disobeying the law that the Creator-God wrote in their hearts, they have deserved his judgment. The emphasis falls on the fourth sin—an offense that brings God's long patience to an end and opens the floodgates of judgment.

First Amos proclaims the Lord's judgment on Damascus, the ancient capital of Aram (Syria). Ever since the days of the Judges, hostility smoldered between Israel and the Arameans. Sometimes it was a matter of border conflicts; then again the fights would flare up into full-scale warfare. Already in the time of King Jehu, the founder of Jeroboam II's dynasty, "the LORD began to reduce the size of Israel. Hazael overpowered the Israelites throughout their territory east of the Jordan in all the land of Gilead" (2 Kings 10:32,33). In the years of Jeroboam II's grandfather Jehoahaz, the Israelite armies were reduced to "fifty horsemen, ten chariots and ten thousand foot soldiers, for the king of Aram had destroyed the rest and made them like the dust at threshing time" (2 Kings 13:7). Apparently the Arameans cruelly plundered the Israelite territories east of the Jordan—"threshed" them the way farmers had their oxen pull iron-toothed threshing sledges over cut grain to beat out the kernels.

Jeroboam II's father, Jehoash, recovered the Israelite towns from the Arameans (2 Kings 13:25). King Jeroboam II himself led successful expeditions eastward into Gilead (Amos 6:13) and also acquired more territory to the north and south. Israel now controlled both Damascus and the way to Hamath (2 Kings 14:25-28). It would be natural for the prophet's Israelite audience to shout their approval when Amos speaks to an Israelite audience of avenging fire consuming the house of the onetime Aramean King Hazael and the fortresses built by Hazael's son, Ben-Hadad (2 Kings 13:22,24); when he prophesies that the gate-bar of Damascus will be broken to open the city before invading armies; when he foretells destruction for the Aramean rulers of the Aven valley and Beth Eden, places north of Damascus; and when he prophesies, "The people of Aram will go into exile to Kir [Mesopotamia?]" (verse 5). The Arameans were Israel's historic enemies.

From Damascus in the northeast, Amos shifts the attention of his Israelite listeners to four of the Philistine cities in southwestern Canaan. Samson, Saul, and David fought the Philistines. King Uzziah broke down the walls of the Philistine cities Gath and Ashdod (2 Chronicles 26:6). Sometime during that long history of hostilities, the Philistines must have captured some Israelite communities and cruelly sold not only the soldiers but also all the civilian inhabitants to the Edomites, who carried on an international trade in slaves. Amos announces God's fiery judgment on the Philistine cities of Gaza, Ashdod, Ashkelon, and Ekron. The Lord will let enemies burn these cities, kill their rulers, and exterminate their population as a punishment for the Philistines' sins against Israel. The prophet's Israelite audience would applaud again. The sovereign Lord is Israel's God. He will protect his people and also avenge them when they are wronged by enemy nations.

We do not hear of long series of hostilities between the Israelites and their Phoenician neighbors to the northwest. Solomon made a treaty with Hiram king of Tyre: in exchange for cedar lumber and skilled labor for his building projects, he provided grain and olive oil to the Tyrian king (1 Kings 5:10-12). Solomon also ceded 20 towns in Galilee to Tyre. Something must have happened to cool that long-standing friendship. The Tyrians disregarded their treaty of brotherhood with Israel and "sold whole communities of captives to Edom" (verse 9), just as the Philistines did. Amos proclaims to his Israelite audience that the Lord's fiery judgment will also destroy the walls and fortresses of Tyre.

All of these judgments upon Syria, Philistia, and Tyre will be fulfilled. Assyrian armies under their aggressive rulers Tiglath Pileser III (also known in the Bible as Pul), Shalmaneser V, and Sennacherib will overrun Syria and Canaan, including Philistia, in 734–732 B.C. Damascus will be the first city to experience the fulfillment of the Lord's judgment: it falls to the armies of Tiglath-Pileser III in 732 B.C., about two decades after the ministry of Amos. Tyre lasts much longer, but it is finally captured by Alexander the Great more than four centuries after Amos prophesies its end. Slowly but surely the Lord carries out the judgment foretold by his prophet.

The prophet has not said so yet, but the same Assyrian armies that will overpower Damascus and Philistia will also tear down the walls of the Israelite capital, Samaria, and burn its palaces. The end is near for Israel too, not only for its enemies. Amos is preparing his Israelite audience to hear this message. By first proclaiming the Lord's judgment upon the sins of Israel's hostile neighbors, the prophet gains a hearing for the message of judgment upon God's own people. By holding up the sins of other nations, he is preparing them to see themselves in the clear light of God's law.

Judgment on Israel's heathen cousins

¹¹This is what the LORD says:

> "For three sins of Edom,
> > even for four, I will not turn back my wrath.
> Because he pursued his brother with a sword,
> > stifling all compassion,
> because his anger raged continually
> > and his fury flamed unchecked,
> ¹² I will send fire upon Teman
> > that will consume the fortresses of Bozrah."

¹³This is what the LORD says:

> "For three sins of Ammon,
> > even for four, I will not turn back my wrath.
> Because he ripped open the pregnant women of Gilead
> > in order to extend his borders,
> ¹⁴ I will set fire to the walls of Rabbah
> > that will consume her fortresses
> amid war cries on the day of battle,
> > amid violent winds on a stormy day.
> ¹⁵ Her king will go into exile,
> > he and his officials together,"

> > > > > > > says the LORD.

2 This is what the LORD says:
> "For three sins of Moab,
> > even for four, I will not turn back my wrath.
> Because he burned, as if to lime,
> > the bones of Edom's king,
> ² I will send fire upon Moab
> > that will consume the fortresses of Kerioth.
> Moab will go down in great tumult
> > amid war cries and the blast of the trumpet.
> ³ I will destroy her ruler
> > and kill all her officials with him,"

> > > > > > > says the LORD.

The Edomites were descendants of Jacob's twin brother, Esau (Genesis 36), and the Bible traces the descent of the Ammonites and Moabites to Abraham's nephew Lot (Genesis 19:36-38). After announcing his judgment upon Israel's foreign heathen neighbors, Aram, Philistia, and Tyre, the Lord now turns to three hostile, heathen "cousins" of his chosen people. It is almost as if a lion is stalking Israel, circling closer and closer, because the judgment the Lord especially has in mind is intended for God's chosen people.

Enmity between the Edomites and Israelites began with their ancestors. Jacob stole the birthright of his twin brother, Esau; Esau planned to kill Jacob (Genesis 27). Esau, also called Edom, settled in harsh, dry Arabah, south of the Dead Sea. The Edomites stood in the way of Israel when Moses brought his people out of Egypt. In response to a request for passage through their territory, Edom answered, "You may not pass through here; if you try, we will march out and attack you with the sword" (Numbers 20:18). The Edomite territories south of the Dead Sea bordered on the land of Judah. David garrisoned soldiers throughout Edom (2 Samuel 8:14), but the Edomites rebelled and were only subdued again about one generation before the ministry of Amos (2 Kings 14:10). Although Edom was Jacob's brother, "his anger raged continually and his fury flamed unchecked" (Amos 1:11) against Israel for generation after generation. Amos therefore proclaims the Lord's fiery judgment upon Edom, from Teman (near Petra) in the south to Bozrah in the north.

The Ammonites, descended from Abraham's nephew Lot and so also related by blood to Israel, inhabited territories beyond the Jordan southeast of Gilead and north of the Dead Sea. They oppressed Israel as far back as the days of the judge Jephthah (Judges 10:6-18). Saul won a great victory over the forces of Nahash the Ammonite, who had cruelly threatened to gouge out the right eyes of all the men of Jabesh Gilead (1 Samuel 11). David defeated an Aramean-Ammonite coalition (2 Samuel 10); after he took the Ammonite capital Rabbah, he had the crown of the king of Ammon placed on his own head (2 Samuel 12:26-31). Jehoshaphat, a later king of Judah, defeated Moab and Ammon in the desert near Tekoa, Amos's hometown (2 Chronicles 20). Sometime during the course of these border wars, while they were trying to extend their territories at Israelite expense, the Ammonites must have "ripped open the pregnant women of Gilead" (verse 13) to cut off the future of God's people there. The fact that Amos prophesies exile, a typical Assyrian punishment, for the Ammonite king and his officials makes it seem likely that it will be the Assyrians who carry out the Lord's judgment by storming the walls and burning the fortresses of Rabbah, the Ammonite capital.

Moab, like Ammon a descendant of Lot, settled in the wilderness east of the Dead Sea. When Moses was leading Israel through the wilderness to Canaan, Balak king of Moab hired the prophet Balaam to "put a curse on these people, because they are too powerful for me" (Numbers 22:6). By the Lord's inspiration, Balaam blessed Israel instead (Numbers 23 and 24). Moabite women seduced Israelite men into sexual immorality and the worship of Baal (Numbers 25:1-5), bringing a plague on Israel. After God's people occupied Canaan, they were subject to Moab's King Eglon for 18 years until the judge Ehud delivered them (Judges 3:12-30). David subdued Moab together with the Edomites, Ammonites, and Philistines (2 Samuel 8:12). The kings of Israel and Judah combined to put down a Moabite revolt about a century before the ministry of Amos (2 Kings 3).

The prophet's words do not condemn the Moabites for offenses against Israel. The sin that ends the Lord's patience with Moab is an atrocity committed against Edom. The hatred of the Moabites against Edom flamed so hot that they even abused the body of the Edomite king after his death. They burned his bones and spread the ashes like fertilizer on a field or mixed them into whitewash for their walls. Such inhumanity will bring God's judgment: the burning of Kerioth, east of the Dead Sea, and the death of the Moabite princes. Perhaps the prophet's Israelite audience does not applaud his message of judgment so loudly now, because they are beginning to realize that the Lord's anger flames against all sin, not only when the sin is committed against Israel.

We may sometimes wonder how people who do not have the Bible can know right from wrong. Many people today, like the Arameans, Philistines, Tyrians, Edomites, Ammonites, and Moabites in the time of Amos, grow up in ignorance of the written Ten Commandments. The prophet's words of judgment against Israel's neighbors remind us that God's law requires a decent, upright life of every individual in every nation, "for God does not show favoritism" (Romans 2:11). "When Gentiles, who do not have the law, do by nature things required by the law, they are a law for themselves, even though they do not have the law, since they show that the requirements of the law are written on their hearts, their consciences also bearing witness, and their thoughts now accusing, now even defending them" (Romans 2:14,15). When we use God's Word to remind people that all of us are sinners, their conscience agrees with the accusations of God's law. Of course, people sometimes silence those inner accusations by persistently disregarding them. May God keep the voice of conscience speaking plainly in every human heart, and may all sinners hear it, so that they recognize their need for forgiveness and seek the true God, their only Savior.

Judgment upon Israel's sister-kingdom Judah

⁴This is what the LORD says:

"For three sins of Judah,
 even for four, I will not turn back my wrath.
Because they have rejected the law of the LORD
 and have not kept his decrees,
because they have been led astray by false gods,
 the gods their ancestors followed,
⁵ I will send fire upon Judah
 that will consume the fortresses of Jerusalem."

The idol-worshiping nations around Israel are ripe for judgment because they have disregarded the law written in their hearts, sinning against Israel and against on another. The people of Israel's sister-kingdom Judah, unlike the neighboring heathen, possess the revealed Word of God. Through Moses, the Lord gave them all the decrees of his law and revealed himself to them as the only God and Savior. Instead, they have chosen to worship other gods, from the golden calves at the foot of Mount Sinai to the heathen deities imported by Solomon from nearby nations. On their high places not far from the temple mount, they have worshiped "Ashtoreth the goddess of the Sidonians, and Molech the detestable god of the Ammonites" and "Chemosh the detestable god of Moab" (1 Kings 11:4-8). In Amos's day, King Uzziah "did what was right in the eyes of the LORD. . . . The high places, however, were not removed; the people continued to offer sacrifices and burn incense there" (2 Kings 15:3,4).

In the time of Amos, the people of the Southern Kingdom still take pride in the law of the Lord, in David's city, Jerusalem, and in the temple, the visible sign of the Lord's presence among his people. But Israel's sister-kingdom,

Judah, is becoming more and more like her heathen neighbors. Therefore, the Lord's judgment condemns the city he chose for his temple, no less than Moab's Kerioth or Ammon's Rabbah: "I will send fire upon Judah that will consume the fortresses of Jerusalem" (verse 5). "God does not show favoritism. All who sin apart from the law will also perish apart from the law, and all who sin under the law will be judged by the law. For it is not those who hear the law who are righteous in God's sight, but it is those who obey the law who will be declared righteous" (Romans 2:11-13).

People who know the true God and have his revealed Word sometimes forget the difference between hearing and doing the Word. Jesus said, "Everyone who hears these words of mine *and puts them into practice* is like a wise man who built his house on the rock" (Matthew 7:24). The Holy Spirit, who inspired the Word, also empowers us to believe it. The faith that he creates is a power to change our lives. The people of Judah took pride in possessing the true teaching of the Word of God, but they hung their hearts on other gods and refused to produce the fruits of faith. These things were written for our learning. "You who brag about the law, do you dishonor God by breaking the law?" (Romans 2:23). May we who have the Word today take warning and examine our own hearts and lives! Do we practice what we preach?

The lion's roar has sounded against all the kingdoms around Israel. The prophet's Israelite audience would be glad to hear it. Now it is Israel's turn.

Judgment on Israel

⁶This is what the LORD says:

"For three sins of Israel,
even for four, I will not turn back my wrath.

They sell the righteous for silver,
  and the needy for a pair of sandals.
⁷ They trample on the heads of the poor
  as upon the dust of the ground
  and deny justice to the oppressed.
Father and son use the same girl
  and so profane my holy name.
⁸ They lie down beside every altar
  on garments taken in pledge.
In the house of their god
  they drink wine taken as fines.

After pronouncing the Lord's judgment on six heathen nations and on Israel's sister-people Judah, Amos speaks directly to his Israelite audience. They have probably been nodding in assent to the Lord's righteous judgment, but in so doing they have condemned themselves. Let them consider what is happening in their courts, where justice should reign. When a poor man is in the right, rich Israelites bribe witnesses and judges to condemn him. When a man cannot pay a debt, even if it does not amount to more than the value of a pair of sandals, they sell him into slavery. The rich are treating their poorer fellow Israelites as if they were dirt under their feet, and the courts deny a poor man justice when he complains of such oppression. Israel has forgotten the Lord, who commanded: "Do not defraud your neighbor or rob him. . . . Do not pervert justice. . . . Love your neighbor as yourself" (Leviticus 19:13-18).

The sins of man against his neighbor go hand in hand with a disregard for God. The Israelites are visiting the cult prostitutes at the Canaanite high places. One generation follows the bad example of another: "Father and son use the same girl" (verse 7). In one act they commit both idolatry and fornication, profaning the name of the God who called them to be holy as he is holy. They heap sin upon sin. If an Israelite lent money to a poor man and took his cloak as security, the law required that the garment be returned by sundown "because his cloak is the only covering he has for his body. What else will he sleep in?" (Exodus 22:27) But now an Israelite creditor is keeping the cloak—and sleeping on it in an idol shrine! According to the law, fines imposed for personal injury were to serve as compensation to the injured party (e.g., Exodus 21:22). But now wine given as payment in kind for a fine is being consumed by the Israelite officials, carousing at their idol shrines. Those who despise their neighbor do not love their God either. Hasn't the Lord deserved more than this from his chosen people?

> 9 **"I destroyed the Amorite before them,**
> **though he was tall as the cedars**
> **and strong as the oaks.**
> **I destroyed his fruit above**
> **and his roots below.**
>
> 10 **"I brought you up out of Egypt,**
> **and I led you forty years in the desert**
> **to give you the land of the Amorites.**
> 11 **I also raised up prophets from among your sons**
> **and Nazirites from among your young men.**
> **Is this not true, people of Israel?"**
> **declares the LORD.**
> 12 **"But you made the Nazirites drink wine**
> **and commanded the prophets not to prophesy.**

Amorites is a name sometimes used for all the inhabitants of Canaan before the people of Israel took the land. Some of the Canaanites, like the gigantic Og, king of Bashan (Deuteronomy 3:1-8), must have been very impressive in stature (Numbers 13:28,32,33). "The people who live there are powerful, and the cities are fortified and very large," the Israelite spies reported to Moses (Numbers 13:28). Poetically pictured, and in comparison with the people of Israel coming from the wilderness, they must have seemed as majestic as cedar trees, which sometimes grow to a height of 120 feet, and as strong as oaks. Yet the Lord uprooted the Canaanites and gave their land to his people, just as he had promised Abraham, Isaac, and Jacob.

Even before the conquest of Canaan, the Lord shepherded his people through the wilderness, providing bread from heaven and water from the rocks. After giving his people a home in Canaan, God blessed the Israelites with prophets like Nathan, Elijah, and Elisha, who preached his Word to their generations. Besides, God moved the hearts of some Israelites to dedicate themselves to him as Nazirites. Nazirites took a vow not to drink wine or eat grapes, not to cut their hair, and not to go near a dead body (Numbers 6:1-21). Their unusual diet and appearance during the term of their vow marked them as God-fearing Israelites who had especially consecrated themselves to the Lord. The presence of both prophets and Nazirites among them reminded all the people of Israel that the holy Lord was their God and that they were to be his holy people.

How did the Israelites receive such special signs of God's favor? They polluted the land he gave them with idol worship. They tried to get the Nazirites to drink wine and so break their vows to the Lord. When the prophets called Israel back to the Lord, they would not listen: "You troubler of Israel" was what King Ahab called the prophet Elijah (1 Kings 18:17), and Queen Jezebel tried to kill him (1 Kings 19:2). Again and again God's ungrateful people bit the hand that fed them. Therefore the Lord now pronounces his imminent judgment:

¹³ "Now then, I will crush you
    as a cart crushes when loaded with grain.
¹⁴ The swift will not escape,
    the strong will not muster their strength,
    and the warrior will not save his life.
¹⁵ The archer will not stand his ground,
    the fleet-footed soldier will not get away,
    and the horseman will not save his life.
¹⁶ Even the bravest warriors
    will flee naked on that day,"
                        declares the LORD.

Amos, the shepherd, has seen farmers driving their carts loaded with sheaves of grain over the fields to the threshing floors. Better stay out from under the cart wheels! The Lord now is bearing down on his unheeding people like a heavy grain cart to crush them with his judgment. The instrument of judgment he is preparing is the Assyrian army. Not even the swiftest, strongest, bravest warriors will survive; arrows and chariots and stout Israelite hearts will be no match for the brutal Assyrians, because the Lord will drive them over the land like a heavy cart to crush a people who have deserted him.

How long does the Lord's patience last? In the time before the flood, he gave corrupt humanity a time of grace that lasted 120 years while Noah built the ark (Genesis 6:3). Then came the deluge. The Northern Kingdom lasted a little more than two centuries, beginning with the rebellion of Jeroboam I in 931 B.C. It will stay in existence for another generation after the ministry of Amos, until the Assyrian conquest in 722 B.C.

In our own time, the Lord is patient, "not wanting anyone to perish, but everyone to come to repentance" (2 Peter 3:9). When his will is persistently despised, he still can use a natural disaster or a conquering army to carry out his judgments in this world's history. His Word also tells us that his last judgment is coming, but he does not tell us when. Finally, for everyone in all the nations, "the day of the Lord will come like a thief. The heavens will disappear with a roar; the elements will be destroyed by fire, and the earth and everything in it will be laid bare. Since everything will be destroyed in this way, what kind of people ought you to be?" (2 Peter 3:10,11). May God keep us from abusing his patience! He has given us time to recognize our guilt, to acknowledge that his judgment is right, to know that Christ bore our sins, to trust his promise of forgiveness, and to become the kind of people he wants us to be. May the Lord also use us to call other sinners to repentance! Some will still listen during this time of grace.

PART TWO

Further Messages of Judgment for Israel
(3:1–6:14)

The cause of the judgment

3 Hear this word the LORD has spoken against you, O people of Israel—against the whole family I brought up out of Egypt:

² "You only have I chosen
    of all the families of the earth;
  therefore I will punish you
    for all your sins."
³ Do two walk together
    unless they have agreed to do so?
⁴ Does a lion roar in the thicket
    when he has no prey?
  Does he growl in his den
    when he has caught nothing?
⁵ Does a bird fall into a trap on the ground
    where no snare has been set?
  Does a trap spring up from the earth
    when there is nothing to catch?
⁶ When a trumpet sounds in a city,
    do not the people tremble?
  When disaster comes to a city,
    has not the LORD caused it?

⁷ Surely the Sovereign LORD does nothing
    without revealing his plan
    to his servants the prophets.

> ⁸ **The lion has roared—**
> **who will not fear?**
> **The Sovereign LORD has spoken—**
> **who can but prophesy?**

After his initial threats of judgment on the nations and then a more extended prophecy against Israel (chapters 1 and 2), Amos continues with more messages of judgment (chapters 3 to 6), the first three beginning "Hear this word."

Speaking through his prophet, the Lord addresses the message in chapter 3 to both Israel and Judah, "against the whole family I brought up out of Egypt" (verse 1). When the Lord says, "You only have I *known*"—the word translated "chosen" in the NIV—he is speaking the language of an ancient covenant or treaty between nations. A subject people "knew" their overlord, and he agreed to "know" them as his vassals. Israel was the Lord's chosen people, the nation to which he said at the foot of Mount Sinai: "You yourselves have seen what I did to Egypt, and how I carried you on eagles' wings and brought you to myself. Now if you obey me fully and keep my covenant, then out of all nations you will be my treasured possession. Although the whole earth is mine, you will be for me a kingdom of priests and a holy nation" (Exodus 19:4-6).

The high privilege of being the Creator's chosen people brought blessings that Israel could not begin to count. It also meant a responsibility that the Lord's people neglected and despised. The covenant that promised blessings for obedience also included curses for disobedience (see especially Leviticus 26). Just because the Lord chose Israel to be his own people for his high saving purpose ("you only have I chosen"), the Israelites especially deserved his wrath when they turned from him in unbelief and despised his gifts ("therefore I will punish you").

207

God's New Testament people, the members of the holy Christian church, have received even richer gifts than the people of Israel. A correspondingly high responsibility accompanies this high privilege. Jesus concludes his parable of the faithful and unfaithful stewards by expressing this general principle: "From everyone who has been given much, much will be demanded; and from the one who has been entrusted with much, much more will be asked" (Luke 12:48). With what attitude of heart are we receiving all the treasures—treasures of the Word and treasures of this world—God has entrusted to us, his New Testament people? "Let us be thankful, and so worship God acceptably with reverence and awe, for our 'God is a consuming fire'" (Hebrews 12:28,29).

Amos is leading his listeners up to the truth that Israel's approaching end is not without cause. The disaster that he is announcing will come from the Lord because his people have broken their covenant with him. In verses 3 to 6, the prophet describes a whole series of causes and effects. The cause in each case is invisible, but the observer should realize that an unseen cause lies behind the visible effect.

The known fact that Israel, in the past, walked with the Lord shows that there must have been an agreement or covenant between this people and their God. Now Israel has broken its covenant with the Lord; that is the reason why the words of the Lord's prophet must sound like a lion's roar. But when does a lion roar? He must have captured some prey. When is a bird trapped? When does a snare spring up from the ground? First the trap must have been set, and then it must have enmeshed a bird in its net. When does the watchman's horn sound from the city walls? Not in time of peace, but when the people are trembling before an approaching enemy.

Verse 6 contains this climactic question: When does disaster come to a city? Only if the Lord, the unseen cause, has brought it about. The judgment upon God's people will not happen because of a chance shift in the balance of power between Israel and Assyria. The threatened effect—the fall of Samaria, the exile of the northern ten tribes—should lead Israel to see the unseen cause: the Lord, the ruler of history, is acting as a righteous judge, punishing his people's unfaithfulness in their covenant relationship with him.

Watching the news on TV or reading our daily newspaper, we can easily forget this lesson of cause and effect. An area is ruined by a flood or an earthquake; a population goes hungry because of drought; a city is terrorized by violence in the streets; a nation's armies are defeated by a more powerful enemy: the Scriptures make it clear that there are no chance happenings in God's world. "When disaster comes to a city, has not the LORD caused it?" (verse 6) Or, in the words the LORD spoke through another prophet: "I form the light and create darkness, I bring prosperity and create disaster; I, the LORD, do all these things" (Isaiah 45:7). Although we often cannot understand God's plan, we need to recognize that he continues to make history for nations and for individuals today. Prosperity and disaster come from him.

While God does not appear in person to carry out his judgment, he does announce his plan for the benefit of anyone who will listen. That is the function of his servants, prophets such as Amos: the Lord "does nothing without revealing his plan to his servants the prophets" (verse 7). The prophet himself trembles before the lion's roar. Therefore, he has no choice but to tell the people about their coming destruction. The prophets serve as watchmen for the house of Israel. Can a watchman like Amos who has heard a lion roaring in the streets of his city refuse to warn his fellow citizens?

Jesus is coming again as Lord and judge of the whole human race. To those who trust in him for the forgiveness of sins, he will appear as Savior and deliverer from all evil. Those who reject the forgiveness he won will die an ever-lasting death because of their unbelief in the "eternal fire prepared for the devil and his angels" (Matthew 25:41). The apostles of Jesus realized that. We hear the urgency in their Pentecost appeal: "Repent and be baptized, every one of you, in the name of Jesus Christ for the forgiveness of your sins" (Acts 2:38).

Man's sin is the cause of God's judgment; therefore we must warn sinners that judgment day is coming. God has forgiveness for all sinners in Jesus; therefore we must tell them about the Savior as he commanded: "Go into all the world and preach the good news to all creation. Whoever believes and is baptized will be saved, but whoever does not believe will be condemned" (Mark 16:15,16). May God give us pastors today who will preach his Word with the same urgency shown by the prophets, the apostles, and the Lord Jesus himself. May he help all of his people realize that calling sinners to repentance and sharing the gospel of forgiveness is life's most urgent business.

Witnesses summoned against Israel

⁹ **Proclaim to the fortresses of Ashdod**
and to the fortresses of Egypt:
"Assemble yourselves on the mountains of Samaria;
see the great unrest within her
and the oppression among her people."

¹⁰ **"They do not know how to do right," declares the LORD,**
"who hoard plunder and loot in their fortresses."

Samaria was built on a heavily fortified hill surrounded by higher ranges. Therefore, it was possible to look down into the city from the higher hills nearby. Amos summons witnesses, the people of Egypt and Ashdod, to look down into Israel's capital city. The Egyptians made slaves of the Israelites, and the Philistines of Ashdod were hostile to Israel since the days of Samson and during the reigns of Saul and David. To shame the Israelites, the Lord calls these heathen enemies to witness his people's disgraceful unrighteousness, as if to say: "You have been more unruly than the nations around you and have not followed my decrees or kept my laws. You have not even conformed to the standards of the nations around you" (Ezekiel 5:7).

What will Egypt and Ashdod see inside the walls and gates of well-fortified Samaria? Unrest, because the rich are violently oppressing the poor; and plunder and loot in the palaces, the profits of dishonesty, profiteering, and corruption heaped up at the expense of the needy members of the Lord's people (2:6,7; 5:12; 8:5,6). Although chosen to receive the promise of the Savior and the revelation of God's law, Israel has become a people who "do not know how to do right" (verse 10).

We might wonder why Amos concentrates on the sins of the Israelites against their poor Israelite neighbors when the people are also disregarding the Lord by worshiping idols. From passages such as 4:4,5 and 5:21-23, it is plain that the people of Israel are worshiping very zealously. At least at the official shrines they claim to be worshiping the Lord, although it is plain from the prophecy of Hosea that they also worship Baal. The prophet mentions oppression and injustice because these sins are visible, outward symptoms of unbelief, the inward spiritual disease that infects his people. Their lives show that true faith has withered away in their hearts. Unbelief and impenitence result in disobedience. The nation has broken its covenant with the Lord.

Can Israel still claim to love the Lord? "If anyone says, 'I love God,' yet hates his brother, he is a liar. For anyone who does not love his brother, whom he has seen, cannot love God, whom he has not seen" (1 John 4:20). Jesus calls a life of love, particularly the love of believer for fellow believer, the confession and proof of discipleship: "All men will know that you are my disciples, if you love one another" (John 13:35). Where there is no love, there are no disciples, and people must live and die in fear of God's judgment. "Anyone who hates his brother is a murderer, and you know that no murderer has eternal life in him" (1 John 3:15).

The coming destruction

¹¹Therefore this is what the Sovereign LORD says:

> "An enemy will overrun the land;
> he will pull down your strongholds
> and plunder your fortresses."

¹²This is what the LORD says:

> "As a shepherd saves from the lion's mouth
> only two leg bones or a piece of an ear,
> so will the Israelites be saved,
> those who sit in Samaria
> on the edge of their beds
> and in Damascus on their couches."

¹³"Hear this and testify against the house of Jacob," declares the Lord, the LORD God Almighty.

> ¹⁴ "On the day I punish Israel for her sins,
> I will destroy the altars of Bethel;
> the horns of the altar will be cut off
> and fall to the ground.
> ¹⁵ I will tear down the winter house
> along with the summer house;
> the houses adorned with ivory will be destroyed
> and the mansions will be demolished,"
> declares the LORD.

No enemy appears anywhere on Israel's horizon. The nation under victorious Jeroboam II seems prosperous and secure. People are living a life of luxury in their fortified palaces. Not for long, says the prophet. An enemy will surround Israel on every side, pull down the fortifications in which Samaria trusts, and carry off the plunder that fills the Israelite strongholds. Amos is prophesying the invasion of the Assyrians, who will take Samaria in 722 B.C.

To show how complete the destruction will be, the prophet uses an illustration from his own life as a shepherd. The law said that if a sheep was torn to pieces by a wild animal, the shepherd was to "bring in the remains as evidence and he will not be required to pay for the torn animal" (Exodus 22:13). The Israelites who have lived in luxury will have no more than a piece of a bed or a corner of a couch left. The few poor remnants that Assyria will leave behind will only show that Jeroboam's proud kingdom is torn to bits, like a helpless sheep in the jaws of a lion.

The Lord first marks for punishment the altars of Bethel, where the Israelites brought their sacrifices before a golden bull-calf. Amos is repeating a prophecy that a man of God from Judah made when Jeroboam I dedicated the first altar at Bethel (1 Kings 13:1-3). The altar will be desecrated; the horns of the altar, extensions on the four corners serving as signs of divine power, will be hacked off. The Lord will fulfill this prophecy about a century after the fall of Samaria, when the Judean king Josiah demolishes the altar at Bethel (2 Kings 23:15).

After the altars, Amos mentions the palaces of the rich as the objects of God's judgment. The winter homes of the wealthy, built to catch the December sun; their second homes on the hillsides, open to cool breezes in summer; their mansions full of furniture adorned with costly ivory panels: all will be demolished by the invading Assyrian armies.

The people of Amos' time have forgotten their Creator. Their ears have become dull to the words of the Lord's prophets, calling them to repentance. Amos has presented the proof that Israel is far from God: the hearts of a rich and powerful people have no feeling for the misery of the poor among them. On this evidence the almighty judge condemns them to conquest by a foreign army and oblivion in exile.

No present-day country can be fully compared to ancient Israel. Members of the Christian church, God's people today, are found in many nations, wherever the gospel is proclaimed. But national wealth can lead even Christians to fall into the same self-deception practiced by Israel under Jeroboam II. Whether the map of our country is labeled "United States of America" or "Israel," prosperity and present-day blessings, such as a highly advanced technology, are no assurance of God's continuing favor. In fact, they can easily mask moral rot, which is sure to be followed by God's judgment. Therefore "'let not the wise man boast of his wisdom or the strong man boast of his strength or the rich man boast of his riches, but let him who boasts boast about this: that he understands and knows me, that I am the LORD, who exercises kindness, justice and righteousness on earth, for in these I delight,' declares the LORD" (Jeremiah 9:23,24).

Oppression will bring judgment

4 Hear this word, you cows of Bashan on Mount Samaria,
   you women who oppress the poor and crush the needy
   and say to your husbands, "Bring us some drinks!"
² The Sovereign LORD has sworn by his holiness:
   "The time will surely come
   when you will be taken away with hooks,
      the last of you with fishhooks.

> ³ **You will each go straight out**
> **through breaks in the wall,**
> **and you will be cast out toward Harmon,"**
> declares the LORD.

To show how certainly judgment is coming, the Lord who cannot lie takes an oath by his own holiness. The land of Bashan, east of the Sea of Galilee, was known for the strong bulls (Psalm 22:12) and fat cows that pastured on its hills. Amos pictures the wealthy women of Samaria as such sleek cattle, concerned only with satisfying their own hunger and thirst at the expense of the oppressed poor. The fat cattle will be butchered and their hindquarters hung on meathooks, or they will be led away like fish on a line, their noses pierced by their captors. There will be so many breaks in the fortifications of Israel's capital that its inhabitants will leave the city in any direction, not only through the gate. Their enemies will drive them out into a foreign place with a strange name. (The location of Harmon is not known. It might mean Mount Hermon or Armenia.)

An ironic invitation to worship

> ⁴ **"Go to Bethel and sin;**
> **go to Gilgal and sin yet more.**
> **Bring your sacrifices every morning,**
> **your tithes every three years.**
> ⁵ **Burn leavened bread as a thank offering**
> **and brag about your freewill offerings—**
> **boast about them, you Israelites,**
> **for this is what you love to do,"**
> declares the Sovereign LORD.

The Israelites are practicing the rites of their worship very zealously (see also 5:5,21-23). Amos ironically urges them to "go to it." What they are doing at Bethel and Gilgal, another of their shrines, is sin and not worship in the Lord's sight, because they are not concerned about doing his will.

The law commanded that God's people should offer one-tenth of what their fields, flocks, and herds produced every year (Leviticus 27:30-33) to support the Levites (Numbers 18:23,24). This tithe freed the Levites to serve in the temple. Every third year the Israelites were to set aside the tithe in all their cities to provide for both the Levites and the poor. With heavy irony Amos directs that tithes be brought in every three days (the word translated "years" in the NIV).

The law did not permit any yeast in a burnt offering (Leviticus 2:11). But since the Israelites have disobeyed the Lord in other respects, the prophet suggests that they also burn leavened thank offerings. The essence of "freewill offerings" was that they should be given in heartfelt love for God, in proportion to his blessings (Deuteronomy 16:10). Amos suggests that the givers brag and boast in their presentation ceremonies at the altar, since they evidently love making a religious show more than they love the Lord.

What would Amos say about our church services? Do we worship the Father "in spirit and truth" (John 4:23), or do we expect that the Lord should be satisfied if we merely join the crowd in church on Sunday? Are we concerned about the truth of the message being proclaimed to us, or would we tolerate falsehood mixed with the truth in the sermons we hear and the songs we sing? Do we cheerfully contribute generous gifts as the fruit of thankful hearts, or do we sometimes bring a "freewill" offering because we like to be called good givers? May Christ's people never offer such sacrifices of fools! (Ecclesiastes 5:1).

Israel has not returned to the Lord

⁶ "I gave you empty stomachs in every city
and lack of bread in every town,
yet you have not returned to me,"
declares the Lord.

⁷ "I also withheld rain from you
when the harvest was still three months away.
I sent rain on one town,
but withheld it from another.
One field had rain;
another had none and dried up.
⁸ People staggered from town to town for water
but did not get enough to drink,
yet you have not returned to me,"
declares the Lord.

⁹ "Many times I struck your gardens and vineyards,
I struck them with blight and mildew.
Locusts devoured your fig and olive trees,
yet you have not returned to me,"
declares the Lord.

¹⁰ "I sent plagues among you
as I did to Egypt.
I killed your young men with the sword,
along with your captured horses.
I filled your nostrils with the stench of your camps,
yet you have not returned to me,"
declares the Lord.

¹¹ "I overthrew some of you
as I overthrew Sodom and Gomorrah.
You were like a burning stick snatched from the fire,
yet you have not returned to me,"
declares the Lord.

The law covenant that the Lord made with Israel at Mount
Sinai and renewed when they entered Canaan included

promises of blessing for obedience to his commandments (Deuteronomy 28:1-14) and threats of his curse for disobedience. Moses told his people: "If you do not obey the LORD your God and do not carefully follow all his commands and decrees I am giving you today, all these curses will come upon you and overtake you. . . . The LORD will strike you with wasting disease, with fever and inflammation, with scorching heat and drought, with blight and mildew, which will plague you until you perish. The sky over your head will be bronze, the ground beneath you iron. . . . The LORD will afflict you with the boils of Egypt . . . . Swarms of locusts will take over all your trees and the crops of your land. . . . Because you did not serve the LORD your God joyfully and gladly in the time of prosperity, therefore in hunger and thirst, in nakedness and dire poverty, you will serve the enemies the LORD sends against you. He will put an iron yoke on your neck until he has destroyed you" (Deuteronomy 28:15-48).

Israel experienced such famines, droughts, plagues, and defeats. The Lord's people should have recognized that his hand had turned against them because of their sins. "When disaster comes to a city, has not the LORD caused it?" (3:6). In spite of all the proofs of his disfavor, "you have not returned to me," the Lord accuses (verses 6-11). "To me" here means "all the way back to me." These words form a sad refrain, repeated five times in this chapter. Perhaps Israel has briefly looked in the Lord's direction for help in times of trouble, but the people have persistently refused to take the way of repentance and faith back to the Father's house.

The Lord's old covenant with Israel came to an end when he made a new covenant with us through Jesus his Son. That new covenant, promised already to Abraham, makes a pledge that stands firm forever in the unchanging mercy of

God: "I will forgive their wickedness and will remember their sins no more" (Jeremiah 31:34).

The Lord may use lack of food or drink, sickness, failures of our crops or businesses, defeat in war, or the death of those we love to lead Christians back to him when we need to be reminded that we depend totally on him. Faith requires exercise that only adversity provides, and surely every experience that causes pain and tears reminds us of the power of sin which brought sorrow and death into our fallen world. But in the new covenant that the Father concluded with us through Christ, such experiences are no curse. "There is now no condemnation for those who are in Christ Jesus" (Romans 8:1). Especially in pain and trouble, we are assured that nothing in all creation "will be able to separate us from the love of God that is in Christ Jesus our Lord" (Romans 8:39).

Because Israel has repeatedly refused to be warned about the results of impenitence and unbelief, Amos announces that the Lord's long patience has come to an end.

Prepare to meet your God

12 "Therefore this is what I will do to you, Israel,
    and because I will do this to you,
    prepare to meet your God, O Israel."

13 He who forms the mountains,
    creates the wind,
    and reveals his thoughts to man,
he who turns dawn to darkness,
    and treads the high places of the earth—
    the LORD God Almighty is his name.

All of the plagues that Israel has suffered until now have been forgotten in the brief return of national glory under Jeroboam II. Therefore the Israelites have not returned to the

Lord. They have refused to seek his face, which would shine with favor for a penitent people. Therefore, Israel must now face him as the stern and righteous judge. He does not say what "this" is that he will do to them. The prophet saves until the end of chapter 6, the end of this part of his book, the plainest announcement of how the judge will appear to Israel: he will stir up an enemy against them who will oppress the land from one end to the other. The final curse of the covenant has been spoken: "The LORD will bring a nation against you from far away, from the ends of the earth, like an eagle swooping down. . . . They will lay siege to all the cities throughout your land until the high fortified walls in which you trust fall down. They will besiege all the cities throughout the land the LORD your God is giving you. . . . You will be uprooted from the land. . . . Then the LORD will scatter you among all nations, from one end of the earth to the other" (Deuteronomy 28:49-64). The Northern Kingdom is rushing toward its end. That will be Israel's final meeting with God.

The Lord who speaks this verdict is no puny deity whose territory is limited by national boundaries. The molder of the mountains, the Creator of the wind, the one who holds all history in his hand and can therefore reveal to man his own thoughts for the future: he is also the judge. He rules light and darkness; the high places—where Canaanites and Israelites are worshiping idols—are like stepping-stones for his feet as he passes on his way to judgment: "Prepare to meet your God, O Israel" (verse 12); "the LORD God Almighty is his name" (verse 13).

A lament over Israel

5 Hear this word, O house of Israel, this lament I take up concerning you:

> ² **"Fallen is Virgin Israel,**
> **never to rise again,**

> deserted in her own land,
>   with no one to lift her up."

³This is what the Sovereign LORD says:

> "The city that marches out a thousand strong for Israel
>   will have only a hundred left;
> the town that marches out a hundred strong
>   will have only ten left."

The prophet speaks these verses in the mournful meter of a funeral dirge. God's chosen people had been like a virgin bride betrothed to him. Because she has broken her engagement with the Lord, she will be dishonored and cast aside by the foreign soldiers who take her land. Without him at her side, there will be no one to restore her. Israel will experience total military defeat, as her armies will be decimated. Nine out of ten men who march out to war will be battle casualties.

Seek the Lord and live

⁴This is what the LORD says to the house of Israel:

> "Seek me and live;
> ⁵   do not seek Bethel,
> do not go to Gilgal,
>   do not journey to Beersheba.
> For Gilgal will surely go into exile,
>   and Bethel will be reduced to nothing."
> ⁶ Seek the LORD and live,
>   or he will sweep through the house of Joseph like a fire;
> it will devour,
>   and Bethel will have no one to quench it.

At Bethel, meaning "house of God," the Lord appeared to Jacob (Genesis 28:10-22). At Gilgal the Israelites were

221

circumcised and first celebrated the Passover in the Promised Land (Joshua 5:2-12). Beersheba was once the home of Abraham, and there the Lord also appeared to Isaac (Genesis 26:23,24) and Jacob (Genesis 46:1-3). All these places later became goals for the religious pilgrimages of idol-worshiping Israelites. The Lord warns that these places will share in the destruction and exile he is preparing for the nation of Israel.

Rather than scurrying on pilgrimages, each Israelite ought to have another concern. The Lord, who created everything at the beginning, remains the only source of life for time and eternity. He invites, "Seek me and live" (verse 4). Even though the Lord has spoken his judgment upon Israel as a nation, he still extends his gospel invitation to individuals in God's people. He offers the gift of life to members of a dying nation. The only alternative to life with God is the fiery judgment that threatens "the house of Joseph"—a name for the kingdom of Israel, since Joseph was the ancestor of both Manasseh and Ephraim, the most prominent northern tribe. The coming judgment will also strike the sanctuary at Bethel in spite of its name, which means "house of God."

The life that the Lord offers here is finally and fully provided in the coming of the Savior, who as the Good Shepherd says about the sheep of his flock, "I have come that they may have life, and have it to the full" (John 10:10). Through faith in his Word, those who follow him receive spiritual life that endures from here to eternity, as he promises: "I give them eternal life, and they shall never perish" (John 10:28).

Injustice will bring judgment

> ⁷ **You who turn justice into bitterness**
> **and cast righteousness to the ground**

⁸ (he who made the Pleiades and Orion,
     who turns blackness into dawn
     and darkens day into night,
   who calls for the waters of the sea
     and pours them out over the face of the land—
     the LORD is his name—
⁹ he flashes destruction on the stronghold
     and brings the fortified city to ruin),
¹⁰ you hate the one who reproves in court
     and despise him who tells the truth.

¹¹ You trample on the poor
     and force him to give you grain.
   Therefore, though you have built stone mansions,
     you will not live in them;
   though you have planted lush vineyards,
     you will not drink their wine.
¹² For I know how many are your offenses
     and how great your sins.

   You oppress the righteous and take bribes
     and you deprive the poor of justice in the courts.
¹³ Therefore the prudent man keeps quiet in such times,
     for the times are evil.

¹⁴ Seek good, not evil,
     that you may live.
   Then the LORD God Almighty will be with you,
     just as you say he is.
¹⁵ Hate evil, love good;
     maintain justice in the courts.
   Perhaps the LORD God Almighty will have mercy
     on the remnant of Joseph.

¹⁶Therefore this is what the Lord, the LORD God Almighty,
says:

   "There will be wailing in all the streets
     and cries of anguish in every public square.
   The farmers will be summoned to weep
     and the mourners to wail.

**¹⁷ There will be wailing in all the vineyards,
for I will pass through your midst,"**

says the Lᴏʀᴅ.

As a striking symptom of Israel's disobedience to the terms of the Lord's covenant law, Amos cites the corruption of its legal processes. While the king served as chief justice in his realm, ordinary courts were made up of respected citizens in any town. When Boaz, for example, needed to settle a legal matter, he presented it to ten elders of the city (Ruth 4:1-12). This court sat at the gate of the city and heard the testimony of those involved. According to God's precept, the judges were to "decide the case, acquitting the innocent and condemning the guilty" (Deuteronomy 25:1).

Because any respected Israelite citizen might serve as one of the judges in local matters, the functioning of the courts gave a fair cross section of the people's conception of right and wrong. The clearest test of moral attitudes would present itself when one of the parties in a legal case was a widow, an orphan, or a foreigner. Such persons had no family or fellow citizens to defend them from injustice. Then the judges had to take particular care to give their decision in keeping with the just standard of the Lord, "who shows no partiality and accepts no bribes. He defends the cause of the fatherless and the widow, and loves the alien" (Deuteronomy 10:17,18).

God's law included explicit warnings against letting money talk in court, one way or the other. Fairness and the law should guide the judges; they should favor neither the poor nor the rich in their decisions (Exodus 23:3,6). "Do not accept a bribe, for a bribe blinds those who see and twists the words of the righteous" (Exodus 23:8). Included in the Lord's Ten Commandments was one that clearly applied to all court proceedings: "You shall not give false testimony against your neighbor" (Exodus 20:16).

Amos describes how far the Israelite courts have fallen from measuring up to the Lord's standards. Justice, which should flow clean and sweet, is turning as bitter as wormwood. Righteousness, which should be exalted in legal decisions as in every other aspect of life, is being cast to the ground. In verses 8 and 9, Amos adds a hymn stanza to remind the judges whom they are offending. Israel's lawgiver is the same Lord who created the awesome constellations in the sky, who commands the sun to rise and set each day, who controls the water cycle, lifting water from the sea into the clouds and then pouring it out as rainfall on the fields. When he is displeased by human injustice, he can impose much stronger penalties than fines and imprisonment: like lightning his judgment strikes and destroys the fortifications in which a city trusts.

Injustice pervades Israelite society. The rich, perhaps by charging excessive rent in kind, deprive poor farmers of the grain they need to feed their families. It was a sign of God's grace when he let his people inherit a land that had been developed by the Canaanites: "I gave you a land on which you did not toil and cities you did not build; and you live in them and eat from vineyards and olive groves that you did not plant" (Joshua 24:13). Now just the opposite will happen: "Though you have built stone mansions, you will not live in them; though you have planted lush vineyards, you will not drink their wine" (verse 11). Israel's enemies will inherit the Promised Land.

Of Israel's many offenses against his law, the Lord again singles out the perversion of justice: judges are declaring the innocent party guilty because his opponent has offered a bribe. As a result, a poor man cannot get a hearing in court. The moral climate has become so hostile to justice that prudent men know they cannot get a hearing for any reproof or talk of reform. They would rather keep silent than call down on themselves the spite of their neighbors.

The prophet Amos, like John the Baptist, preaches repentance while he warns of a judgment to come. True repentance, really seeking the Lord, will be accompanied by fruits. The person who seeks the Lord will "seek good, not evil" (verse 14). To say with our mouths "The Lord is with us" is a false and empty claim unless our hearts love his will. Some Israelites might still hate evil and love good. They will testify to their repentance by bucking the tide of injustice in their courts. To such a remnant of Joseph— "Joseph" means the kingdom of Israel—Amos holds out the possibility that "perhaps the LORD God Almighty will have mercy" (verse 15) in the coming judgment.

The Northern Kingdom as a nation, however, is doomed. The prophet shows this by returning in verse 16 to the lamentation that introduced chapter 5. The sad sounds will be heard in every street and square of every town, because the nation will die. Amos pictures a funeral scene in which not only professional mourners will wail, but farmers will be called from their fields to weep, and the vineyards, usually the scene of merry harvest songs and dancing, will be filled instead with laments. The Lord is going to pass among his people for judgment. His coming means the end of the kingdom of Israel.

Amos directed his prophecy to the Old Testament people of God. How does it apply to the church today? Christians look into God's law as a mirror to reflect sin: that is the law's most important purpose (Romans 3:20). But the law also serves as a guide for godly living. God's law requires fairness in all our dealings, particularly when we have power or authority over others. Are parents fair in the treatment of their children, teachers in the administration of their classrooms, employers in the way they regulate and pay their employees? If God has given us wealth, do we see to it that we do not increase it by trampling the poor (verse 11) or misuse it to bend the law in our own favor (verse 12)? We say that we seek the Lord so that we may live (verse 4). Do we apply this in daily life by seeking good, not evil (verse 14)? Do we hate evil and love good (verse 15), or do we live lives of indifference to serious moral issues? When Jesus comes again to judge the world, he tells us that he will point to works of mercy done to our needy fellow believers as the proof of Christian faith (Matthew 25:35-40). Does he find such fruits of faith in our lives?

The judicial process in a present-day nation seems much more complicated than the simple justice that God's law required in ancient Israel. Yet everyone will recognize that the basic principle of fairness is a part of natural law, written into all people's hearts and, to some extent, reflected in every country's laws. A person who has a grievance against his fellow citizen deserves a fair hearing. The person who is accused of a crime deserves a fair trial. British and American legal systems guarantee a man the right to a hearing before a jury of his peers. Such a requirement expresses the same standard of fairness that Israel fulfilled by having cases heard at the city gate by ten respected citizens. Whether the accused is rich or poor should have nothing to do with the outcome. Everyone knows by nature that offering or accepting a bribe is wrong.

Since "righteousness exalts a nation, but sin is a disgrace to any people" (Proverbs 14:34), it must be the concern of every government to administer the law fairly. In some countries a constitution guarantees to every citizen such privileges as choosing representatives to enact laws. Therefore, every citizen must have a concern for the fairness of the laws and the impartial administration of justice in the courts. Even though Christians hold citizenship in the eternal kingdom of Christ, they are also subjects of earthly governments. A letter written by the prophet Jeremiah to the Jews in their Babylonian captivity gives helpful guidance to Christian citizens: "Seek the peace and prosperity of the city to which I have carried you into exile. Pray to the LORD for it, because if it prospers, you too will prosper" (Jeremiah 29:7). By prayer and honest service, Christians will seek the welfare of their communities.

The day of the Lord

> ¹⁸ Woe to you who long
>   for the day of the LORD!
> Why do you long for the day of the LORD?
>   That day will be darkness, not light.
> ¹⁹ It will be as though a man fled from a lion
>   only to meet a bear,
> as though he entered his house
>   and rested his hand on the wall
>   only to have a snake bite him.
> ²⁰ Will not the day of the LORD be darkness, not light—
>   pitch-dark, without a ray of brightness?

When the people of Israel were crying out because of their misery in Egypt, the Lord told Moses, "I have come down to rescue them from the hand of the Egyptians" (Exodus 3:8). Believing Israelites knew that the Lord would come again to save his people. He gave them that hope by promising them a Savior. From this passage in Amos, it is clear that many Israelites in his time are looking forward to the Lord's coming. They call the time when he will come "the day of the LORD" (see also Joel 3:14; Zechariah 14:1; Malachi 4:1-5). They anticipate the dawn of that day because then God will deliver his people from every evil.

But what will the Lord's coming mean for an impenitent people who have forsaken him and broken his covenant? Then his coming to his people can only mean judgment, not deliverance. Amos warns, "That day will be darkness, not light" (verse 18). When they experience any kind of trouble, the Israelites might say, "It looks dark now, but just wait! The day of the LORD will come!" The prophet has a blunt warning for them: if they continue in impenitence, the Lord's coming will mean trouble worse than any they have ever seen. It will mean "out of the frying pan and into the fire." Amos says the Israelites are like a man who runs away from a fierce lion (their present troubles) only to meet a more dangerous bear (the day of the Lord), or like someone who thinks that reaching home (the day of the Lord) means safety at last, but then a poisonous snake (his holy judgment) strikes from a hole in the wall. For people who have broken a covenant with their God, the "day of the LORD" will be pitch-dark indeed. He is coming to bring down the curtain and turn out the lights on the history of the Northern Kingdom.

We New Testament believers also look forward to the coming day of the Lord. "Christ was sacrificed once to take away the sins of many people; and he will appear a second time, not to bear sin, but to bring salvation to those who are waiting for him" (Hebrews 9:28). That day, we know, will mean the end of all sorrow and trouble for God's people. Whenever the Bible speaks to us of that day, it emphasizes not only deliverance from evil but also readiness for judgment. "Be always on the watch," Jesus said (Luke 21:36). Being ready for his coming means daily repentance, faith in him, and living by constant trust in his promises. "So then, dear friends, since you are looking forward to this [day of the Lord], make every effort to be found spotless, blameless and at peace with him" (2 Peter 3:14).

Fake religion is an abomination

²¹ "I hate, I despise your religious feasts;
   I cannot stand your assemblies.
²² Even though you bring me burnt offerings and grain
      offerings,
   I will not accept them.
Though you bring choice fellowship offerings,
   I will have no regard for them.
²³ Away with the noise of your songs!
   I will not listen to the music of your harps.
²⁴ But let justice roll on like a river,
   righteousness like a never-failing stream!

²⁵ "Did you bring me sacrifices and offerings
   forty years in the desert, O house of Israel?
²⁶ You have lifted up the shrine of your king,
   the pedestal of your idols,
   the star of your god—
   which you made for yourselves.
²⁷ Therefore I will send you into exile beyond Damascus,"
   says the LORD, whose name is God Almighty.

The ceremonial law that God gave his people through Moses instituted three annual pilgrimage festivals when every adult male Israelite was to appear before the Lord at the tabernacle or the temple: the Feast of Unleavened Bread, including Passover; the Feast of Harvest, or Firstfruits; and the Feast of Ingathering, or Pentecost (Exodus 23:14-19). The law prescribed sacred assemblies at these and other holy days and on every Sabbath (Leviticus 23). The worship required by God included burnt offerings (Leviticus 1), grain offerings (Leviticus 2), and fellowship, or peace offerings (Leviticus 3). King David adorned Israel's worship by having some of the Levites sing joyful psalms, accompanied by harps and other musical instruments (1 Chronicles 15:16).

All of Israel's worship was designed to express faith in the Lord and willing obedience to him. The festivals acknowledged that the Lord had delivered his people from bondage in Egypt and that he was providing for all their needs in the land he gave them. The sacrifices were a promise from the Lord of his perfect sacrifice for all their sins. Offerings also symbolized thanksgiving and devotion to him as Israel's God. Songs and instrumental music expressed praise to the Lord for all his wonderful works.

But now the Israelites are going through the motions of worship without faith, without their hearts' devotion, with no will to praise the Lord for his salvation. They think they can follow a set of formulas to guarantee the favor of their God. In their opinion, going to his sanctuary for festivals and assemblies is a way of staying on the right side of the Lord even while disobeying his commandments in their daily life. Amos has recited the evidence of Israel's insincerity: injustice in the courts and unrighteousness in men's treatment of their fellowmen. The just and righteous Lord despises such "worship."

There is a kind of adoration that he gladly accepts. God's people truly praise him as their Savior when they trust in him alone for their salvation. They glorify him on earth when they treat one another fairly. Justice should roll on among them constantly, like a cleansing, nourishing stream. God's people worship him when they do not turn righteousness on again, off again, like a desert wadi holding water for only a few days after a rain. Righteousness in their lives should reflect the Lord's own constant righteousness: "Let justice roll on like a river, righteousness like a never-failing stream!" (verse 24). Worship is life, and life is worship. When the Lord's people approach him daily in repentance and faith, then the lives they live in their homes and workplaces will agree with their sacrifices of praise and thanksgiving in his temple. Then the Lord will also be pleased to receive their temple worship, because it comes from hearts that belong to him.

The ordinances of Israel's worship do not regulate the worship of Christians today. Living in a new covenant established at the death of Christ, we are free to establish our own worship forms, days to hear the Word, sacrifices of thanksgiving, liturgies, and hymns of praise (Colossians 2:16,17). God is pleased to accept our worship when it comes from penitent, faith-filled hearts.

But if ever we think of our liturgies, hymns, and offerings as a way to stay on the right side of the Lord while caring nothing about his will for our daily lives at home and on the job, then he says to us as he said to Israel, "I hate, I despise your religious feasts; I cannot stand your assemblies" (verse 21). "Such ceremonies are highly dangerous to the worshiper because he is attempting to stifle his moral and social conscience by all the 'business' of religion. Amos would say to us:

> I loathe and despise your communion services;
>> your matins and vespers give me no pleasure.
> You may bring me the paltry percentage of your
>> income,
>> and I shall not so much as look at it.
> I don't want to hear the songs of your liturgies;
>> my ears are closed to your organ music.
> Instead, let justice roll on like a mighty river,
>> and integrity flow like a never-failing stream."*

According to verses 25 and 26, the apostasy that Amos is pointing out in the Northern Kingdom is nothing new in

---

* B. Backer, "Foundations of Worship" (paper presented to Minnesota District Pastoral Conference, Lake City, MN, 1977).

Israel's history. Some of the Israelites have just been going through the motions of worship ever since God ordained the law at Mount Sinai. Even though they built the tabernacle, carried it with them in the wilderness, and brought sacrifices there for 40 years on the way to Canaan, even then their whole hearts did not belong to the Lord. Amos says that during the wilderness wandering, the people also carried with them other worship paraphernalia devoted to idols. The words translated *king, shrine,* and *pedestal* in verse 26 may also be names of heathen deities. Already in ancient times, Israel stubbornly resisted God's Holy Spirit. The Christian martyr Stephen makes this point to the unbelieving Jews in Acts 7:42,43 by quoting Amos 5:25-27.

Such persistent idolatry and disobedience can have only one outcome. In each section of his book, Amos has added additional details to his inspired description of the coming judgment. He has mentioned captivity and exile before (4:2; 5:11). Now he adds the Lord's word about the prisoners' destination: "I will send you into exile beyond Damascus" (verse 27). This must mean captivity in Assyria.

The people should have no doubt about who is imposing such a severe sentence. It is "the LORD, whose name is God Almighty" who is sending them into exile. He who so abundantly blessed his people according to his promise also meant what he said when he threatened through Moses, "If you do not obey the LORD your God . . . just as it pleased the LORD to make you prosper and increase in number, so it will please him to ruin and destroy you. You will be uprooted from the land you are entering to possess. Then the LORD will scatter you among all nations, from one end of the earth to the other" (Deuteronomy 28:15,63,64).

The new covenant of grace that God made with us in the death of Jesus Christ contains no threats. It is a promise to forgive all sins freely because Jesus shed his blood on the cross. God extends his gospel invitation to all sinners: "Come to the cross, trust Christ, and live" (TLH 377:8). "Whoever believes in him is not condemned" (John 3:18).

On the other hand, "whoever does not believe stands condemned already because he has not believed in the name of God's one and only Son" (John 3:18). Outside the Lord's covenant of grace, there is no salvation. Old Testament believers like Abraham were also saved through faith in the promised seed, not by keeping the commandments of the Sinai covenant. But why did the Israelites break the Lord's commandments? Why did they worship false gods, mistreat their fellowmen, and then refuse to repent when the Lord sent his prophets to call them back to him? Israel's disobedience was rooted in unbelief. They would not trust in the Lord for his salvation. They wanted to choose their own gods and to follow their own desires. This sad example of God's love rejected, his salvation despised, should make us run to Jesus and cling to his cross. How earnestly we will avoid everything that would lead us away from the Word of our God, his Savior, and his way of salvation! How urgently we will invite others to hear the Word with us because it is the only means God uses to lead sinners to repentance and faith in Christ.

Woe to the complacent

6 Woe to you who are complacent in Zion,
      and to you who feel secure on Mount Samaria,
   you notable men of the foremost nation,
      to whom the people of Israel come!
   ² Go to Calneh and look at it;
      go from there to great Hamath,
      and then go down to Gath in Philistia.

Are they better off than your two kingdoms?
  Is their land larger than yours?
³ You put off the evil day
  and bring near a reign of terror.
⁴ You lie on beds inlaid with ivory
  and lounge on your couches.
You dine on choice lambs
  and fattened calves.
⁵ You strum away on your harps like David
  and improvise on musical instruments.
⁶ You drink wine by the bowlful
  and use the finest lotions,
  but you do not grieve over the ruin of Joseph.
⁷ Therefore you will be among the first to go into exile;
  your feasting and lounging will end.

Uzziah king of Judah in Jerusalem and Jeroboam II king of Israel in Samaria, together with the other leaders of their lands, must be feeling quite pleased with themselves as they survey their kingdoms from their fortresses on Mount Zion and on the mountain of Samaria. No foreign enemies threaten Israel or Judah on any side. The kings and their courts sit secure in their well-fortified capitals, holding audience for the people who come to Jerusalem and Samaria seeking justice or favors.

The Lord shatters their self-satisfaction with a word of woe. He suggests that the great men of Jerusalem and Samaria consider some cities that have met defeat or destruction: Calneh, not certainly known to us today but probably a place in Syria and not the Mesopotamian city mentioned in Genesis chapter 10; once-mighty Hamath, which lost its southern territories to Jeroboam II (2 Kings 14:28); and Gath, the Philistine city whose walls Uzziah broke down (2 Chronicles 26:6). What happened to those once great cities could happen to Samaria or Jerusalem as well.

Satan knows how to distract human beings from contemplating unpleasant topics such as sin and the coming judgment. Amos describes the high luxury in which the Israelite leaders are living. The wealth gained through military victories and profitable commerce has purchased comforts for their homes. The average Israelite house had little furniture. At night people slept on the floor or on an earthen shelf, wrapped in their cloaks. Now the nation's wealthy are sleeping on beds inlaid with carved panels of ivory, while by day they sprawl on soft couches. In the average ancient Israelite diet, meat was reserved for special celebrations. Now the wealthy are feasting regularly on choice cuts of lamb and veal. Their days and nights are occupied with parties and entertainment, times to strum stringed instruments, drink large quantities of wine, and perfume one's body with choice ointments. No pleasure seems to be lacking.*

What is missing, says the prophet, is spiritual concern on the part of the people's leaders. The kingdom that seems so fortunate is actually ruined, because it has decayed from within. This society that thinks it is enjoying health and prosperity is actually sick unto death. Yet the kings and their leading citizens distract themselves with pleasures and entertainment. They refuse to grieve for the fact that "Joseph"—the Northern Kingdom that includes the tribes of Ephraim and Manasseh, Joseph's sons—is morally rotten and ruined. Very well, Amos says: let the notable men of Israel lead their people—into captivity. Let Israel's feasting and lounging be replaced by the bitter experience of exile far from the Promised Land.

---

* Amos may be describing a pagan ritual. See Philip J. King, "The *Marzeah* Amos Denounces," *Biblical Archaeology Review* 15, 4 (July-August, 1988), 34-44.

It is not difficult for us in prosperous times to look around and see an all-consuming concern for pleasure in the citizens of our country. We need to remember that Amos is speaking to God's chosen people Israel, and that today his words apply particularly to Christians. We who call ourselves disciples of Jesus in this favored land also enjoy the prosperity of our times. We buy comfortable furniture, eat and drink at expensive restaurants, listen to beautiful music on fine stereo systems.

We say that our wealth is a gift of God. But is it also true that we do not grieve over the ruin of his church? Are we unconcerned whether our pastors are teaching what the Bible teaches, as long as our congregation has an impressive physical plant? Do we take no measures to protect even our own families against the moral laxity that rules the world? Do we wrap ourselves so tightly in a soft cocoon of luxury that we live unaware of people suffering for lack of food, clothing, and a roof over their heads? Do we spend so generously on ourselves that little is left to give for preaching the good news among those who have not heard it? Then Jesus reproves our unbelief and warns us with the words he said to the unbelieving elders of the Jews: "I tell you that the kingdom of God will be taken away from you and given to a people who will produce its fruit" (Matthew 21:43).

The Lord abhors the pride of Israel

⁸The Sovereign LORD has sworn by himself—the LORD God Almighty declares:

> "I abhor the pride of Jacob
>   and detest his fortresses;
> I will deliver up the city
>   and everything in it."

⁹If ten men are left in one house, they too will die. ¹⁰And if a relative who is to burn the bodies comes to carry them out of the

house and asks anyone still hiding there, "Is anyone with you?" and he says, "No," then he will say, "Hush! We must not mention the name of the LORD."

> ¹¹ For the LORD has given the command,
> and he will smash the great house into pieces
> and the small house into bits.

> ¹² Do horses run on the rocky crags?
> Does one plow there with oxen?
> But you have turned justice into poison
> and the fruit of righteousness into bitterness—
> ¹³ you who rejoice in the conquest of Lo Debar
> and say "Did we not take Karnaim by our own
> strength?"

> ¹⁴ For the LORD God Almighty declares,
> "I will stir up a nation against you, O house of Israel,
> that will oppress you all the way
> from Lebo Hamath to the valley of the Arabah."

The Lord who established his covenant with Israel now appears as a plaintiff bearing witness that Israel deserves to be destroyed. He takes an oath, swearing by himself because there is no higher authority. His testimony: Israel is guilty of pride, the sin that has been called the complete anti-God state of mind. Instead of trusting and praising their God, the Israelites feel completely self-sufficient. In this court the Lord acts not only as plaintiff but also as judge. He imposes the death penalty: Samaria, the capital and leading city of the Northern Kingdom, will be delivered to its enemies and destroyed, together with its population and all its wealth.

In verses 9 and 10, Amos presents one scene from the destruction of the city. A house is left where the family before the war included ten men. Such a house would seem well able to defend itself against any enemy. But not one of those men will escape alive. A relative comes to show the dead a final token of respect. Perhaps because the whole city is filled with corpses, burial is difficult and the bodies are to be burned. A trembling fugitive has taken refuge in this house of death. There is a quick conversation.

Relative: "Is anyone still with you in the house?"

Fugitive: "No! Shh! We must not mention the name of the Lord." He is so terrified by the horrors he has experienced that he does not want to call the Lord's attention to this house. He is afraid that the avenging God will finish off even the few who have so far escaped death.

There are grounds for such fear. All the people of Israel were delivered from Egypt, were fed in the wilderness, were blessed with a home in the Promised Land. Whether or not they were true children of Abraham by faith in the Promised Seed, they all shared in many of the earthly blessings of the covenant, since Israel as a nation was blessed. Now Israel as a nation is being judged, and the whole population must share in the judgment. The judge has already passed sentence. Foreign armies will carry out Israel's execution just as he wills. Though the conquerors do not know it, the Lord is their almighty commander. Upon his order they will smash the great house and the small house (verse 11)—in other words, the dwellings of both rich and poor.

Anyone who wants to reach some goal or accomplish some project must proceed prudently. A horseman, for example, who wants to arrive at his destination in one piece does not race his animal pell-mell over rocky cliffs. A farmer who wants to prepare soil for planting does not have his oxen plow on rocky mountainsides. (Another reading in verse 12, dividing one of the Hebrew words in two, brings out the same point: "Does one plow the sea with oxen?") Yet the Israelites have proceeded as foolishly as reckless riders or unthinking plowmen. Justice in the courts should heal the ills of their society, but they have perverted justice and turned it to poison. Works of righteousness should flourish among God's people like sweet grapes in a well-tended vineyard. Instead, Israel's life bears fruit as bitter as wormwood.

Though they live in unrighteousness, Jeroboam II and his people are filled with insolent pride over the conquests their armies have won. Lo Debar and Karnaim, mentioned in verse 13, were cities on the east side of the Jordan, probably taken by Jeroboam's forces when they marched against Syria (2 Kings 14:28). *Lo Debar* means "nothing" and *Karnaim* means "horns," a symbol of strength. By naming these particular cities, Amos mocks Israel's foolish national pride. It is as if the Israelites are saying, "Our might is stronger than strength! Look! We have taken No-town!"

The inspired prophet has gradually painted a picture of the coming judgment, one detail after another. The Israelites will experience military defeat (2:14,15). Their altars and their homes will be destroyed (3:14,15). They will meet the Lord God, their Creator, coming to be their judge (4:12,13). They will be exiled beyond Damascus (5:27). Now Amos speaks for the Lord to say that he, God Almighty himself, will ally himself with the enemy side: "I will stir up a nation against you" (verse 14). The invaders will oppress the whole land from Lebo Hamath, Jeroboam's northern boundary, to the valley of the Arabah, south of the Dead Sea, the southern limit of Israelite control (2 Kings 14:25). Added to earlier details, this can only mean invasion by the Assyrians, their army under the Lord's all-controlling command.

In 722 B.C. the Assyrian king took Samaria after a three-year siege and deported the Israelites to Mesopotamia (2 Kings 17:6). About 700 B.C. Assyrian armies spread like a flood over the Southern Kingdom as well (Isaiah 8:7,8).

King Sennacherib captured all the fortified cities of Judah and laid siege to Jerusalem (2 Kings 18:13-37). The capital only escaped destruction by the Lord's miraculous deliverance (2 Kings 18 and 19).

Israel's unique blessings and unique responsibilities have their parallels in the present-day life of the Christian church. Israel's moral decay, accompanied by pride in earthly successes, gave evidence of unbelieving hearts that did not trust in the Lord for his salvation, impenitent hearts that cared nothing for doing his will. Amos describes an equation for the death of God's people: inward moral decay + pride in outward success = destruction.

Do we as a church point with pride at impressive buildings while failing to show love to fellow believers who need our help? Do we congratulate ourselves over the success of an ecclesiastical or educational program without caring how it serves God's will to save all men? Do we as Christian individuals comfort ourselves by pointing to our social standing or more than adequate income without coming to grips with the sins that are widening the gap between us and our God? Paul was addressing Christians and Christian churches when he wrote, "Do not be deceived: God cannot be mocked. A man reaps what he sows. The one who sows to please his sinful nature, from that nature will reap destruction; the one who sows to please the Spirit, from the Spirit will reap eternal life" (Galatians 6:7,8).

PART THREE

Five Visions and Messages of Judgment
(7:1–9:10)

The Lord gave his Word to Amos in such a way that the prophet saw the coming judgment (1:1). The third main part of the book of Amos contains five visions.

Visions of locusts and fire

7 This is what the Sovereign LORD showed me: He was preparing swarms of locusts after the king's share had been harvested and just as the second crop was coming up. ²When they had stripped the land clean, I cried out, "Sovereign LORD, forgive! How can Jacob survive? He is so small!"

³So the LORD relented.

"This will not happen," the LORD said.

⁴This is what the Sovereign LORD showed me: The Sovereign LORD was calling for judgment by fire; it dried up the great deep and devoured the land. ⁵Then I cried out, "Sovereign LORD, I beg you, stop! How can Jacob survive? He is so small!"

⁶So the LORD relented.

"This will not happen either," the Sovereign LORD said.

As a part of the prophet's call, perhaps even before he begins to preach in Israel, the Lord shows Amos two visions. In both of them, the judgment has already begun. In the first vision, the king's servants have taken the early cutting of hay and the field is just greening up again when the Lord sends a locust plague. Locusts can totally consume everything green in areas extending over many square miles (see the Introduction to Joel in this volume). The locust swarm strips all the young grass from the fields and is ready to attack the vineyards, olive trees, and orchards. In love for the people of Israel, Amos intercedes with God. He prays that the Lord would forgive Israel's sins and have pity on such an insignificant people. The Lord answers, "This will not happen" (verse 3), and he removes the locusts without carrying his judgment to its conclusion.

In the second vision too, the destruction has already begun. This time a word is used to describe a court case in progress. The Lord appears as executioner. Armed with the same consuming fire that burned on Mount Sinai (Exodus 24:17), he demands punishment for Israel's disobedience. The fire licks up the Mediterranean Sea and is ready to devour the land of Canaan, perhaps by searing the fields with a severe drought. Again the prophet intercedes for his people, and again the Lord relents.

A spokesman of the Lord like Amos must be disgusted by the immorality of Israel. He condemns the people's unbelief and sin in no uncertain terms. Yet he loves his people and does not want them to be destroyed. His reaction to these two visions of approaching judgment shows that the prophet has a heart for the people of Israel. He does not share the foolish illusions of greatness that fill the minds of Jeroboam II and his leaders: Israel is, compared with Egypt or Assyria, an insignificant bit player on the stage of world history. Besides, the nation has forgotten its God-given mission and well deserves punishment. Yet Amos loves the Lord's people and intercedes for them when he sees them in danger of destruction.

The Lord gives believers the insight to discern when their nation is decaying morally or when their church is growing indifferent to its mission in the world. Conscientious Christians are disgusted by the moral decay and spiritual carelessness they see around them. Yet love's way is to intercede for church and nation, to pray for the Lord's forgiveness and a further time of grace. Such prayers reflect the heart of God and go to his heart, because he says, "I take no pleasure in the death of anyone. . . . Repent and live!" (Ezekiel 18:32).

A vision of a plumb line

⁷This is what he showed me: The Lord was standing by a wall that had been built true to plumb, with a plumb line in his hand. ⁸And the LORD asked me, "What do you see, Amos?"

"A plumb line," I replied.

Then the Lord said, "Look, I am setting a plumb line among my people Israel; I will spare them no longer.

⁹ "The high places of Isaac will be destroyed
    and the sanctuaries of Israel will be ruined;
        with my sword I will rise against the house of Jeroboam."

In this third vision, the Lord himself appears, standing next to a wall. To impress the vision on Amos, he asks the prophet what he sees. Amos sees a plumb line in God's hand. The lead weight that the Lord is holding on a cord shows that the wall, once vertical, has now sagged out of plumb. A careful stonemason or bricklayer would tear it down and start his building over.

The meaning of the vision is clear. The Lord is picturing himself as a mason laying brick or stone. The wall represents Israel, the people he created to receive his covenant. The plumb line is his law, the standard laid down at Mount Sinai for Israel's life as his covenant people. The law reveals Israel's sin: the people are like a sagging, crooked wall, ready to be torn down. "I will spare them no longer," the Lord says (verse 8).

On their high places throughout the land and in the calf sanctuaries at Bethel and Dan, the people of Israel have been flaunting their unfaithfulness to the Lord. These shrines will be destroyed by the invading Assyrians. Israel's leader, both in the nation's successful military campaigns and also in the people's abandonment of the Lord's law, has been Jeroboam II. Therefore, the Lord says, "With my sword I will rise against the house of Jeroboam" (verse 9). Jeroboam's royal line will come to a bloody end.

This time the prophet remains silent and does not intercede for his people. The Lord has measured Israel, found his people wanting, and announced his decision: "I will spare them no longer" (verse 8). Amos is not allowed to protest or intercede.

Jeroboam II completed his 41-year reign and died in 753 B.C., a few years after Amos finished his ministry. He was succeeded by his son Zechariah, who also "did not turn away from the sins of Jeroboam [I] son of Nebat" (2 Kings 15:9). After a six-month reign, Zechariah was assassinated, and the royal house of Jeroboam II—the dynasty of Jehu—came to its bloody end. No doubt Shallum, Zechariah's assassin, thought that he was acting to carry out his own plan to become the next king of Israel. Actually, his sword carried out the Lord's judgment announced by his prophets Amos and Hosea (Amos 1:4).

"Through the law we become conscious of sin" (Romans 3:20). Too often God's people forget this first function of the Ten Commandments in their lives. If we live in daily repentance, we will constantly measure what we think, say, and do by the plumb line of the Lord's law. Such daily self-examination will prevent any kind of self-righteousness, because the outcome will always be the same: our lives are "out of line," like a crooked wall ready to be torn down.

Those who think that they can save themselves by keeping God's commandments are insolently asking to have their sinful lives measured by his all-seeing eye against the perfect vertical of his plumb line. His final righteous judgment will not spare them.

How can we escape the Lord's judgment? The perfect life of Jesus Christ fully measured up to his Father's holy standard, and that life was lived for us. When his Spirit gives us faith through Baptism and the Word, God writes down his verdict on the holy, loving life of Christ next to our names. Jesus lived and died in our place "so that in him we might become the righteousness of God" (2 Corinthians 5:21). "There is now no condemnation for those who are in Christ Jesus" (Romans 8:1).

Amos and Amaziah

¹⁰**Then Amaziah the priest of Bethel sent a message to Jeroboam king of Israel: "Amos is raising a conspiracy against you in the very heart of Israel. The land cannot bear all his words. ¹¹For this is what Amos is saying:**

> **" 'Jeroboam will die by the sword,**
> **and Israel will surely go into exile,**
> **away from their native land.' "**

¹²**Then Amaziah said to Amos, "Get out, you seer! Go back to the land of Judah. Earn your bread there and do your prophesying there. ¹³Don't prophesy anymore at Bethel, because this is the king's sanctuary and the temple of the kingdom."**

From this passage we know that Amos is prophesying at Bethel, an official sanctuary where the Israelites come to pay their homage to the golden calf erected by Jeroboam I. Perhaps it is the time of the royal festival, and pilgrim Israelites have come from all over the Northern Kingdom to

Bethel or Dan, in order to show their loyalty to Israel's king (1 Kings 12:32,33). The prophet's prediction of judgment against the royal house sounds like treason to Amaziah, the high priest who supervises the official worship at Bethel.

(Amaziah's name means "The Lord is strong." Israelites, like other ancient people, often included the name of their deity in their own personal names. Amaziah's name thus testifies that, even while the Israelites broke God's First Commandment by worshiping at the calf-shrine, they still thought they were serving the Lord there.)

In his message to Jeroboam II, Amaziah slightly misquotes Amos. The prophet has threatened death to "the house of Jeroboam," not to the king personally. The priest, however, does not miss the main point of the prophet's message: defeat and exile for the people of Israel (5:27; 6:7; 7:9). Without waiting for a response from the king, Amaziah proceeds on his own authority to expel this foreign prophet. Amos has come to Bethel from Tekoa in the Southern Kingdom. Amaziah has nothing against a man earning his living by prophesying, but Amos, he says, should do his work among his own countrymen. A Judean prophet, the priest thinks, should not strain Israelite hospitality by preaching his rude message of judgment against Jeroboam II in Bethel, the king's own sanctuary.

Those who preach and confess God's Word today will also meet opposition. In countries that have no religious liberty, the state may oppose the preaching of God's law and gospel. In lands where citizens enjoy freedom of conscience, opposition arises from public opinion. Jesus warned his disciples: "No servant is greater than his master. If they persecuted me, they will persecute you also. . . . They will treat you this way because of my name, for they do not know the One who sent me" (John 15:20,21).

247

¹⁴Amos answered Amaziah, "I was neither a prophet nor a prophet's son, but I was a shepherd, and I also took care of sycamore-fig trees. ¹⁵But the LORD took me from tending the flock and said to me, 'Go, prophesy to my people Israel,' ¹⁶Now then, hear the word of the LORD. You say,

> "'Do not prophesy against Israel,
> and stop preaching against the house of Isaac.'

¹⁷"Therefore this is what the LORD says:

> "'Your wife will become a prostitute in the city,
> and your sons and daughters will fall by the sword.
> Your land will be measured and divided up,
> and you yourself will die in a pagan country.
> And Israel will certainly go into exile,
> away from their native land.'"

By forbidding Amos to prophesy, Amaziah has set himself directly against the Lord. Amos did not make his own decision to preach against the people of Israel. He is not one of the "sons of the prophets," a member of a "company of prophets" like those who attached themselves to Elijah and Elisha (2 Kings 2:3) to study at the feet of the older spokesmen of the Lord. If it were left to the personal choice of Amos, he would still be feeding his flocks at Tekoa (1:1), or he might be tending to a grove of sycamore-fig trees at some oasis near the Mediterranean or Dead Sea. That is how he earned his bread before he was called to prophesy. He was a layman, not a "professional" prophet.

It was the Lord who said to Amos, "Go, prophesy to my people Israel" (verse 15). Therefore Amos will not be silent, even if his words offend the king of Israel or if the king's high priest commands him to stop preaching. In fact, Amos emphatically repeats that Israel will go into exile in a faraway land. He sharpens the point of his message: the judgment will come during Amaziah's lifetime. Invading enemy soldiers will dishonor the high priest's wife, treating her like a prostitute. The priest's own sons and daughters will be among the casualties when their city falls. Amaziah's fields and gardens will be measured out by heathen surveyors and distributed as booty to foreign conquerors. He himself will die in exile in a pagan land. Amos calls Assyria "an unclean land"— "a pagan country" in the NIV—(verse 17), that is, a country where the people do not know the laws of Moses, about what is ceremonially clean or unclean for God's people.

People who preach and teach the Word of God must be sure of their message. Only under one condition can our preachers and teachers today share the assurance that Amos showed in Bethel: they must be certain that the message is God's and not just their own. Then each of them can boldly say as Luther did, "Here I stand; I cannot do otherwise. God help me."

The whole church must always be concerned for studying, teaching, and applying the words of the Bible. That must also be our concern as we train the next generation of pastors and teachers. Faithfulness to the Word is also their prime duty as they carry out their ministry, serving as representatives of the church that has called them. They must remember that the call comes from Christ through his church. They are servants of Christ, and then also servants of his congregation. When they preach the pure gospel and administer the sacraments for us according to Christ's institution, we should faithfully hear them, honor them, and confess the truth with them, even when such a confession means taking a stand against earthly authorities and popular opinion.

A vision of ripe fruit

8 **This is what the Sovereign LORD showed me: a basket of ripe fruit. ²"What do you see, Amos?" he asked.**

"A basket of ripe fruit," I answered.

Then the LORD **said to me, "The time is ripe for my people Israel; I will spare them no longer.**

³**"In that day," declares the Sovereign** LORD, **"the songs in the temple will turn to wailing. Many, many bodies—flung everywhere! Silence!"**

To fix his message in the minds of the prophet and his listeners, the Lord sometimes plays with the sound of words. The Hebrew word for "summer" or "fruit that ripens in summer" is *qa'yits;* the word for "end" is *qeyts.* Both words have the same consonants. God gives Amos this vision of summer fruit to tell the people of Israel that the end has come for their nation. The ripe fruit means that Israel is ripe for destruction. The Lord will put off his judgment no longer.

With a few brief strokes, the Lord paints a picture of the fall of Israel. In the days of Jeroboam II, the land is full of the songs of temple singers, praising Baal and the other fertility deities, or offering to the Lord the false worship at the calf-shrines. All those songs will turn to wails of terror and sorrow as the Assyrians besiege the Israelite fortresses and capture them. There will be so many corpses that the people will fling them out into the streets or over the city walls. Even someone who strains his ears in the stillness after the battle will hear only dead silence. No one will be left to cry or the survivors will not dare raise their voices for fear of calling down further punishment from the Lord (see also 6:10).

If Israel's fate is already sealed, why does the Lord send Amos to preach? (1) He shows that his judgment is just. We could compare the way a judge might read the charge and formally announce the finding of the jury before pronouncing sentence on a guilty criminal. (2) By warning about the coming destruction of Israel as a nation, he summons individuals out of the doomed people to repent, much as Peter did when he preached in Jerusalem: "Save yourselves from this corrupt generation (Acts 2:40). (3) "These things happened to them as examples and were written down as warnings for us" (1 Corinthians 10:11). Knowing the sad history of Israel should make us beware of repeating it.

The greed of Israel's merchants

⁴ Hear this, you who trample the needy
and do away with the poor of the land,

⁵saying,

"When will the New Moon be over
that we may sell grain,
and the Sabbath be ended
that we may market wheat?"—
skimping the measure,
boosting the price
and cheating with dishonest scales,
⁶ buying the poor with silver
and the needy for a pair of sandals,
selling even the sweepings with the wheat.

Amos addresses some parts of his prophecy to particular elements of the Israelite people, for example, the wealthy women (4:1-3) or the complacent leaders (6:1-7). He also proclaims judgment to all Israel (2:6-16) or even to both kingdoms, Israel and Judah (3:1-15). In the present verses he turns to the greedy merchant class. Their offense is not wealth itself but the way they are gaining it at the expense of their needy fellow-countrymen. They treat the poor like dirt under their feet.

Evidently these merchants observe the forms of worship. They join the religious assemblies when the new moon announces the beginning of another month (Numbers 10:10; 28:14). They close their grain stalls in the marketplaces to rest on the Sabbath days, according to the law (Exodus 20:10). Yet all the time their hearts are not in their worship. Rather, they are itching for the days of rest and worship to pass so that they can get back to making money.

Do we sometimes neglect worship in order to make extra income on overtime pay, so that we can spend it on luxuries? Do we occupy our minds with thoughts of profit and loss even while our mouths pray and sing hymns? Do we go to church reluctantly or participate in public worship halfheartedly because "time is money," and we do not like to spend it feeding our souls on the Word of God? Do we couple such disrespect for the Lord with a lack of concern for our needy fellowmen? Then we have become like these Israelite merchants.

The particular kind of business that Amos uses as an example is the sale of grain, since bread was the common people's staff of life. Grain was sold by the ephah, a measure containing a little more than half a bushel. When a customer bought grain, he paid with bits of silver, balanced on the merchant's scales with a shekel weight (two-fifths of an ounce). These greedy and dishonest Israelite merchants in Jeroboam's time are selling their wheat in skimpy baskets holding less than a full ephah. Then they weigh the price in silver against shekel weights that are heaver than customary (see Deuteronomy 25:13-16). Besides, they also cheat their customers by using unbalanced scales.

Honesty will be one of the marks of those who follow the Lord. A Christian merchant will want to give good measure and a quality product for a fair price. He will not package or advertise deceptively and excuse himself by saying, "Let the buyer beware." "Each of you should look not only to your own interests, but also to the interests of others" (Philippians 2:4).

In order to get enough food for himself, his wife, and his children, a poor Israelite may be forced to sell himself and his family into slavery. He may be so needy that he will sell himself for the price of a pair of sandals, just to have enough to eat. Even then, Amos says, the grain he brings home from the marketplace may not make good bread, because the merchants sweep up what has fallen to the ground and mix the sweepings with the wheat.

Already in the first sermon Amos addressed to Israel, the Lord pointed to the unrighteous treatment of the poor as a symptom of the nation's impenitence (2:6). The Lord's law commanded: "Do not be hardhearted or tight-fisted toward your poor brother. . . . Give generously to him and do so without a grudging heart; then because of this the LORD your God will bless you in all your work and in everything you put your hand to. There will always be poor people in the land. Therefore I command you to be openhanded toward your brothers and toward the poor and needy in your land" (Deuteronomy 15:7-11). The Lord does not disregard how his people treat their poor fellowmen, particularly their poor fel-lowmembers of the people of God. "For he will deliver the needy who cry out, the afflicted who have no one to help" (Psalm 72:12).

In both Old and New Testaments, the Lord puts himself at the side of and in the place of the poor. "He who is kind to the poor lends to the LORD," he says (Proverbs 19:17). On the Last Day, Jesus will say to his believers who fed the hungry, gave hospitality to the needy, clothed the naked, comforted the sick, and visited the prisoners in jail, "What-ever you did for one of the least of these brothers of mine, you did for me" (Matthew 25:40). Do our lives show such evidence of faith in him?

Earthquake, darkness, and mourning

⁷The LORD has sworn by the Pride of Jacob: "I will never forget anything they have done.

⁸ "Will not the land tremble for this,
and all who live in it mourn?
The whole land will rise like the Nile;
it will be stirred up and then sink
like the river of Egypt."

⁹"In that day," declares the Sovereign LORD,

"I will make the sun go down at noon
and darken the earth in broad daylight.
¹⁰ I will turn your religious feasts into mourning
and all your singing into weeping.
I will make all of you wear sackcloth
and shave your heads.
I will make that time like mourning for an only son
and the end of it like a bitter day."

Earlier in this book, the Lord took an oath by himself (6:8). Here he swears the same kind of oath again, calling himself the "Pride of Jacob." Rather than boasting of their own accomplishments, the true people of God will glory in their Savior. The Israelites, however, have proven their impenitence and unbelief by disregarding the Lord's justice and righteousness. Therefore the Lord swears this terrifying oath: "I will never forget anything they have done" (verse 7).

In speaking of the coming judgment, Amos describes several events together, just as Jesus predicted the fall of Jerusalem and the world's final judgment almost in the same breath (Luke 21:5-36). One sign of the judgment will be an earthquake. The Nile River rises at flood stage and then sinks down again. In the same way, the ground beneath men's feet will heave and fall. This frightening event took place two years after Amos predicted it (1:1; see also Zechariah 14:5).

Another sign of judgment will be darkness at noon. Amos may be predicting an eclipse of the sun. (According to Assyrian records, a total solar eclipse took place in 763 B.C.) Events such as earthquakes and eclipses confirm the fact that the prophet truly is a spokesman for the Creator and judge of the world. All his prophecies of judgment for Israel will come true (see Deuteronomy 18:21,22).

Darkness beginning at noon accompanied the sufferings and death of Jesus on the cross (Matthew 27:45). "The earth shook and the rocks split" when Jesus died (Matthew 27:51). God was speaking his angry judgment on the sins of the world that his Son was bearing. "There will be famines and earthquakes" before Jesus returns (Matthew 24:7). The darkening of the sun, moon, and stars will also announce the second coming of Christ to judge the world (Mark 13:24). The Lord reminds mankind that the pattern of life as we know it now, with the earth standing firm underfoot, with darkness following light every 24 hours, is not eternal. This world will not stand forever, and history is aimed toward a final judgment.

For impenitent Israel the coming day of judgment will be a day of wrath and mourning. Amos returns to the note of lamentation he struck in chapter 5. Mourning will replace happy songs and festivals. Everyone will put on sackcloth, the coarse material that the people wore as mourning dress. They will shave their heads—a mourning custom forbidden by the law (Deuteronomy 14:1), but apparently adopted by Israel from the heathen. So bitter will the day of judgment be that it can only be compared to a day when parents mourn the death of an only son. The kingdom of Israel will die.

How dark the picture becomes when men forsake their God! If impenitence and unbelief take the place of faith in human hearts, then fear must also take the place of hope for the future. When Jesus described the signs of the Last Day he said, "Men will faint from terror, apprehensive of what is coming on the world" (Luke 21:26). Those who live in repentance and faith will experience the same events with a totally different reaction: "When these things begin to take place, stand up and lift up your heads, because your redemption is drawing near" (Luke 21:28).

A famine of the Word

> [11] "The days are coming," declares the Sovereign LORD,
>   "when I will send a famine through the land—
> not a famine of food or a thirst for water,
>   but a famine of hearing the words of the LORD.
> [12] Men will stagger from sea to sea
>   and wander from north to east,
> searching for the word of the LORD,
>   but they will not find it.

> [13] "In that day

> "the lovely young women and strong young men
>   will faint because of thirst.
> [14] They who swear by the shame of Samaria,
>   or say, 'As surely as your god lives, O Dan,'
>   or, 'As surely as the god of Beersheba lives'—
> they will fall,
>   never to rise again."

No other nation enjoyed the privileges of the Israelites. Israel was "entrusted with the very words of God" (Romans 3:2). Yet the time will come for this people, the Lord says, when they will be totally deprived of his Word. Like thirst-crazed, dying men they will stagger from the Mediterranean to the Dead Sea and from Galilee to Gilead looking for a message from the Lord, but they will not hear it. The strong young men and women seem to be best equipped to survive famine and thirst, but they too will become faint for a lack of the Word and will finally fall.

The reason for the famine of the Word is plain. Instead of fearing the Lord their God, serving him only and taking their oaths by his name, the people have followed other gods, the gods of the people around them (Deuteronomy 6:13,14). They now swear their oaths by the "shame of Samaria"—an idol god—or by the golden calf image that Jeroboam I set up at Dan, or by the god they worship with their pilgrimages to Beersheba (see also 5:5). When God raises up prophets from among their sons, they command them not to prophesy (2:11,12).

People who refuse to hear the Word of the Lord finally *cannot* hear it, because God takes his Word away. Commenting on Paul's words, "Now is the time of God's favor, now is the day of salvation" (2 Corinthians 6:2), Luther said: "The preaching of the gospel is not an eternal, lasting, continual teaching, but it is like a passing shower which travels on. Some ground is watered and another place stays dry. It does not return and also does not stand still. Then the hot sun comes and licks up the moisture that remains." If we neglect the Word and refuse to follow our Savior's leading, the gospel will pass on to others like a summer shower and will not return to us and our children. The time to hear, believe, and follow the Word is *now*, while we live in the day of God's favor!

A vision of destruction

9 **I saw the Lord standing by the altar, and he said:**

> **"Strike the tops of the pillars**
> **so that the thresholds shake.**

> Bring them down on the heads of all the people;
>> those who are left I will kill with the sword.
> Not one will get away,
>> none will escape.
> ² Though they dig down to the depths of the grave,
>> from there my hand will take them.
> Though they climb up to the heavens,
>> from there I will bring them down.
> ³ Though they hide themselves on the top of Carmel,
>> there I will hunt them down and seize them.
> Though they hide from me at the bottom of the sea,
>> there I will command the serpent to bite them.
> ⁴ Though they are driven into exile by their enemies,
>> there I will command the sword to slay them.
> I will fix my eyes upon them
>> for evil and not for good."

In this fifth and final vision, the Lord shows the prophet a judgment of destruction that no one in Israel will escape. The Lord himself appears, standing next to the altar in one of the sanctuaries where the Israelites worship their idols. He comes to destroy both the temple and those who worship there. All the powers of nature must obey the Lord. In this vision he is again predicting the earthquake that will occur two years after the ministry of Amos (1:1; 8:8). Centuries later the people will still remember this terrible event (Zechariah 14:5).

But the earthquake will be only a beginning of sorrows. The Lord will kill the remnant of the nation with the sword of the Assyrians. No one will escape. Verses 2 to 4 are a picture of fugitives scrambling to the farthest corners of creation to evade the judgment. But there is no way to escape the Lord's avenging hand, not in the depths of the grave or in the highest heavens, not on top of Mount Carmel or on the bottom of the Mediterranean. Even gigantic monsters in the sea must obey their Creator's will, and his will is to destroy Israel. Even exile from Canaan will not be the end of the judgment. The nation must utterly perish, so even exiles will die by the sword. The Lord speaks a harsh and terrifying word of judgment: "I will fix my eyes upon them for evil and not for good" (verse 4). This is the end of a people who reject the Lord.

The omniscience and omnipresence of God must strike terror into the hearts of those who become his enemies through unbelief. If God knows everything and is present everywhere, there simply is no escaping him, in time or in eternity. Think what it means, on the other hand, to have such a God for our friend and Father! He knows our needs better than we do. He is with us always, and we are with him, for time and for eternity. His believers thankfully confess: "Where can I go from your Spirit? Where can I flee from your presence? If I go up to the heavens, you are there; if I make my bed in the depths, you are there. If I rise on the wings of the dawn, if I settle on the far side of the sea, even there your hand will guide me, your right hand will hold me fast" (Psalm 139:7-10).

A hymn of praise to the Lord

> [5] The Lord, the LORD Almighty,
>   he who touches the earth and it melts,
>   and all who live in it mourn—
>   the whole land rises like the Nile,
>   then sinks like the river of Egypt—
> [6] he who builds his lofty palace in the heavens
>   and sets its foundation on the earth,
>   who calls for the waters of the sea
>   and pours them out over the face of the land—
>   the LORD is his name.

Three times Amos interrupts the flow of his prophecy with what sounds like a stanza of a hymn of praise that he is composing or quoting: "He who forms the mountains" (4:13), "He who made the Pleiades and Orion" (5:8), and now "He who touches the earth and it melts." Each stanza includes the refrain "The LORD (God Almighty) is his name." Each time the hymn immediately follows a strong word of judgment on the Israelite nation. Israel should remember that the Lord whose covenant has been broken is no mere local or national deity but the almighty Creator and preserver of the universe.

In verse 5 the prophet again predicts the earthquake with the same words he used in 8:8. Men will mourn because the ground that has always seemed so solid under their feet will rise like the Nile at flood stage and then sink, melting away like a heap of mud in a downpour. More easily than a human builder erects his house, the Lord built the whole visible world, the sky like a domed roof above, its foundation set on the earth at the horizon all around. (The word translated "lofty palace" may mean simply "stairs"; people built their houses with outside stairways, enabling them to walk or sit on the roof.) At God's almighty Word, water evaporates from the sea, turns to clouds and then gushes down on the land as rain (see also 5:8).

Believers live on close terms with Almighty God. He encourages us to call him "Father," and his eternal Son, the Word through whom all things were made (John 1:3), is true man, our brother. If familiarity ever begins to breed contempt, we need to hear passages like this one. If men and human accomplishments begin to look great and God looks small in our eyes, then let the prophets remind us of his majesty: "He sits enthroned above the circle of the earth, and its people are like grasshoppers. He stretches out the heavens like a canopy, and spreads them out like a tent to live in" (Isaiah 40:22). This is the God who invites us to call him "Father." This omnipotent Creator sent his Son to become one of us, to die for us on earth so that we can live with him in heaven forever.

Only a remnant will be saved

> 7 "Are not you Israelites
>> the same to me as the Cushites?"
>>> declares the LORD.
> "Did I not bring Israel up from Egypt,
>> the Philistines from Caphtor
>> and the Arameans from Kir?
> 8 "Surely the eyes of the Sovereign LORD
>> are on the sinful kingdom.
> I will destroy it
>> from the face of the earth—
> yet I will not totally destroy
>> the house of Jacob,"
>>> declares the LORD.
> 9 "For I will give the command,
>> and I will shake the house of Israel
>> among all the nations
> as grain is shaken in a sieve,
>> and not a pebble will reach the ground.
> 10 All the sinners among my people
>> will die by the sword,
> all those who say,
>> 'Disaster will not overtake or meet us.'

At the beginning of this book, the Lord spoke his messages of judgment against the nations around Israel. Then his fist came down on his own people: they deserve his anger even more because they have become worse than the heathen. Of all the people the Israelites knew, the ones most obviously Gentiles and not Hebrews were the inhabitants of Cush, south of Egypt, the black-skinned Ethiopians. They appeared to be the "most foreign" foreigners. Yet now the Lord puts the question to the people he chose out of all the nations to be his treasured possession, "Are not you Israelites the same to me as the Cushites?" (verse 7).

It is true that the Lord brought the people of Israel up from Egypt and gave them the land of Canaan as proof of his love, to keep his promises to Abraham. Yet if the Israelites will look around them, they will observe that other nations have also migrated from place to place. The Lord of the nations brought the Philistines over the sea from Caphtor (Crete?) to settle on the Mediterranean coast between Canaan and Egypt. He brought the Arameans from Kir in Mesopotamia to inhabit Damascus (see also 1:5). In no way can Israel prove from the external facts of history that it is God's chosen people. What sets Israel apart is the grace of God and the covenant he made with the fathers. Now it is a fact to be observed that God's chosen people are no longer his own through faith. They have broken their covenant with the Lord and made themselves worse than the heathen. They have no special claim on his blessings.

When God sent his Son to earth, he sent him first to his chosen Old Testament people. The Jews in the time of Jesus still took pride in pointing to their descent from Abraham, but they would not receive the Savior whom God sent as Abraham's promised seed. John the Baptist, a preacher of repentance like Amos, showed that being physical descendants of Abraham, like participation in the exodus from Egypt, did not insure a blessing. The Jews needed to believe the message God was sending them, as Abraham did, and to trust his messenger. John told them: "Do not think you can say to yourselves, 'We have Abraham as our father.' I tell you that out of these stones God can raise up children for Abraham. The ax is already at the root of the trees, and every tree that does not produce good fruit will be cut down and thrown into the fire" (Matthew 3:9,10).

We also have no claim on the mercy of God. His choosing us for his own is a matter of pure grace. To say "I am an orthodox Christian" or "I am a Bible-believing Lutheran," as if God must then pay attention and bless us, is as foolish as the Jews' claim: "We are descendants of Abraham," or "The Lord brought our fathers out of Egypt." The grace of God is not something we inherit through the history of our church, just as it is not something we can earn by what we do. God's grace becomes our own only through Spirit-worked faith. Those who trust God's promises live in daily repentance, and true repentance bears good fruit.

The Lord has already announced, "I will fix my eyes upon them for evil and not for good" (verse 4). This threat applies particularly to "the sinful kingdom" of Israel, which he is about to destroy. Nevertheless, together with this threat a gospel promise begins to dawn: the Lord "will not totally destroy the house of Jacob" (verse 8). He will leave a remnant in order to fulfill his promises.

The prophet uses the picture of grain in a sieve. A farmer shakes and whirls the wheat or barley. Sand and fine pebbles that remain after winnowing fall through the screen to the ground, so that only pure grain is left. Israel will be carried off to Assyria, and somewhat over a century later, Judah will be exiled to Babylon. Even though most of the people will be sifted out by being scattered among the nations, the Lord will bring back a purified remnant after the captivity (see also Isaiah 10:21,22; 17:3). Through the remnant that returns to the Promised Land, he will send his Savior when his time fully comes.

There is one more clap of thunder before Amos lets sunshine burst through the clouds at the end of his book. Even when disaster strikes, there will still be some who take pride in their own strength (6:13) and think they are beyond the reach of God's avenging arm. No, says the Lord, the judgment will involve them all: "All the sinners among my people will die by the sword" (verse 10). Yet by addressing the sinners among his people, the Lord leaves open the possibility that a few souls, "like a burning stick snatched from the fire" (4:11), will hear the prophet's warning and repent. Even in Israel a remnant may be saved through faith.

After hearing so many prophecies of judgment, the believing reader is glad to see the gleam of good news in these verses. A prophet who represented the Lord in Israel in the eighth century B.C. had to preach the law. With good reason Israel's Lord could say that all day long he had stretched out his hands to an obstinate people (Isaiah 65:2,3). Yet the Lord never forgot the promise he made to Abraham, Isaac, and Jacob long before he gave his commandments to Moses. Even when most of his people forsook him, he graciously saved a remnant in order to keep his promises.

Each of us can look back on times when we have neglected the spiritual opportunities God offered us. We ignored the warnings of his Word, broke his commandments, refused to listen to the voice of conscience, and went our own stubborn, sinful way. Yet again and again he called us to repentance. Even today his mercy is still calling us. The Lord's patience dare never be a reason for continuing to despise his mercy by devoting ourselves to our sins and refusing to hear his voice. But in the long-suffering mercy he showed Israel, we find the assurance that his grace is also sufficient for us in spite of our unworthiness.

> "Though great our sins and sore our woes,
>> His grace much more aboundeth.
> His helping love no limit knows,
>> Our utmost need it soundeth."
>
> (TLH 329:5)

PART FOUR

A Promise of Blessing in the Last Days
(9:11-15)

The restoration of the house of David

> ¹¹ "In that day I will restore
> David's fallen tent.
> I will repair its broken places,
> restore its ruins,
> and build it as it used to be,
> ¹² so that they may possess the remnant of Edom
> and all the nations that bear my name,"
> declares the LORD, who will do these things.

King David wanted to build a house of worship for the Lord in Jerusalem to replace the tabernacle. Through the prophet Nathan, the Lord revealed that David's son would build the temple: "When your days are over and you rest with your fathers, I will raise up your offspring to succeed you, who will come from your own body, and I will establish his kingdom. He is the one who will build a house for my Name, and I will establish the throne of his kingdom forever. . . . Your house and your kingdom will endure forever before me; your throne will be established forever" (2 Samuel 7:12-16). Thus the Lord assured David that his son Solomon would build the temple. This promise, however, included much more: another "Son of David" would sit on his throne forever, so that David's house—his royal family—would reign over an everlasting kingdom.

When Jeroboam I tore the ten tribes away from the Davidic kings in Jerusalem, the house of David seemed to be falling to ruin. The destruction of Jerusalem and the exile of Judah in 586 B.C. would be another severe blow to the house of David. After the return from exile, Persian governors ruled the land of Judah. Then it fell under the power of Greek, Syrian, and Roman rulers. When Jesus was born, the Roman-appointed king in Jerusalem was Herod the Great, an Idumean (Edomite). The Magi had to ask this foreign ruler, "Where is the one who has been born king of the Jews?" (Matthew 2:2). The royal family of David had fallen to ruin. His house resembled a hut with gaps in its walls or a tent that had collapsed.

The Lord promises that David's fallen tent will be rebuilt. The angel Gabriel announced the fulfillment of this promise when he said to the Virgin Mary: "You will be with child and give birth to a son, and you are to give him the name Jesus. He will be great and will be called the Son of the Most High. The Lord God will give him the throne of his father David, and he will reign over the house of Jacob forever; his kingdom will never end" (Luke 1:31-33). Accordingly, "that day" in which the Lord promises to rebuild David's fallen tent will begin with the birth of Christ and will continue through the New Testament era into eternity. Jesus is the everlasting King who will restore David's fallen house to glory.

The eternal kingdom of David's greater Son will have even broader boundaries than the united kingdom of Israel in the golden age under David and Solomon. People like the remnant of the Edomites, inveterate enemies of Israel, will belong to the people of God, not as vanquished enemies but as fellow heirs of the Lord's blessing. According to verse 12, the Edomites will be joined in the Lord's family by

267

other Gentile nations, all of those whom God calls by his name, that is, the ones he adopts as his children through Baptism and faith in Christ.

When Paul and Barnabas returned from their first mission journey in Cyprus and Asia Minor, they reported back to the Jewish congregations how God "had opened the door of faith to the Gentiles" (Acts 14:27). This question arose: must Gentile believers be circumcised? Must they be required to obey the ceremonial law of Moses if they are to become members of God's people? James recognized that the Lord was "taking from the Gentiles a people for himself" (Acts 15:14). He quoted Amos 9:11,12 in Acts 15:16-18 to show that in the Old Testament God prophesied the spread of the Christian church among the Gentiles. The prophets said nothing about imposing circumcision or the other Old Testament ceremonies on these converts. Through the spread of the gospel among the Gentiles, the Lord was carrying out his eternal plan of salvation for all nations.

We cannot thank God enough that he not only graciously opens his kingdom to members of his ancient people Israel but also calls Gentiles into the Christian church. Without Christ the Gentiles were "excluded from citizenship in Israel and foreigners to the covenants of the promise, without hope and without God in the world" (Ephesians 2:12). God's kingdom is his own; he may include in it whomever he wants. By dying for the sins of the world, Jesus made believing Gentiles equal citizens in his kingdom with believing Israelites: "You who once were far away have been brought near through the blood of Christ" (Ephesians 2:13).

The blessings of "that day"

¹³"The days are coming," declares the LORD,

"when the reaper will be overtaken by the plowman
and the planter by the one treading grapes.

> **New wine will drip from the mountains**
> **and flow from all the hills.**
> ¹⁴ **I will bring back my exiled people Israel;**
> **they will rebuild the ruined cities and live in them.**
> **They will plant vineyards and drink their wine;**
> **they will make gardens and eat their fruit.**
> ¹⁵ **I will plant Israel in their own land,**
> **never again to be uprooted**
> **from the land I have given them,"**
>
> **says the LORD your God.**

This prophecy includes three features of the coming days: (1) superabundant harvests; (2) the return of the exiles to their cities, vineyards, and gardens; and (3) the everlasting occupation of the land by God's people Israel.

First, it is a picture of abundance beyond imagination. Farmers in Canaan usually plowed in October, when the early rains began to soften the parched ground. They harvested their grain crop in May and June. Try to imagine a crop so abundant that the harvesters will still be reaping grain in the field when the plowmen are ready to break up the ground for a new crop! Grapes in Canaan would be picked and pressed out to make wine in late summer. Imagine vineyards producing so many grapes that the harvesters will still be treading the winepresses in October, at planting time!

Vineyards in Canaan were often planted on hillsides (Isaiah 5:1), which might be terraced. In or near the vineyard would be a winepress, a pit where the harvesters pressed out the grape juice with their feet. The juice would then flow down from the press into a second, smaller collecting pit. Try to imagine such a bountiful crop of luscious grapes that the juice will overflow the winepresses and drip down the hillsides!

A second aspect of the "coming days" will be the return of God's exiled people to their own land. Before Israel entered Canaan, Moses told the people that God was showing his undeserved favor to them by giving them a land with large, flourishing cities they did not build, houses filled with all kinds of good things they did not provide, wells they did not dig, and vineyards and olive groves they did not plant (Deuteronomy 6:10,11). When Amos announced God's coming judgment, he told the Israelites that they would not enjoy the fruits of their own labors. Though they had built stone mansions, they would not live in them. Though they had planted lush vineyards, they would not drink their wine (5:11). The coming days will see a restoration of Israel's fortunes. God's people will return from their exile to live in their own rebuilt cities, drink wine from their vineyards, and eat fruit from their gardens.

A third and final aspect of the "coming days" will be Israel's permanent occupation of the land. When he exiled his people to Mesopotamia, it was as if the Lord roughly uprooted the vine that he planted in Canaan and transplanted it to another place. His restored people will not have to endure such an experience again. They will be planted in their own land forever. To all eternity they will be the Lord's people, and he will be their God.

What do these words mean? The Lord did bring a remnant of Judah back from captivity in Babylon. Yet the returning Jews enjoyed nothing like the prosperity described in these verses. Neither did they remain in their land forever. The Romans destroyed Jerusalem in A.D. 70 and again in 135. During the following years, most of the Jews were scattered all over the Mediterranean world.

We will find the clue to the understanding of these promises in the New Testament. When the Lord says, "In that day I will restore David's fallen tent," we have seen that he points forward to the coming of David's Son, the Messiah. These verses that begin "The days are coming" are a further description of the New Testament era.

Jesus, in the New Testament, teaches us that he does not reign over his people on earth as a glorious king in a visible earthly kingdom. He reigns by the gospel in the hearts of those who are brought to faith by his Word. "My kingdom is not of this world," he said (John 18:36). "For this reason I was born, and for this I came into the world, to testify to the truth. Everyone on the side of truth listens to me" (John 18:37). The blessings of his kingdom are the blessings of salvation revealed by his Word. In Amos' words the Lord is not promising his people earthly houses, abundant grain, and a surplus of wine but the forgiveness of sins and eternal life. The prophets picture the future blessings of Christ's reign—the blessings of salvation—in terms of the past blessings enjoyed by the people of Israel in the land of Canaan— houses, grain, fruit, and wine.

Christians should read Amos 9:13-15 with the understanding firmly in mind that the prophet is describing the blessings we have in the kingdom of Christ. We enjoy God's gifts in an abundance beyond imagination: forgiveness of sins, the status of sons and daughters in his family, comfort in every trouble, confidence to pray, the joy of worship, the privilege of serving him, assurance that he will keep us in faith, help against temptation, victory over death, everlasting life.

The Lord promised the blessings of his kingdom to the descendants of Abraham, the people of Israel. But the descendants of Abraham who receive the blessing are not just the people who have the physical blood of father Abraham in their veins. Abraham believed the Lord's promises, and

271

"those who believe are children of Abraham" (Galatians 3:7), whether or not they are his physical descendants. Paul shows in the New Testament that "those who have faith are blessed with Abraham, the man of faith" (Galatians 3:9). All believers, Jews and Gentiles, are the true Israel of God.

To have all the blessings of salvation in Christ, it is not necessary for Christians to own a house, vineyard, and garden in the land of Israel. We enjoy God's gift of salvation through faith in Christ, not by residence in a particular city or country. Wherever God's people live in the world, they enjoy the abundance of blessings that Jesus brought, as he promised: "I have come that they may have life, and have it to the full" (John 10:10).

With this understanding of the abundant life that the prophet promises, we can also see what it means to live in the Promised Land forever. This everlasting occupation of the land must also be understood as an Old Testament picture of the New Testament future. For God's people to be planted in their own land—really his land—forever, never again to be uprooted, means that they will enjoy everlasting life with the Lord. "Never again will they hunger; never again will they thirst" (Revelation 7:16). Through faith Christians look forward to "the resurrection of the body and the life everlasting." "We will be with the Lord forever" (1 Thessalonians 4:17).

The book of Amos closes with the words "says the Lord your God." Once more the prophet reminds us that he proclaims not his own words but the words and promises of God. After all his messages of judgment, he also preaches the gospel once more by calling the Lord "your God." The prophet Amos and his believing listeners know: "The Lord is our God and we are his people."

Let the prophet speak to us today. God made us his own by redeeming us from all sins through the blood of his Son.

We enjoy all the blessings of Jesus Christ in his everlasting kingdom. May we serve the Lord our God with pure hearts in his church on earth and praise him forever in heaven.

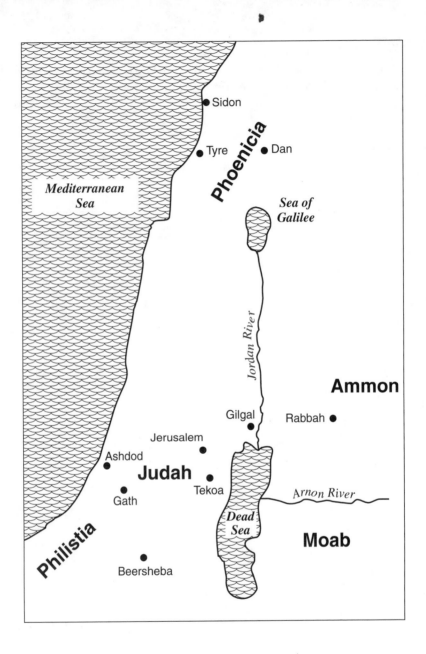